THE HISTORY OF
JOSEPH SMITH
BY HIS MOTHER

JOSEPH SMITH, THE PROPHET

THE HISTORY OF
JOSEPH SMITH
BY HIS MOTHER

BIOGRAPHICAL SKETCHES OF JOSEPH SMITH,
THE PROPHET, AND HIS PROGENITORS
FOR MANY GENERATIONS

THE COMPLETE AND UNABRIDGED
1853 - FIRST EDITION

BY

LUCY MACK SMITH
MOTHER OF THE PROPHET

First Published in Liverpool in
1853

————

Copyright 2020

————

ISBN: 978-8630756206

————

NOTE: The numbers in brackets correspond
to the page numbers of the original.

TABLE OF CONTENTS

———

CHAPTER 52

CHAPTER 53

CHAPTER 54

APPENDIX

PREFACE

THE following pages, embracing biographical sketches and the genealogy of Joseph Smith, the Prophet, and his Progenitors, were mostly written previous to the death of the Prophet, and under his personal inspection.

Most of the historical items and occurrences related have never before been published. They will therefore be exceedingly interesting to all Saints, and sincere inquirers after the Truth, affording them the privilege of becoming more extensively acquainted with the private life and character of one of the greatest Prophets that ever lived upon the earth. Independent of this, the events which have occurred in connection with the history of this remarkable family, are, in themselves, of the most marvellous kind, and of infinite importance in their bearings upon the present and future generations.

No events that have happened since the first advent of our Saviour, are of more thrilling interest than those connected with the history of the Prophet, Joseph Smith. Every incident relating to his life, or the lives of his progenitors, will be eagerly sought after by all future generations. The geographical, [xiv] mechanical, and other scientific discoveries of modern ages, sink into insignificance, compared with the importance of those discoveries made by this great man. They are designed by the Almighty to produce the greatest moral and physical revolutions which the inhabitants of this globe ever witnessed — revolutions which, through the judgments of God, will utterly overthrow and destroy all governments and kingdoms that will not become subject to Christ.

Under these infinitely important considerations, the following pages are recommended to the careful and candid perusal of all nations.

ORSON PRATT [15]

JOSEPH SMITH, THE PROPHET AND HIS PROGENITORS

CHAPTER 1

SOLOMON MACK, THE FATHER OF LUCY MACK—EXTRACT FROM HIS
NARRATIVE

MY father, Solomon Mack, was born in the town of Lyme, New London
county, state of Connecticut, Sept. 26, 1735. His father, Ebenezer Mack,
was a man of considerable property, and lived in good style,
commanding all the attention and respect which are ever shown to those
who live in fine circumstances, and habits of strict morality. For a length
of time he fully enjoyed the fruits of his industry. But this state of things
did not always continue, for a series of misfortunes visited my
grand-parents, by which they were reduced to that extremity, that a once
happy and flourishing family were compelled to disperse, and throw
themselves upon the charity of a cold, unfeeling world.

My father was taken into the family of a neighbouring farmer, where
he remained until he was nearly twenty-one years of age, about which
time he enlisted in the service of his country.

I have a sketch of my father's life, written by himself, in which is
detailed an account of his several campaigns, and many of his
adventures, **[16]** while in the army. From this I extract the following:—

"At the age of twenty-one years, I left my master. Shortly after which,
I enlisted in the services of my country, under the command of Captain
Henry, and was annexed to the regiment commanded by Col. Whiting.

"From Connecticut, we marched to Fort Edwards, in the state of New
York. We were in a severe battle, fought at Half-way Brook in 1755.
During this Expedition, I caught a heavy cold, which rendered me unfit
for business until the return of warm weather. I was carried the ensuing
spring to Albany.

"In the year 1757, I had two teams in the King's service, which were employed in carrying the General's baggage. While thus engaged I went one morning as usual to yoke my team, but three of my oxen were missing. When this came to the knowledge of the officer, he was very angry, and drawing his sword, threatened to run it through me. He then ordered me to get three other oxen, which I accordingly did, and proceeded with the baggage to Fort Edwards, and the next day I returned in order to find my missing oxen.

"While I was performing this trip, the following circumstance occurred. About half way from Stillwater to Fort Edwards, I espied four Indians nearly thirty rods distant, coming out of the woods; they were armed with scalping knives, tomahawks, and guns. I was alone, but about twenty rods behind me was a man by the name of Webster. I saw my danger, and that there was no way to escape, unless I could do it by stratagem; so I rushed upon them, calling in the mean time at the top of my voice, Rush on! rush on, my boys! we'll have the devils. The only weapon I had, was a walking staff, yet I ran toward them, and as the other man appeared just at that instant, it gave them a terrible fright, and I saw no more of them.

"I hastened to Stillwater the next day, as aforementioned, and finding my oxen soon after I arrived there, I returned the same night to Fort-Edwards, a distance of seven miles, the whole of which was a dense forest.

"In 1758, I enlisted under Major Spenser, and went immediately over Lake George, with a company who crossed in boats, to the western side, where we had a [17] bloody and hot engagement with the enemy, in which Lord Howe fell at the onset of the battle. His bowels were taken out and buried, but his body was embalmed, and carried to England.

"The next day we marched to the breastworks, but were unsuccessful, being compelled to retreat with a loss of five hundred men killed, and as many more wounded.

"In this contest I narrowly escaped — a musket ball passed under my chin, within half an inch of my neck. The army then returned to Lake George, and, on its way thither, a large scouting party of the enemy came round by Skeenesborough, and, at the Half-way Brook, destroyed a large number of both men and teams. Upon this, one thousand of our men were detached to repair immediately to Skeenesborough in pursuit of them; but when we arrived at South Bay, the enemy were entirely out of our reach.

"The enemy then marched to Ticonderoga, New York, in order to procure supplies, after which they immediately pursued us, but we eluded them by hastening to Wood-Creek, and thence to Fort Ann, where we arrived on the 13th day of the month. We had but just reached this place, when the sentry gave information that the enemy were all around us, in consequence of which we were suddenly called to arms. Major Putman led the company, and Major Rogers brought up the rear. We marched but three quarters of a mile, when we came suddenly upon a company of Indians that were lying in ambush. Major Putman marched his men through their ranks, whereupon the Indians fired, which threw our men into some confusion. Major Putman was captured by them, and would have been killed by an Indian, had he not been rescued by a French lieutenant.

"The enemy rose like a cloud, and fired a whole volley upon us, and, as I was in the foremost rank, the retreat of my company brought me in the rear, and the tomahawks and bullets flew around me like hail stones. As I was running, I saw not far before me a windfall, which was so high that it appeared to me insurmountable, however, by making great exertions, I succeeded in getting over it. Running a little farther, I observed a man who had in this last conflict been badly wounded, and the Indians were close upon him; nevertheless I turned aside for the purpose of assisting him, and succeeded in getting him into the midst of our army, in safety. [18]

"In this encounter, a man named Gersham Bowley, had nine bullets shot through his clothes, but received no personal injury. Ensign Worcester received nine wounds, was scalped and tomahawked, notwithstanding which, he lived, and finally recovered.

"The above engagement commenced early in the morning, and continued until about three o'clock, p.m., in which half of our men were either killed, wounded, or taken prisoners. In consequence of this tremendous slaughter we were compelled to send to Fort Edwards for men, in order to assist in carrying our wounded, which were about eighty in number.

"The distance we had to carry them, was nearly fourteen miles. To carry so many thus far, was truly very fatiguing, insomuch, that when we arrived at the place of destination, my strength was about exhausted.

"I proceeded immediately to Albany, for the purpose of getting supplies, and returned again to the army as soon as circumstances would admit.

"Autumn having now arrived I went home, where I tarried the ensuing winter.

"In the spring of 1759, the army marched to Crown-point, where I received my discharge. In the same year, I became acquainted with an accomplished young woman, a school teacher, by the name of Lydia Gates. She was the daughter of Nathan Gates, who was a man of wealth, living in the town of East Haddam, Connecticut. To this young woman I was married shortly after becoming acquainted with her.

"Having received a large amount of money for my services in the army, and deeming it prudent to make an investment of the same in real estate, I contracted for the whole town of Granville, in the state of New York. On the execution of the deed, I paid all the money that was required in the stipulation, which stipulation also called for the building of a number of log houses. I accordingly went to work to fulfil this part of the contract, but after laboring a short time, I had the misfortune to cut my leg, which subjected me, during that season, to the care of the physician. I hired a man to do the work, and paid him in advance, in order to fulfil my part of the contract; but he ran away with the money, without performing the labor, and the consequence was, I lost the land altogether. **[19]**

"In 1761, we moved to the town of Marlow, where we remained until we had four children. When we moved there, it was no other than a desolate and dreary wilderness. Only four families resided within forty miles. Here I was thrown into a situation to appreciate more fully the talents and virtues of my excellent wife; for, as our children were deprived of schools, she assumed the charge of their education, and performed the duties of an instructress as none, save a mother, is capable of. Precepts accompanied with examples such as hers, were calculated to make impressions on the minds of the young, never to be forgotten.

"She, besides instructing them in the various branches of an ordinary education, was in the habit of calling them together both morning and evening, and teaching them to pray; meanwhile urging upon them the necessity of love towards each other, as well as devotional feelings towards Him who made them.

"In this manner my first children became confirmed in habits of piety, gentleness, and reflection, which afforded great assistance in guiding those who came after them, into the same happy channel. The education of my children would have been a more difficult task, if they had not inherited much of their mother's excellent disposition.

"In 1776, I enlisted in the service of my country, and was for a considerable length of time in the land forces, after which, I went with my two sons, Jason and Stephen, on a privateering expedition, commanded by Captain Havens. Soon after we set sail, we were driven upon Horseneck. We succeeded, however, in getting some of our guns on shore, and bringing them to bear upon the enemy, so as to exchange many shots with them; yet they cut away our rigging, and left our vessel much shattered.

"We then hauled off, and cast anchor; but, in a short time we espied two row-gallies, two sloops, and two schooners. We quickly weighed anchor, and hauled to shore again, and had barely time to post four cannon[s] in a position in which they could be used, before a sanguinary contest commenced. The balls from the enemy's guns, tore up the ground, cutting asunder the saplings in every direction. One of the row-gallies went round a point of land with the view of hemming us in, but we killed forty **[20]** of their men, with our small arms, which caused the enemy to abandon their purpose.

"My son Stephen, in company with the cabin boys, was sent to a house not far from the shore, with a wounded man. Just as they entered the house, an eighteen-pounder followed them. A woman was engaged in frying cakes, at the time, and being somewhat alarmed, she concluded to retire into the cellar, saying, as she left, that the boys might have the cakes, as she was going below.

"The boys were highly delighted at this, and they went to work cooking, and feasting upon the lady's sweet cakes, while the artillery of the contending armies was thundering in their ears, dealing out death and destruction on every hand. At the head of this party of boys, was Stephen Mack, my second son, a bold and fearless stripling of fourteen.

"In this contest, the enemy was far superior to us in point of numbers, yet we maintained our ground, with such valour, that they thought it better to leave us, and accordingly did so. Soon after which, we hoisted sail, and made for New London.

"When hostilities had ceased, and peace and tranquillity were again restored, we freighted a vessel for Liverpool. Selling both ship and cargo in this place, we embarked on board Captain Foster's vessel, which I afterwards purchased; but, in consequence of storms and wrecks, I was compelled to sell her, and was left completely destitute.

"I struggled a little longer to obtain property, in making adventures, then returned to my family, after an absence of four years, about pennyless. After this, I determined to follow phantoms no longer, but devote the rest of my life to the service of God, and my family."

I shall now lay aside my father's journal, as I have made such extracts as are adapted to my purpose, and take up the history of his children. [21]

———————

CHAPTER 2

HISTORY OF JASON MACK

JASON, my oldest brother, was a studious and manly boy. Before he had attained his sixteenth year he became what was then called a *Seeker*, and believing that by prayer and faith the gifts of the Gospel, which were enjoyed by the ancient disciples of Christ, might be attained, he labored almost incessantly to convert others to the same faith. He was also of the opinion that God would, at some subsequent period, manifest his power as he had anciently done—in signs and wonders.

At the age of twenty he became a preacher of the Gospel. And in a short time after this he formed an acquaintance with a young woman of wealthy parentage.[1] She was the pride of the place in which she resided, not so much on account of her splendid appearance, as the soundness of her mind, and her stately deportment, joined with an unaffected mildness of disposition, and a condescension of manners, which were admirably suited to the taste and principles of my brother. Jason became deeply in love with her, insomuch that his heart was completely hers, and it would have been as easy to have convinced him that he could

———————

[1] The name of this young woman was Esther Bruce; she was from the state of New Hampshire.

exist without his head, as that he could live and enjoy life, without being united with her in marriage. These feelings, I believe, were mutual, and Jason and she entered into an engagement to be married, but, as they were making arrangements for the solemnization of their nuptials, my father received a letter from Liverpool, containing information that a large amount of money was collected for him, and that it was ready for his reception. [22]

On account of this intelligence it was agreed that the marriage of my brother, as my father desired that he should accompany him to Liverpool, should be deferred until their return. Accordingly, my brother left his affianced bride, with a heavy heart, and with this promise, that he would write to her and his sister conjointly, at least once in three months during his absence. In three months after his departure, according to agreement, a letter arrived, which indeed met with a very warm reception, but it was never followed by another from him. A young man who kept the post-office where she received her letters, formed in his heart a determination to thwart my brother, if possible, in his matrimonial prospects, in order to obtain the prize himself. He commenced by using the most persuasive arguments against her marrying my brother; but not succeeding in this, he next detained his letters, and then reproached him for neglecting her. Being still unsuccessful, he forged letters purporting to be from a friend of Jason, which stated that he (Jason Mack) was dead, and his friends might cease to expect him. He then urged his suit again, but she still rejected him, and continued to do so until within four months of Jason's return, when she concluded that she had wronged the young man, and that he was really more worthy than she had expected. The time also which Jason was to be absent having expired without his return, she believed that the reports concerning his death must be true. So she accepted the hand of this young man, and they were united in the bonds of matrimony.

As soon as Jason arrived he repaired immediately to her father's house. When he got there she was gone to her brother's funeral; he went in, and seated himself in the same room where he had once paid his addresses to her. In a short time she came home; when she first saw him she did not know him, but when she got a full view of his countenance she recognized him, and instantly [23] fainted. From this time forward she never recovered her health, but, lingering for two years, died the victim of disappointment.

Jason remained in the neighbourhood a short time, and then went to sea, but he did not follow the sea a great while. He soon left the main, and commenced preaching, which he continued until his death.

CHAPTER 3

LOVISA AND LOVINA MACK

THE history of Lovisa and Lovina, my two oldest sisters, is so connected and interwoven that I shall not attempt to separate it.

They were one in faith, in love, in action, and in hope of eternal life. They were always together, and when they were old enough to understand the duties of a Christian, they united their voices in prayer and songs of praise to God. This sisterly affection increased with their years, and strengthened with the strength of their minds. The pathway of their lives was never clouded with a gloomy shadow until Lovisa's marriage, and removal from home, which left Lovina very lonely.

In about two years after Lovisa's marriage she was taken very sick, and sent for Lovina. Lovina, as might be expected, went immediately, and remained with her sister during her illness, which lasted two years, baffling the skill of the most experienced physicians; but at the expiration of this time she revived a little, and showed some symptoms of recovery.

I shall here relate a circumstance connected with her sickness, which may try the credulity of some of my readers, yet hundreds were eye witnesses, and **[24]** doubtless many of them are now living, who, if they would, could testify to the fact which I am about to mention.

As before stated, after the space of two years she began to manifest signs of convalescence, but soon a violent re-attack brought her down; again, and she grew worse and worse, until she became entirely speechless, and so reduced that her attendants were not allowed to even turn her in bed. She took no nourishment except a very little rice water. She lay in this situation three days and two nights. On the third night, about two o'clock, she feebly pronounced the name of Lovina, who had all the while watched over her pillow, like an attendant angel, observing every change and symptom with the deepest emotion. Startled at hearing the sound of Lovisa's voice, Lovina now bent over the emaciated form of her sister, with thrilling interest, and said, "my sister! my sister! what will you?"

Lovisa then said emphatically, "the Lord has healed me, both soul and body—raise me up and give me my clothes, I wish to get up."

Her husband told those who were watching with her, to gratify her, as in all probability it was a revival before death, and he would not have her crossed in her last moments.

They did so, though with reluctance, as they supposed she might live a few moments longer, if she did not exhaust her strength too much by

19

exerting herself in this manner.

Having raised her in bed, they assisted her to dress; and although, when they raised her to her feet, her weight dislocated both of her ancles, she would not consent to return to her bed, but insisted upon being set in a chair, and having her feet drawn gently in order to have her ancle joints replaced. She then requested her husband to bring her some wine, saying, if he would do so she would do quite well for the present.

Soon after this, by her own request, she was assisted to cross the street to her father-in-law's, who **[25]** was at that time prostrated upon a bed of sickness. When she entered the house he cried out in amazement, "Lovisa is dead, and her spirit is now come to warn me of my sudden departure from this world." "No, father," she exclaimed, "God has raised me up, and I have come to tell you to prepare for death." She conversed an hour or so with him, then, with the assistance of her husband and those who attended upon her that night, she crossed the street back again to her own apartment.

When this was noised abroad, a great multitude of people came together, both to hear and see concerning the strange and marvellous circumstance which had taken place. She talked to them a short time, and then sang a hymn, after which she dismissed them, promising to meet them the next day at the village church, where she would tell them all about the strange manner in which she had been healed.

The following day, according to promise, she proceeded to the church, and when she arrived there a large congregation had collected. Soon after she entered, the minister arose and remarked, that as many of the congregation had doubtless come to hear a recital of the strange circumstance which had taken place in the neighbourhood, and as he himself felt more interested in it than in hearing a Gospel discourse, he would open the meeting and then give place to Mrs. Tuttle.

The minister then requested her to sing a hymn; she accordingly did so, and her voice was as high and clear as it had ever been. Having sung, she arose and addressed the audience as follows: — "I seemed to be borne away to the world of spirits, where I saw the Saviour, as through a veil, which appeared to me about as thick as a spider's web, and he told me that I must return again to warn the people to prepare for death; that I must exhort them to be watchful as well as prayerful; that I must declare faithfully unto them their accountability before God, and the certainty of their being **[26]** called to stand before the judgment seat of Christ; and that if I would do this, my life should be prolonged." After which, she spoke much to the people upon the uncertainty of life.

When she sat down, her husband and sister, also those who were with her during the last night of her sickness, arose and testified to her appearance just before her sudden recovery.

Of these things she continued to speak boldly for the space of three years. At the end of which time she was seized with the consumption which terminated her earthly existence.

A short time before Lovisa was healed in the miraculous manner before stated, Lovina was taken with a severe cough which ended in consumption. She lingered three years. During which time she spoke with much calmness of her approaching dissolution, contemplating death with all that serenity which is characteristic of the last moments of those who fear God, and walk uprightly before him. She conjured her young friends to remember that life upon this earth cannot be eternal. Hence the necessity of looking beyond this vale of tears, to a glorious inheritance, "where moths do not corrupt, nor thieves break through and steal."

The care of Lovina, during her illness, devolved chiefly upon myself. The task, though a melancholy one, I cheerfully performed, and, although she had much other attention, I never allowed myself to go an hour, at a time, beyond the sound of her voice while she was sick. A short time before she breathed out her last moments, which was in the night, she awakened me, and requested that I would call father and mother, for she wished to see them, as she would soon be gone. When they came, she said, "Father and mother, now I am dying, and I wish you to call my young associates, that I may speak to them before I die." She then requested me to place her in a chair, and as soon as the young people who were called in, were seated, she commenced speaking. After talking a short time to [27] them, she stopped, and, turning to her mother, said, "Mother, will you get me something to eat? it is the last time you will ever bring me nourishment in this world." When my mother had complied with her request, she eat a small quantity of food, with apparent appetite, then gave back the dish, saying, "There, mother, you will never get me anything to eat again."

After which, she turned to the company, and proceeded with her remarks, thus:—"I do not know when I received any material change of heart, unless it was when I was ten years old. God, at that time, heard my prayers, and forgave my sins; and ever since then I have endeavored to serve him according to the best of my abilities. And I have called you here to give you my last warning—to bid you all farewell, and beseech you to endeavor to meet me where parting shall be no more."

Shortly after this, holding up her hands, and looking upon them as one would upon a trifling thing unobserved before, she said, with a smile upon her countenance, "See, the blood is settling under my nails."

Then, placing the fingers of her left hand across her right, she continued thus, "'Tis cold to there—soon this mortal flesh will be food for worms." Then, turning to me, she said, "Now, sister Lucy, will you help me into bed."

I did as I was directed, carrying her in my arms just as I would a child. Although I was but thirteen years old, she was so emaciated that I could carry her, with considerable ease.

As I was carrying her to bed, my hand slipped. At this she cried out, "Oh! Sister, that hurt me." This, indeed, gave me bitter feelings. I was well assured, that this was the last sad office I should ever perform for my sister, and the thought that I had caused her pain in laying her on her death bed, wounded me much.

Soon after this, she passed her hand over her face, and again remarked, "My nose is now quite cold." Then, slightly turning and straightening herself in [28] bed, she continued, "Father, mother, brother, sister, and dear companions, all farewell, I am going to rest—prepare to follow me; for

> "Death! 'tis a melancholy day
> To those that have no God,
> When the poor soul is forced away
> To seek her last abode.
>
> "In vain to heaven she lifts her eyes;
> But guilt, a heavy chain,
> Still drags her downwards from the skies,
> To darkness, fire, and pain.
>
> "Awake and mourn, ye heirs of hell,
> Let stubborn sinners fear;
> You must be driven from earth, and dwell
> A long FOR EVER there!
>
> "See how the pit gapes wide for you,
> And flashes in your face;
> And thou, my soul, look downward too,
> And sing recovering grace.
>
> "He is a God of sov'reign love,
> Who promised heaven to me,
> And taught my thoughts to soar above,
> Where happy spirits be.
>
> "Prepare me, Lord, for thy right hand,
> Then come the joyful day;
> Come, death, and some celestial band,
> To bear my soul away."

After repeating this hymn, she folded her hands across her breast, and then closed her eyes for ever.

Having led my readers to the close of Lovina's life, I shall return to Lovisa, of whom there only remains the closing scene of her earthly career.

In the course of a few months subsequent to the death of sister Lovina, my father received a letter from South Hadley, stating, that Lovisa was very low of the consumption, and that she earnestly desired him to come and see her as soon as possible, as she expected to live but a short time.

My father set out immediately, and when he arrived there, he found her in rather better health than he expected. In a few days after he got there, she resolved in her heart to return with him at all hazards. To this her father unwillingly consented, and, after making the requisite preparations, they started for Gilsum. [29]

They travelled about four miles, and came to an inn kept by a man by the name of Taff. Here her father halted, and asked her if she did not wish to tarry a short time to rest herself. She replied in the affirmative. By the assistance of the landlord, she was presently seated in an easy chair. My father then stepped into the next room to procure a little water and wine for her. He was absent but a moment; however, when he returned it was too late, her spirit had fled from its earthly tabernacle to return no more, until recalled by the trump of the Archangel.

My father immediately addressed a letter to mother, informing her of Lovisa's death, lest the shock of seeing the corpse unexpectedly should overcome her. And as soon as he could get a coffin, he proceeded on his journey for Gilsum, a distance of fifty miles.

She was buried by the side of her sister Lovina, according to her own request.

The following is part of a hymn composed by herself, a few days previous to her decease:—

> "Lord, may my thoughts be turned to thee;
> Lift thou my heavy soul on high;
> Wilt thou, O Lord, return to me
> In mercy, Father, ere I die!
> My soaring thoughts now rise above—
> Oh fill my soul with heavenly love.

> "Father and mother, now farewell;
> And husband, partner of my life,
> Go to my father's children, tell
> That lives no more on earth thy wife;
> That while she dwelt in cumbrous clay,
> For them she prayed both night and day.

"My friends, I bid you all adieu;
    The Lord hath called, and I must go—
And all the joys of this vain earth,
    Are now to me of little worth;
'Twill be the same with you as me,
    When brought as near eternity."

Thus closes this mournful recital, and when I pass with my readers into the next chapter, with them probably may end the sympathy aroused by this rehearsal, but with me it must last while life endures. [30]

_____

CHAPTER 4

LOT OF STEPHEN MACK

MY brother Stephen, who was next in age to Jason, was born in the town of Marlow, June 15, 1766.

I shall pass his childhood in silence, and say nothing about him until he attained the age of fourteen, at which time he enlisted in the army, the circumstances of which were as follows:—

A recruiting officer came into the neighbourhood to draft soldiers for the revolutionary war, and he called out a company of militia to which my brother belonged, in order to take therefrom such as were best qualified to do military duty. My brother, being very anxious to go into the army at this time, was so fearful that he would be passed by on account of his age, that the sweat stood in large drops on his face, and he shook like an aspen leaf. Fortunately, the officer made choice of him among others, and he entered the army, and continued in the service of his country until he was seventeen. During this time he was in many battles, both on land and sea, and several times narrowly escaped death by famine; but, according to his own account, whenever he was brought into a situation to fully realize his entire dependance upon God, the hand of Providence was always manifested in his deliverance.

Not long since, I met with an intimate acquaintance of my brother Stephen, and requested him to furnish me such facts as were in his possession in relation to him; and he wrote the following brief, yet comprehensive account, for the gratification of my readers:—

"I, Horace Stanly, was born in Tunbridge, Orange county, Vermont, August 21, 1798. I have been personally acquainted with Major Mack and his family ever since I can remember, as I lived in the same township, [31] within one mile and a half of the Major's farm, and two miles from his store, and eight miles from Chelsea, the county seat of

Orange county; where he conducted the mercantile and tinning business.

"My eldest brother went to learn the tinning business of the Major's workmen. The Major being a man of great enterprize, energetic in business, and possessed of a high degree of patriotism, launched forth on the frontiers at Detroit, in the year 1800 (if I recollect rightly), where he immediately commenced trading with the Indians.

"He left his family in Tunbridge, on his farm, and while he was engaged in business at Detroit he visited them—sometimes once in a year, in eighteen months, or in two years, just as it happened.

"I visited Detroit November 1, 1820, where I found the Major merchandising upon quite an extensive scale, having six clerks in one store; besides this, he had many other stores in the territory of Michigan, as well as in various parts of Ohio.

"His business at Pontiac was principally farming and building, but in order to facilitate these two branches of business, he set in operation a saw and flour mill, and afterwards added different branches of mechanism. He made the turnpike road from Detroit to Pontiac at his own expense. He also did considerable other public work, for the purpose of giving employment to the poor.

"He never encouraged idleness, or the man above his business. In 1828, having been absent from Detroit a short time, I returned. The Major was then a member of the Council of the territory, and had acted a very conspicuous part in enhancing its prosperity and enlarging its settlement; and it was a common saying, that he had done much more for the territory than any other individual.

"In short, the Major was a man of talents of the first order. He was energetic and untiring. He always encouraged industry, and was very cautious how he applied his acts of charity.

"Respectfully by

"HORACE STANLY."

My brother was in the city of Detroit in 1812, the year in which Hull surrendered the territory to the British Crown. My brother, beings somewhat [32] celebrated for his prowess, was selected by General Hull to take the command of a company, as Captain. After a short service in this office, he was ordered to surrender. At this his indignation was roused to the highest pitch. He broke his sword across his knee; and, throwing it into the lake, exclaimed that he would never submit to such a disgraceful compromise while the blood of an American continued to run through his veins.

This drew the especial vengeance of the army upon his head; and his property, doubtless, would have been sacrificed to their resentment, had they known the situation of his affairs. But this they did not know, as his housekeeper deceived them by a stratagem, related by Mr. Stanly, as follows:—

"At the surrender of Detroit, not having as yet moved his family hither, Major Mack had an elderly lady, by the name of Trotwine, keeping house for him. The old lady took in some of the most distinguished British officers as boarders. She justified them in their course of conduct towards the Yankees, and, by her shrewdness and tact, she gained the esteem of the officers, and thus secured through them the good will of the soldiery, so far as to prevent their burning (what they supposed to be) her store and dwelling, both of which were splendid buildings.

"The Major never forgot this service done him by the old lady, for he ever afterwards supported her handsomely."

Thus was a great amount of goods and money saved from the hands of his enemies. But this is not all: the news came to her ears that they were about to burn another trading establishment belonging to the Major, and, without waiting to consult him, she went immediately to the store, and took from the counting-room several thousand dollars, which she secreted until the British left the city. The building and goods were burned.

As soon as the English left the territory, he recommenced business, and removed his family from Tunbridge to Detroit. Here they remained but a short time, when he took them to Pontiac; and, as [33] soon as they were well established or settled in this place, he himself went to the city of Rochester, where he built a saw-mill.

But, in the midst of his prosperity, he was called away to experience another state of existence, with barely a moment's warning, for he was sick only four days from the time he was first taken ill until he died; and even on the fourth day, and in the last hour of his illness, it was not supposed to be at all dangerous, until his son, who sat by his bed side, discovered that he was dying.

He left his family with an estate of fifty thousand dollars, clear of encumbrance.

_____

CHAPTER 5

LYDIA MACK, THIRD DAUGHTER OF SOLOMON MACK

OF my sister Lydia I shall say but little; not that I loved her less, or that she was less deserving of honourable mention; but she seemed to float more with the stream of common events than those who have occupied the foregoing pages: hence fewer incidents of a striking character are furnished for the mind to dwell upon.

She sought riches and obtained them; yet in the day of prosperity she remembered the poor, for she dealt out her substance to the needy, with a liberal hand, to the end of her days, and died the object of their affection. As she was beloved in life, so she was bewailed in death. **[34]**

CHAPTER 6

DANIEL MACK—HE RESCUES THREE MEN FROM A WATERY GRAVE

DANIEL comes next in order. He was rather worldly minded, yet he was not vicious; and if he had any peculiar trait of character, it was this—he possessed a very daring and philanthropic spirit, which led him to reach forth his hand to the assistance of those whose lives were exposed to danger, even to the hazard of his own life. For instance; he, in company with several others, was once standing on the bank of Miller's River, in the town of Montague, when one of the number proposed taking a swim. Daniel objected, saying it was a dangerous place to swim in, yet they were determined, and three went in; but, going out into the stream rather too far, they were overpowered by the current, and a kind of eddy which they fell into, and they sunk immediately.

At this, Daniel said, "Now, gentlemen, these men are drowning: who will assist them at the risk of his life?" No one answered. At this, he sprang into the water, and, diving to the bottom, found one of them fastened to some small roots. Daniel took hold of him, and tore up the roots to which he was clinging, and brought him out, and then told the bystanders to get a barrel, for the purpose of rolling him on it, in order to make him disgorge the water which he had taken. He then went in again, and found the other two in the same situation as the first, and saved them in like manner.

After rolling them a short time on barrels, he took them to a house, and gave them every possible attention, until they had so far recovered as to be able to speak. As soon as they could talk, one of them, fixing his eyes upon Daniel, said, "Mr. Mack, we have reason to look upon you as our saviour, for you have delivered us from a watery tomb; and I **[35]** would that I could always live near you. We are now assured that you have not only wisdom to counsel, but, when men have spurned your advice, you have still that greatness of soul which leads you to risk your own life to save your fellow man. No, I will never leave you as long as I live, for I wish to convince you that I ever remember you, and that I will never slight your counsel again."

In this they were all agreed, and they carried out the same in their future lives.

CHAPTER 7

SOLOMON MACK

MY youngest brother, Solomon, was born and married in the town of Gilsum, state of New Hampshire, where he is *still living;* and although he is now very aged, he has never travelled farther than Boston, to which place his business leads him twice a year.

He has gathered to himself in this rocky region, fields, flocks, and herds, which multiply and increase upon the mountains. He has been known at least twenty years, as Captain Solomon Mack, of Gilsum; but, as he lives to speak for himself, and as I have to do chiefly with the dead, and not the living, I shall leave him, hoping that, as he has lived peaceably with all men, he may die happily.

I have now given a brief account of all my father's family, save myself; and what I have written has been done with the view of discharging an obligation which I considered resting upon me, inasmuch as they have all passed off this stage of action, except myself and youngest brother. And seldom do I meet with an individual with whom I **[36]** was even acquainted in my early years, and I am constrained to exclaim—"The friends of my youth! where are they?" The tomb replies, "Here are they!" But, through my instrumentality,

> "Safely truth to urge her claims, presumes
> On names now found alone on books and tombs."

CHAPTER 8

EARLY LIFE OF LUCY MACK—HER MARRIAGE WITH JOSEPH SMITH

I SHALL now introduce the history of my own life. I was born in the town of Gilsum, Cheshire county, state of New Hampshire, on the eighth of July, 1776.

When I arrived at the age of eight years, my mother had a severe fit of sickness. She was so low that she, as well as her friends, entirely despaired of her recovery. During this sickness she called her children around her bed, and, after exhorting them always to remember the instructions which she had given them—to fear God and walk uprightly before Him, she gave me to my brother Stephen, requesting him to take care of me, and bring me up as his own child, then bade each of us farewell.

This my brother promised to do; but, as my mother shortly

recovered, it was not necessary, and I consequently remained at my father's house until my sister Lovisa was married. Some time after this event I went to South Hadley, to pay Lovisa, who was living there, a visit.

I returned home to my parents in about six months, and remained with them in Gilsum until the death of Lovina. Soon after which, my brother Stephen, who was living at Tunbridge, Vermont, came to my father's on a visit; and he insisted so earnestly on my accompanying him home, that my parents consented. The grief occasioned by the [37] death of Lovina was preying upon my health, and threatened my constitution with serious injury, and they hoped that to accompany my brother home might serve to divert my mind, and thus prove a benefit to me. For I was pensive and melancholy, and often in my reflections I thought that life was not worth possessing.

In the midst of this anxiety of mind, I determined to obtain that which I had heard spoken of so much from the pulpit—a change of heart.

To accomplish this, I spent much of my time in reading the Bible, and praying; but, notwithstanding my great anxiety to experience a change of heart, another matter would always interpose in all my meditations—If I remain a member of no church, all religious people will say I am of the world; and if I join some one of the different denominations, all the rest will say I am in error. No church will admit that I am right, except the one with which I am associated. This makes them witnesses against each other; and how can I decide in such a case as this, seeing they are all unlike the Church of Christ, as it existed in former days!

While I remained at Tunbridge, I became acquainted with a young man by the name of Joseph Smith, to whom I was subsequently married.

I continued with my brother one year, then went home. I was at home but a short time, when my brother came after me again, and insisted so hard upon my returning with him, that I concluded to do so. And this time I remained with him until I was married, which took place the next January. [38]

CHAPTER 9

SEVEN GENERATIONS OF THE SMITH FAMILY—FOUR GENERATIONS OF THE MACK FAMILY

HERE, I would like to give the early history of my husband, for many facts might be mentioned, that doubtless would be highly interesting;

but, as I am not capable of giving them in order, I shall decline making the attempt, and in the place thereof shall insert a transcript from the record of his family, beginning with Samuel Smith, who was the son of Robert and Mary Smith, who came from England.

The above Samuel Smith, was born Jan. 26,1666, in Toppsfleld, Essex county, Massachusetts; and was married to Rebecca Curtis, daughter of John Curtis, Jan. 25, 1707.

Children of Samuel and Rebecca Smith

NAMES	BORN	MARRIED	DIED
Phebe	Jan. 8, 1708.	To Steph. Averel	
1st Mary. . . .	Aug. 14, 1711. . .	To Amos Towne	
2nd Samuel .	Jan. 26, 1714. . . .	To Priscilla Gould	Nov. 14, 1785.
Rebecca	Oct. 1, 1715	To John Batch	
Elizabeth . . .	July 8, 1718	To Elizer Gould	March, 1753.
Hephzibah. .	May 12, 1722 . . .	To Wm. Gallop	Nov. 15, 1774.
Robert.	Apr. 25, 1724		
Susanna	May 2, 1726	. . . .	May 5, 1741.
Hannah	Apr. 5. 1729	To John Peabody	Aug. 17, 1764.

1st Samuel Smith died July 12, 1748.
His wife Rebecca Smith, March 2, 1753.

Children of 2nd Samuel, and 1st Priscilla Smith, which Samuel was the son of 1st Samuel and Rebecca Smith.

NAMES	BORN	MARRIED	DIED
Priscilla	Sept. 26, 1735. . .	To Jacob Kimball Sept. 15, 1755.	
3rd Samuel .	Oct. 28, 1737 . . .	To Rebecca Towne Jan. 2, 1760.	
Vasta.	Oct. 5, 1739	To Solomon Curtis Sept. 15, 1763. The 2nd time to Jacob Hobbs, 1767.	
Susanna	Jan. 24, 1742. . . .	To Isaac Hobbs 1767.	[39]
1st Asael. . . .	Mar. 1, 1744. . . .	To Mary Duty, Feb. 12, 1761.	

Children of 1st Asael and Mary Smith; which Asael was the son of 2nd Samuel and Priscilla Smith.

NAMES	BORN	MARRIED	DIED
1st Jesse. . . .	Apr. 20, 1768 . .	To Hanh. Peabody Jan. 20, 1792.	
Priscilla. . . .	Oct. 27, 1769. . .	To John C. Walker Aug. 24, 1796.	
1st Joseph . .	July 12, 1771. . .	To Lucy Mack Jan. 24, 1796.	Sep. 14, 1840.
2nd Asael . .	May 21, 1773 . .	Betsy Schillinger Mar. 21, 1802.	
Mary	June 4, 1775 . . .	To Israel Pearce.	
4th Samuel .	Sept. 15, 1777 . .		
1st Silas	Oct. 1, 1779. . . .	To Ruth Stevens Jan. 29, 1805. The second time to Mary Atkins, March 4, 1828.	
1st John. . . .	July 16, 1781. . .	To Clarissa Lyman Sept. 11, 1815	
3rd Susanna	May 18, 1783		
Stephen. . . .	Apr. 17, 1785 . .	. . . .	July 25, 1802.
Sarah	May 17, 1789 . .	To Joseph Sanford Oct. 15, 1809	May 27, 1824.

Children of 1st. Jesse and Hannah Smith; which Jesse was the son of 1st. Asael and Mary Smith.

Benjamin G. was born May 2, 1793
Eliza,   "   "   Mar. 9, 1795
Ira,   "   "   Jan. 30,1797
Harvy,   "   "   Apr. 1, 1799
Harriet,   "   "   Apr. 8, 1801
Stephen,   "   "   May 2, 1803
Mary,   "   "   May 4, 1805
Catherine,   "   "   July 13, 1807
Royal,   "   "   July 2, 1809
Sarah,   "   "   Dec. 16, 1810 **[40]**

Children of John C. and Priscilla Waller; which Priscilla was the daughter of 1st. Asael Smith.

Calvin C.	was	born	June 6, 1797
Dolly,	"	"	Oct. 16, 1799
Marshall,	"	"	March 18, 1801
Royal,	"	"	Nov. 29, 1802
Dudley C.	"	"	Sept. 29, 1804
Bushrod,	"	"	Oct. 18, 1806
Silas B.	"	"	Jan. 1, 1809
Sally P.	"	"	Oct. 31, 1810
John H.	"	"	Sept. 9. 1812

Children of 1st. Joseph and Lucy Smith; which Joseph was the son of the 1st. Asael and Mary Smith.

NAMES	BORN	MARRIED	DIED
Alvin	Feb. 11, 1799	. . . .	Nov. 19, 1824
Hyrum	Feb. 8, 1800 Tunbridge, Vermont	To Jerusha Barden, Nov. 2, 1826 Manchester, N.Y. To Mary Fielding, 1837.	Murdered by a mob, June 27, 1844, in Carthage Jail, Hancock co. Illinois, while under the protection of Gov. Thomas Ford.
Sophronia	May 18, 1803 Tunbridge, Vermont.	To Calvin Stodard Dec. 2, 1827, Palmyra, N.Y.	
2nd Joseph	Dec. 23, 1805 Sharon, Windsor co., Vermont	To Emma Hale, daughter of Isaac Hale, in South Bainbridge, Chenango county, New York, Jan. 18, 1827	Murdered by a mob, June 27, 1844, in Carthage Jail, Hancock co. Illinois, while under the protection of Gov. Thomas Ford.[41]
5th Samuel	Mar. 13, 1808 Tunbridge, Vermont	To Mary Bailey, Aug, 18, 1834. To Levira Clark, Apr. 29, 1842.	July 30, 1844 of a fever, occasioned by over exertion in getting away from a mob, when his brothers were killed.
Ephriam . . .	Mar. 13, 1810	. . . .	Mar. 24 1810.

William ...	Mar. 13, 1811 Royalton, Vermont	To Caroline Grant daughter of Joshua Grant, Feb. 14, 1833.	
Catherine .	July 8, 1812 Lebanon, N. Hamphsire	To Wilkins J. Salisbury, Jan. 8, 1831.	
Don Carlos	Mar. 25, 1816	To Agnes Coolbrith July 30, 1835, Kirtland, Ohio.	Aug. 7, 1841
Lucy	July 18, 1821	To Arthur Miliken, June 4, 1840, Nauvoo.	

Children of 2nd Asael and Betsy Smith; which Asael was the son of 1st Asael and Mary Smith.

Elias,	was	born	Sept. 6, 1804
Emily,	"	"	Sept. 1, 1806
2nd Jesse J.	"	"	Oct. 6, 1808
Esther	"	"	Sept. 20, 1810
Mary J.	"	"	April 28, 1813
Julia P.	"	"	March 4, 1815
Martha,	"	"	June 8, 1817
2nd Silas	"	"	June 5, 1822

Children of Israel and Mary Pearce; which Mary was the daughter of 1st Asael and Mary Smith.

Eunice,	was	born	April 29, 1799
Miranda,	"	"	June 17, 1803
Horace,	"	"	June 8, 1805
John S.	"	"	March 6, 1807
Susan,	"	"	June 20, 1809 [42]
Mary,	"	"	April 25, 1811
Laura,	"	"	Feb. 8, 1814
Eliza A.	"	"	Sept. 2, 1817

Children of 1st Silas and Ruth Smith; which Silas was the son of 1st Asael and Mary Smith.

Charles,	was	born	Nov. 11, 1806
Charity,	"	"	April 1, 1808
Curtis S.	"	"	Oct. 29, 1809
6th Samuel,	"	"	Oct. 3, 1811
Stephen,	"	"	Jan. 8, 1815
Susan,	"	"	Oct. 19, 1817
3rd Asael,	"	"	Oct. 12, 1819

Children by his second wife Mary Smith.

Silas L.	was	born	Oct. 20, 1830
John A.	"	"	July 6, 1832
Nathaniel J.	"	"	Dec. 2, 1834

Children of 1st John and Clarissa Smith; which John was the son of 1st Asael and Mary Smith.

George A.	was	born	June 26, 1817
Caroline	"	"	June 6, 1820
2nd John L.	"	"	Nov. 17, 1823

Children of Hyrum and Jerusha Smith; which Hyrum was the son of 1st Joseph and Lucy Smith.

Lovina,	was	born	Sept. 16, 1827
Mary,	"	"	June 27, 1829
John,	"	"	Sept. 22, 1832
2nd Hyrum,	"	"	April 27, 1834
Jerusha,	"	"	Jan. 13, 1836
Sarah,	"	"	Oct. 2, 1837

Children of Hyrum Smith and Mary, his second wife.

4th Joseph,	was	born	Nov. 13, 1838
Martha,	"	"	May 14, 1841

Children of 2nd Joseph, the Prophet, and Emma Smith; which Joseph was the son of 1st Joseph and Lucy Smith.

Julia M. Smith, adopted daughter, was born April 30, 1831.

3rd Joseph,	was born	Nov. 6, 1832 **[43]**
Frederick G. W.	" "	June 20, 1836
Alexander,	" "	June 2, 1838
Don Carlos,	" "	June 13, 1840
David H.	" "	Nov. 18, 1844

Children of 5th. Samuel Smith and Mary, his first wife; which Samuel was the son of 1st. Joseph and Lucy Smith.

Susanna B.	was born	Oct. 27, 1835
Mary B.	" "	March. 27, 1837
Samuel H. B.	" "	Aug. 1, 1838
Lucy B.	" "	Jan. 31, 1841

Mary Smith died Jan. 25th, 1841.

Children of Samuel Smith and Levira, his second wife.

Levira A. C.	was born	April, 29, 1842
Lovisa C.	" "	Aug. 28, 1843
Lucy J. C.	" "	Aug. 20, 1844

Children of William and Caroline Smith; which William was the son of 1st Joseph and Lucy Smith.

Mary Jane	was born	Jan. 1835
Caroline L.	" "	Aug. 1836

Children of Don Carlos and Agnes Smith; which Don Carlos was the son of 1st Joseph and Lucy Smith.

Agnes C.	was born	Aug. 1, 1836
Sophronia,	" "	1838
Josephine D.	" "	March 10, 1841

Children of Calvin and Sophronia Stodard.

Eunice,	was born	March 22, 1830
Maria,	" "	April 12, 1832

Children of Wilkins J. and Catharine Salisbury; which Catharine was the daughter of 1st. Joseph Smith.

Elizabeth,	was	born	April 9,1832
Lucy,	"	"	Oct. 3, 1834
Solomon J.	"	"	Sept. 18, 1835
Alvin,	"	"	June 7, 1838
Don C.	"	"	Oct. 25, 1841
Emma C.	"	"	March 25, 1844 [44]

Arthur and Lucy Miliken have one son, named Don Carlos Miliken. Geo. A. Smith, son of 1st. John Smith, was married to Bathsheba Bigler, July 25, 1841.

Children of George A. and Bathsheba Smith.

George Albert,	was	born	July 7, 1842
Bathsheba,	"	"	Aug. 14, 1844

Having now given all the names belonging to the family of Smith, I shall take up another lineage, namely, that of the Mack family, commencing with my grandfather Ebenezer Mack. Ebenezer Mack had three sons, Elisha, Samuel, and Solomon, and one daughter named Hypsebeth. His son Solomon was born in the town of Lyme, state of Connecticut, Sept. 26, 1735; was married to a young woman by the name of Lydia Gates, in the year 1759. This Lydia Gates was born in East Haddam, state of Connecticut, Sept. 3,1735.

The following are the names of the children of 1st. Solomon and Lydia Mack; which Solomon was the son of Ebenezer and Hannah Mack.

Jason Mack.	Lovisa Mack.
Stephen Mack.	Lovina Mack.
Daniel Mack.	Lydia Mack.
2nd. Solomon Mack,	Lucy Mack.

Children of 2nd Solomon Mack; which Solomon was the son of 1st Solomon Mack.

Calvin,	was	born	Nov. 28, 1797
Orlando,	"	"	Sept. 23, 1799
Chilon,	"	"	July 26, 1802
3rd Solomon,	"	"	May 23, 1805

Amos,	"	"	May 1, 1807
Dennis,	"	"	Oct. 18, 1809
Merrill,	"	"	Sept. 14, 1812
Esther,	"	"	April 2, 1815
Rizpath,	"	"	June 5, 1818 [45]

CHAPTER 10

A PRESENT OF ONE THOUSAND DOLLARS, FROM JOHN MUDGET AND STEPHEN MACK, TO THE AUTHOR

SOON after I was married, I went with my husband to see my parents, and as we were about setting out on this visit, my brother Stephen, and his partner in business, John Mudget, were making some remarks in regard to my leaving them, and the conversation presently turned upon the subject of giving me a marriage present. "Well," said Mr. Mudget, "Lucy ought to have something worth naming, and I will give her just as much as you will."

"Done," said my brother, "I will give her five hundred dollars in cash."

"Good," said the other, "and I will give her five hundred dollars more."

So they wrote a cheque on their bankers for one thousand dollars, and presented me with the same. This cheque I laid aside, as I had other means by me sufficient to purchase my housekeeping furniture.

Having visited my father and mother, we returned again to Tunbridge, where my companion owned a handsome farm, upon which we settled ourselves, and began to cultivate the soil. We lived on this place about six years, tilling the earth for a livelihood.

In 1802 we rented our farm in Tunbridge, and moved to the town of Randolph, where we opened a mercantile establishment. When we came to this place we had two children, Alvin and Hyrum. [46]

CHAPTER 11

SICKNESS IN RANDOLPH

WE had lived in Randolph but six months when I took a heavy cold, which caused a severe cough. To relieve this, every possible exertion was made, but it was all in vain. A hectic fever set in, which threatened to prove fatal, and the physician pronounced my case to be confirmed consumption. During this sickness my mother watched over me with much anxiety, sparing herself no pains in administering to my comfort, yet I continued to grow weaker and weaker, until I could scarcely endure even a footfall upon the floor, except in stocking-foot, and no one was allowed to speak in the room above a whisper.

While I was in this situation a Methodist exhorter came to see me. On coming to the door, he knocked in his usual manner, and his knocking so agitated me that it was a considerable length of time before my nerves became altogether quieted again. My mother motioned him to a chair, and in a whisper informed him of my situation, which prevented his asking me any questions. He tarried some time, and while he sat he seemed deeply to meditate upon the uncertainty of my recovering; in the mean time, he showed a great desire to have conversation with me respecting my dying.

As he thus sat pondering, I fancied to myself that he was going to ask me if I was prepared to die, and I dreaded to have him speak to me, for then I did not consider myself ready for such an awful event, inasmuch as I knew not the ways of Christ; besides, there appeared to be a dark and lonesome chasm, between myself and the Saviour, which I dared not attempt to pass.

I thought I strained my eyes, and by doing so I could discern a faint glimmer of the light that [47] was beyond the gloom which lay immediately before me.

When I was meditating upon death, in this manner, my visitor left, soon after which my husband came to my bed, and took me by the hand, and said, "Oh, Lucy! my wife! my wife! you must die! The doctors have given you up; and all say you cannot live."

I then looked to the Lord, and begged and pleaded with him to spare my life, in order that I might bring up my children, and be a comfort to my husband. My mind was much agitated during the whole night. Sometimes I contemplated heaven and heavenly things; then my thoughts would turn upon those of earth—my babes and my companion.

During this night I made a solemn covenant with God, that, if he would let me live, I would endeavour to serve him according to the best of my abilities. Shortly after this, I heard a voice say to me, "Seek, and ye shall find; knock, and it shall be opened unto you. Let your heart be comforted; ye believe in God, believe also in me."

In a few moments my mother came in, and, looking upon me, she said, "Lucy, you are better."

I replied, as my speech returned just at that instant, "Yes, mother, the Lord will let me live, if I am faithful to the promise which I made to him, to be a comfort to my mother, my husband, and my children." I continued to gain strength, until I became quite well as to my bodily health; but my mind was considerably disquieted. It was wholly occupied upon the subject of religion. As soon as I was able, I made all diligence in endeavouring to find some one who was capable of instructing me more perfectly in the way of life and salvation.

As soon as I had strength sufficient, I visited one Deacon Davies, a man whom I regarded as exceedingly pious; and, as he was apprised of my sudden and miraculous recovery, I expected to hear about the same which I had heard from my mother—"The Lord has done a marvellous work; let His [48] name have the praise thereof." But, no: from the time I arrived at his house until I left I heard nothing, except, "Oh, Mrs. Smith has come—help her in—run, build a fire, make the room warm—fill the tea-kettle—get the great arm-chair," &c., &c. Their excessive anxiety concerning my physical convenience and comfort, without being seasoned with one word in relation to Christ or godliness, sickened and disgusted me, and I returned home very sorrowful and much disappointed.

From my anxiety of mind to abide the covenant which I had made with the Lord, I went from place to place, for the purpose of getting information, and finding, if it were possible, some congenial spirit who could enter into my feelings, and thus be able to strengthen and assist me in carrying out my resolutions.

I heard that a very devout man was to preach the next Sabbath in the Presbyterian Church; I therefore went to meeting, in the full expectation of hearing that which my soul desired—the Word of Life. When the minister-commenced speaking, I fixed my mind with deep attention upon the spirit and matter of his discourse; but, after hearing him through, I returned home, convinced that he neither understood nor appreciated the subject upon which he spoke, and I said in my heart that there was not then upon earth the religion which I sought. I therefore determined to examine my Bible, and, taking Jesus and his disciples for my guide, to endeavour to obtain from God that which man could neither give nor take away. Notwithstanding this, I would hear all that could be said, as well as read much that was written, on the subject of religion; but the Bible I intended should be my guide to life and salvation. This course I pursued a number of years. At length I considered it my duty to be baptized, and, finding a minister who was willing to baptize me, and leave me free in regard to joining any religious denomination, I stepped forward and yielded obedience to this ordinance; after [49] which I continued to read the Bible as formerly, until my eldest son had attained his twenty-second year.

CHAPTER 12

JOSEPH SMITH, SENIOR, LOSES HIS PROPERTY AND BECOMES POOR—RECEIVES A VISIT FROM JASON MACK—THE HISTORY OF THE LATTER CONCLUDED

MY husband, as before stated, followed merchandising for a short period in the town of Randolph. Soon after he commenced business in this place, he ascertained that crystalized gensang root sold very high in China, being used as a remedy for the plague, which was then raging there.

He therefore concluded to embark in a traffic of this article, and consequently made an investment of all the means which he commanded, in that way and manner which was necessary to carry on a business of this kind, viz., crystalizing and exporting the root. When he had obtained a quantity of the same, a merchant by the name of Stevens, of Royalton, offered him three thousand dollars for what he had; but my husband refused his offer, as it was only about two-thirds of its real value, and told the gentleman that he would rather venture shipping it himself.

My husband, in a short time, went to the city of New York, with the view of shipping his gensang, and finding a vessel in port which was soon to set sail, he made arrangements with the captain to this effect—that he was to sell the gensang in China, and return the avails thereof to my husband; and this the captain bound himself to do, in a written obligation.

Mr. Stevens, hearing that Mr. Smith was making arrangements to ship his gensang, repaired immediately to New York, and, by taking some pains, [50] he ascertained the vessel on board of which Mr, Smith had shipped his gensang; and having some of the same article on hand himself, he made arrangements with the captain to take his also, and he was to send his son on board the vessel to take charge of it.

It appears, from circumstances that afterwards transpired, that the gensang was taken to China, and sold there to good advantage, or at a high price, but not to much advantage to us, for we never received any thing, except a small chest of tea, of the avails arising from this adventure.

When the vessel returned, Stevens the younger also returned with it, and when my husband became apprized of his arrival, he went immediately to him and made inquiry respecting the success of the captain in selling his gensang. Mr. Stevens told him quite a plausible tale, the particulars of which I have forgotten; but the amount of it was, that the sale had been a perfect failure, and the only thing which had been brought for Mr. Smith from China was a small chest of tea, which chest had been delivered into his care, for my husband.

In a short time after this, young Stevens hired a house of Major Mack, and employed eight or ten hands, and commenced the business of crystalizing gensang. Soon after engaging in this business, when he had got fairly at work, my brother, Major Mack, went to see him, and, as it happened, he found him considerably intoxicated. When my brother came into his presence, he spoke to him thus, "Well, Mr. Stevens, you are doing a fine business; you will soon be ready for another trip to China." Then observed again, in a quite indifferent manner, "Oh, Mr. Stevens, how much did brother Smith's adventure bring?" Being under the influence of liquor, he was not on his guard, and took my brother by the hand and led him to a trunk; then opening it, he observed, "There, sir, are the proceeds of Mr. Smith's gensang!" exhibiting a large amount of silver and gold. [51]

My brother was much astounded at this; however, he disguised his feelings, and conversed with him a short time upon different subjects, then returned home, and about ten o'clock the same night he started for Randolph, to see my husband.

When Mr. Stevens had overcome his intoxication, he began to reflect upon what he had done, and making some inquiry concerning my brother, he ascertained that he had gone to Randolph. Mr. Stevens, conjecturing his business—that he had gone to see my husband respecting the gensang adventure, went immediately to his establishment, dismissed his hands, called his carriage, and fled with his cash for Canada, and I have never heard any thing concerning him since.

My husband pursued him a while, but finding pursuit vain, returned home much dispirited at the state of his affairs. He then went to work to overhaul his accounts, in order to see how he stood with the world; upon which he discovered that, in addition to the loss sustained by the China adventure, he had lost about two thousand dollars in bad debts. At the time he sent his venture to China he was owing eighteen hundred dollars in the city of Boston, for store goods, and he expected to discharge the debt at the return of the China expedition; but, having invested almost all his means in gensang, the loss which he suffered in this article rendered it impossible for him to pay his debt with the property which remained in his hands. The principal dependence left him, in the shape of property, was the farm at Tunbridge, upon which we were then living, having moved back to this place immediately after his venture was sent to China. This farm, which was worth about fifteen hundred dollars, my husband sold for eight hundred dollars, in order to make a speedy payment on the Boston debt; and, as I had not used the check of one thousand dollars, which my brother and Mr. Mudget gave me, I added it to the eight hundred dollars obtained for the farm, and by this means the whole debt was liquidated. [52]

While we were living on the Tunbridge farm, my brother Jason made us a visit. He brought with him a young man by the name of William Smith, a friendless orphan, whom he had adopted as his own son, and, previous to this time, had kept constantly with him; but he now thought best to leave him with us, for the purpose of having him go to school. He remained with us, however, only six months before my brother came again and took him to New Brunswick, which they afterwards made their home, and where my brother had gathered together some thirty families, on a tract of land which he had purchased for the purpose of assisting poor persons to the means of sustaining themselves. He planned their work for them, and when they raised anything which they wished to sell, he took it to market for them. Owning a schooner himself, he took their produce to Liverpool, as it was then the best market.

When Jason set out on the above-mentioned visit to Tunbridge, he purchased a quantity of goods, which he intended as presents for his friends, especially his mother and sisters; but, on his way thither, he found so many objects of charity, that he gave away not only the goods, but most of his money. On one occasion, he saw a woman who had just lost her husband, and who was very destitute; he gave her fifteen dollars in money, and a full suit of clothes for herself and each of her children, which were six in number.

This was the last interview I ever had with my brother Jason, but, twenty years later, he wrote the following letter to my brother Solomon, and that is about all the intelligence I have ever received from him since I saw him: —

"South Branch of Ormucto, Province of New Brunswick, June 30, 1835.

"My Dear Brother Solomon, — You will, no doubt, be surprised to hear that I am still alive, although in an absence of twenty years I have never written to you before. But I trust you will forgive me when I tell you [53] that, for most of the twenty years, I have been so situated that I have had little or no communication with the lines, and have been holding meetings, day and night, from place to place; besides, my mind has been so taken up with the deplorable situation of the earth, the darkness in which it lies, that, when my labours did call me near the lines, I did not realize the opportunity which presented itself of letting you know where I was. And, again, I have designed visiting you long since, and annually have promised myself that the succeeding year I would certainly seek out my relatives, and enjoy the privilege of one pleasing interview with them before I passed into the valley and shadow of death. But last, though not least, let me not startle you when I say, that, according to my early adopted principles of the power of faith, the Lord has, in his exceeding kindness, bestowed upon me the gift of healing by the prayer of faith, and the use of such simple means as seem congenial to the human system; but my chief reliance is upon him who organized us at the first, and can restore at pleasure that which is disorganized.

"The first of my peculiar success in this way was twelve years since, and from nearly that date I have had little rest. In addition to the incessant calls which I, in a short time had, there was the most overwhelming torrent of opposition poured down upon me that I ever witnessed. But it pleased God to take the weak to confound the wisdom of the wise. I have in the last twelve years seen the greatest manifestations of the power of God in healing the sick, that, with all my sanguinity, I ever hoped or imagined. And when the learned infidel has declared with sober face, time and again, that disease had obtained such an ascendancy that death could be resisted no longer, that the victim must wither beneath his potent arm, I have seen the almost lifeless clay slowly but surely resuscitated, and revive, till the pallid monster fled so far that the patient was left in the full bloom of vigorous health. But it is God that hath done it, and to him let all the praise be given.

"I am now compelled to close this epistle, for I must start immediately on a journey of more than one hundred miles, to attend a heavy case of sickness; so God be with you all. Farewell!

"JASON MACK." [54]

The next intelligence we received concerning Jason, after his letter to brother Solomon, was, that he, his wife, and oldest son, were dead, and this concludes my account of my brother Jason.

CHAPTER 13

THE AUTHOR'S DREAM

WHILE we were living in the town of Tunbridge, my mind became deeply impressed with the subject of religion; which, probably, was occasioned by my singular experience during my sickness at Randolph. I began to attend Methodist meetings, and, to oblige me, my husband accompanied me; but when this came to the ears of his father and oldest brother, they were so displeased, and said so much in regard to the matter, that my husband thought it best to desist. He said that he considered it as hardly worth our while to attend the meetings any longer, as it would prove of but little advantage to us; besides this, it

gave our friends such disagreeable feelings. I was considerably hurt by
this, yet I made no reply. I retired to a grove not far distant, where I
prayed to the Lord in behalf of my husband—that the true Gospel might
be presented to him, and that his heart might be softened so as to receive
it, or, that he might become more religiously inclined. After praying
some time in this manner, I returned to the house, much depressed in
spirit, which state of feeling continued until I retired to my bed. I soon
fell asleep, and had the following dream:—

I thought that I stood in a large and beautiful meadow, which lay a
short distance from the house in which we lived, and that everything
around me wore an aspect of [55] peculiar pleasantness. The first thing
that attracted my special attention in this magnificent meadow, was a
very pure and clear stream of water, which ran through the midst of it;
and as I traced this stream, I discovered two trees standing upon its
margin, both of which were on the same side of the stream. These trees
were very beautiful, they were well proportioned, and towered with
majestic beauty to a great height. Their branches, which added to their
symmetry and glory, commenced near the top, and spread themselves
in luxurious grandeur around. I gazed upon them with wonder and
admiration; and after beholding them a short time, I saw one of them
was surrounded with a bright belt, that shone like burnished gold, but
far more brilliantly. Presently, a gentle breeze passed by, and the tree
encircled with this golden zone, bent gracefully before the wind, and
waved its beautiful branches in the light air. As the wind increased, this
tree assumed the most lively and animated appearance, and seemed to
express in its motions the utmost joy and happiness. If it had been an
intelligent creature, it could not have conveyed, by the power of
language, the idea of joy and gratitude so perfectly as it did; and even
the stream that rolled beneath it, shared, apparently, every sensation felt
by the tree, for, as the branches danced over the stream, it would swell
gently, then recede again with a motion as soft as the breathing of an
infant, but as lively as the dancing of a sunbeam. The belt also partook
of the same influence, and as it moved in unison with the motion of the
stream and of the tree, it increased continually in refulgence and
magnitude, until it became exceedingly glorious.

I turned my eyes upon its fellow, which stood opposite; but it was
not surrounded with the belt of light as the former, and it stood erect
and fixed as a pillar of marble. No matter how strong the wind blew
over it, not a leaf was stirred, not a bough was bent; but obstinately stiff
it stood, scorning alike the zephyr's breath, or the power of the mighty
storm.

I wondered at what I saw, and said in my heart, What can be the
meaning of all this? And the interpretation given me was, that these
personated my husband and his oldest brother, Jesse Smith; that the
stubborn and unyielding tree was like Jesse; that the other, more pliant
and flexible, was like Joseph, my husband; that the breath of heaven,

which passed over them, was the [56] pure and undefiled Gospel of the Son of God, which Gospel Jesse would always resist, but which Joseph, when he was more advanced in life, would hear and receive with his whole heart, and rejoice therein; and unto him would be added intelligence, happiness, glory, and everlasting life.

CHAPTER 14

FIRST VISION OF JOSEPH SMITH, SENIOR—THE BOX—SECOND VISION—THE TREE AND THE SPACIOUS BUILDING

AFTER selling the farm at Tunbridge, we moved only a short distance, to the town of Royalton. Here we resided a few months, then moved again to Sharon, Windsor county, Vermont. In the latter place, my husband rented a farm of my father, which he cultivated in the summer, teaching school in the winter. In this way my husband continued labouring for a few years, during which time our circumstances gradually improved, until we found ourselves quite comfortable again.

In the meantime we had a son, whom we called Joseph, after the name of his father; he was born December 23, 1805. I shall speak of him more particularly by and by.

We moved thence to Tunbridge. Here we had another son, whom we named Samuel Harrison, born March 13, 1808. We lived in this place a short time, then moved to Royalton, where Ephraim was born, March 13, 1810. We continued here until we had another son, born March 13, 1811, whom we called William.

About this time my husband's mind became much excited upon the subject of religion; yet he would not subscribe to any particular system of faith, but [57] contended for the ancient order, as established by our Lord and Saviour Jesus Christ, and his Apostles.

One night my husband retired to his bed, in a very thoughtful state of mind, contemplating the situation of the Christian religion, or the confusion and discord that were extant. He soon fell into a sleep, and before waking had the following vision, which I shall relate in his own words, just as he told it to me the next morning:—

"I seemed to be travelling in an open, barren field, and as I was travelling, I turned my eyes towards the east, the west, the north, and the south, but could see nothing save dead fallen timber. Not a vestige of life, either animal or vegetable, could be seen; besides, to render the scene still more dreary, the most death-like silence prevailed, no sound of anything animate could be heard in all the field. I was alone in this gloomy desert, with the exception of an attendant spirit, who kept constantly by my side. Of him I inquired the meaning of what I saw, and why I was thus travelling in such a dismal place. He answered thus: 'This field is the world, which now lieth inanimate and dumb, in regard to the true religion, or plan of salvation; but travel on, and by the wayside you will find on a certain log a box, the contents of which, if you eat thereof, will make you wise, and give unto you wisdom and understanding.' I carefully observed what was told me by my guide, and proceeding a short distance, I came to the box. I immediately took it up, and placed it under my left arm; then with eagerness I raised the lid, and began to taste of its contents; upon which all manner of beasts, horned cattle, and roaring animals, rose up on every side in the most threatening manner possible, tearing the earth, tossing their horns, and bellowing most terrifically all around me, and they finally came so close upon me, that I was compelled to drop the box, and fly for my life. Yet, in the midst of all this I was perfectly happy, though I awoke trembling."

From this forward, my husband seemed more confirmed than ever, in the opinion that there was no order or class of religionists that knew any more concerning the Kingdom of God, than those of the [58] world, or such as made no profession of religion whatever.

In 1811, we moved from Royalton, Vermont, to the town of Lebanon, New Hampshire. Soon after arriving here, my husband received another very singular vision, which I will relate:—

"I thought," said he, "I was travelling in an open, desolate field, which appeared to be very barren. As I was thus travelling, the thought suddenly came into my mind that I had better stop and reflect upon what I was doing, before I went any further. So I asked myself, 'What motive can I have in travelling here, and what place can this be?' My guide, who was by my side, as before, said, 'This is the desolate world; but travel on.' The road was so broad and barren, that I wondered why I should travel in it; for, said I to myself, 'Broad is the road, and wide is the gate that leads to death, and many there be that walk therein; but narrow is the way, and straight is the gate that leads to everlasting life, and few there be that go in thereat.' Travelling a short distance further, I came to a narrow path. This path I entered, and, when I had travelled a little way in it, I beheld a beautiful stream of water, which ran from the east to the west. Of this stream I could see neither the source nor yet the termination; but as far as my eyes could extend I could see a rope, running along the bank of it, about as high as a man could reach, and beyond me, was a low, but very pleasant, valley, in which stood a tree, such as I, had never seen before. It was exceedingly handsome, insomuch that I looked upon it with wonder and admiration. Its beautiful branches spread themselves somewhat like an umbrella, and it bore a kind of fruit, in shape much like a chestnut bur, and as white as snow, or, if possible, whiter. I gazed upon the same with considerable interest, and as I was doing so, the burs or shells commenced opening and shedding their particles, or the fruit which they contained, which was of dazzling whiteness. I drew near, and began to eat of it, and I found it delicious beyond description. As I was eating, I said in my heart, 'I cannot eat this alone, I must bring my wife and children, that they may partake with me.' Accordingly, I went and brought my family, which consisted of a wife and seven children, and we all commenced eating, and praising God for this blessing. We were exceedingly [59] happy, insomuch that our joy could not easily be expressed. While thus engaged, I beheld a spacious building standing opposite the valley which we were in, and it appeared to reach to the very heavens. It was full of doors and windows, and they were all filled with people, who were very finely dressed. When these people observed us in the low valley, under the tree, they pointed the finger of scorn at us, and treated us with all manner of disrespect and contempt. But their contumely we utterly disregarded. I presently turned to my guide, and inquired of him the meaning of the fruit that was so delicious. He told me it was the pure love of God, shed abroad in the hearts of all those who love him, and keep his commandments. He then commanded me to go and bring the rest of my children. I told him that we were all there. 'No,' he replied, 'look yonder, you have two more, and you must bring them also.' Upon raising my eyes, I saw two small children, standing some distance off. I immediately went to them, and brought them to the tree; upon which they commenced eating with the rest, and we all rejoiced together. The more we eat, the more we seemed to desire, until we even got down upon our knees, and scooped it up, eating it by double handfulls. After feasting in this manner a short time, I asked my guide what was the meaning of the spacious building which I saw. He replied, 'It is Babylon, it is Babylon, and it must fall. The people in the doors and windows are the inhabitants thereof, who scorn and despise the Saints of God, because of their humility.' I soon awoke, clapping my hands together for joy."

———

CHAPTER 15

SICKNESS AT LEBANON—SOPHRONIA'S MIRACULOUS RECOVERY

WE moved, as before-mentioned, to the town of Lebanon, New Hampshire. Here we settled ourselves down, and began to contemplate, with joy and satis[60]faction, the prosperity which had attended our recent exertions; and we doubled our diligence, in order to obtain more of this world's goods, with the view of assisting our children, when they should need it; and, as is quite natural, we looked forward to the decline of life, and were providing for its wants, as well as striving to procure those things which contribute much to the comfort of old age.

As our children had, in a great measure, been debarred from the privilege of schools, we began to make every arrangement to attend to this important duty. We established our second son Hyrum in an academy at Hanover; and the rest, that were of sufficient age, we were sending to a common school that was quite convenient. Meanwhile, myself and companion were doing all that our abilities would admit of for the future welfare and advantage of the family, and were greatly blessed in our labours.

But this state of things did not long continue. The typhus fever came in Lebanon, and raged tremendously. Among the number seized with this complaint were, first, Sophronia; next Hyrum, who was taken while at school, and came home sick; then Alvin; in short, one after another was taken down, till all of the family, with the exception of myself and husband, were prostrated upon a bed of sickness.

Sophronia had a heavy siege. The physician attended upon her eighty-nine days, giving her medicine all the while; but on the ninetieth day, he said she was so far gone, it was not for her to receive any benefit from medicine, and for this cause he discontinued his attendance upon her. The ensuing night, she lay altogether motionless, with her eyes wide open, and with that peculiar aspect which bespeaks the near approach of death. As she thus lay, I gazed upon her as a mother looks upon the last shade of life in a darling child. In this moment of distraction, my husband and myself clasped our hands, fell upon our knees by the bed[61]side, and poured out our grief to God, in prayer and supplication, beseeching him to spare our child yet a little longer.

Did the Lord hear our petition? Yes, he most assuredly did, and before we rose to our feet, he gave us a testimony that she should recover. When we first arose from prayer, our child had, to all appearance, ceased breathing. I caught a blanket, threw it around her, then, taking her in my arms, commenced pacing the floor. Those present remonstrated against my doing as I did, saying, "Mrs. Smith, it is all of no use; you are certainly crazy, your child is dead." Notwithstanding, I would not, for a moment, relinquish the hope of again seeing her breathe and live.

This recital, doubtless, will be uninteresting to some; but those who have experienced in life something of this kind are susceptible of feeling, and can sympathize with me. Are you a mother who has been bereft of a child? Feel for your heart-strings, and then tell me how I felt with my expiring child pressed to my bosom! Would you at this trying moment feel to deny that God had "power to save to the uttermost all who call on Him"! I did not then, neither do I now.

At length she sobbed. I still pressed her to my breast, and continued to walk the floor. She sobbed again, then looked up into my face, and commenced breathing quite freely. My soul was satisfied, but my strength was gone. I laid my daughter on the bed, and sunk by her side, completely overpowered by the intensity of my feelings.

From this time forward Sophronia continued mending, until she entirely recovered. [62]

CHAPTER 16

THE SUFFERINGS OF JOSEPH SMITH, JUNIOR, WITH A FEVER SORE—
EXTRACTION OF LARGE FRAGMENTS OF BONE FROM ONE OF HIS LEGS

JOSEPH, our third son, having recovered from the typhus fever, after something like two weeks' sickness, one day screamed out while sitting in a chair, with a pain in his shoulder, and, in a very short time, he appeared to be in such agony, that we feared the consequence would prove to be something very serious. We immediately sent for a doctor. When he arrived, and had examined the patient, he said that it was his opinion that this pain was occasioned by a sprain. But the child declared this could not be the case, as he had received no injury in any way whatever, but that a severe pain had seized him all at once, of the cause of which he was entirely ignorant.

Notwithstanding the child's protestations, still the physician insisted, that it must be a sprain, and consequently, he anointed his shoulder with some bone linament; but this was of no advantage to him, for the pain continued the same after the anointing as before.

When two weeks of extreme suffering had elapsed, the attendant physician concluded to make closer examination; whereupon he found that a large fever sore had gathered between his breast and shoulder. He immediately lanced it, upon which it discharged fully a quart of matter.

As soon as the sore had discharged itself, the pain left it, and shot like lightning (using his own terms) down his side into the marrow of the bone of his leg, and soon became very severe. My poor boy, at this, was almost in despair, and he, cried out "Oh, father! the pain is so severe, how can I bear it!"

His leg soon began to swell, and he continued to suffer the greatest agony for the space of two weeks longer. During this period, I carried him much of [63] the time in my arms, in order to mitigate his suffering as much as possible; in consequence of which, I was taken very ill myself. The anxiety of mind that I experienced, together with physical overexertion, was too much for my constitution, and my nature sunk under it.

Hyrum, who was rather remarkable for his tenderness and sympathy, now desired that he might take my place. As he was a good, trusty boy, we let him do so; and, in order to make the task as easy for him as possible, we laid Joseph upon a low bed, and Hyrum sat beside him, almost day and night, for some considerable length of time, holding the affected part of his leg in his hands, and pressing it between them, so that his afflicted brother might be enabled to endure the pain, which was so excruciating, that he was scarcely able to bear it.

At the end of three weeks, we thought it advisable to send again for the surgeon. When he came, he made an incision of eight inches, on the front side of the leg, between the knee and ankle. This relieved the pain in a great measure, and the patient was quite comfortable until the wound began to heal, when the pain became as violent as ever.

The surgeon was called again, and he this time enlarged the wound, cutting the leg even to the bone. It commenced healing the second time, and as soon as it began to heal, it also began to swell again, which swelling continued to rise till we deemed it wisdom to call a council of surgeons; and when they met in consultation, they decided that amputation was the only remedy.

Soon after coming to this conclusion, they rode up to the door, and were invited into a room, apart from the one in which Joseph lay. They being seated, I addressed them thus: "Gentlemen, what can you do to save my boy's leg?" They answered, "We can do nothing; we have cut it open to the bone, and find it so affected that we consider his leg incurable, and that amputation is absolutely necessary in order to save his life." **[64]**

This was like a thunder bolt to me. I appealed to the principal surgeon, saying, "Dr. Stone, can you not make another trial? Can you not, by cutting around the bone, take out the diseased part, and perhaps that which is sound will heal over, and by this means you will save his leg? You will not, you must not, take off his leg, until you try once more. I will not consent to let you enter his room until you make me this promise."

After consulting a short time with each other, they agreed to do as I had requested, then went to see my suffering son. One of the doctors, on approaching his bed, said, "My poor boy, we have come again." "Yes," said Joseph, "I see you have; but you have not come to take off my leg, have you, sir?" "No," replied the surgeon, "it is your mother's request that we make one more effort, and that is what we have now come for."

The principal surgeon, after a moment's conversation, ordered cords to be brought to bind Joseph fast to a bedstead; but to this Joseph objected. The doctor, however, insisted that he must be confined, upon which Joseph said very decidedly, "No, doctor, I will not be bound, for I can bear the operation much better if I have my liberty." "Then," said Dr. Stone, "will you drink some brandy?"

"No," said Joseph, "not one drop."

"Will you take some wine?" rejoined the doctor. "You must take something, or you can never endure the severe operation to which you must be subjected."

"No," exclaimed Joseph, "I will not touch one particle of liquor, neither will I be tied down; but I will tell you what I will do—I will have my father sit on the bed and hold me in his arms, and then I will do whatever is necessary in order to have the bone taken out." Looking at me, he said, "Mother, I want you to leave the room, for I know you cannot bear to see me suffer so; father can stand it, but you have carried me so much, and watched over me so long, you are almost worn out." Then looking up [65] into my face, his eyes swimming in tears, he continued, "Now, mother, promise me that you will not stay, will you? The Lord will help me, and I shall get through with it."

To this request I consented, and getting a number of folded sheets, and laying them under his leg, I retired, going several hundred yards from the house in order to be out of hearing.

The surgeons commenced operating by boring into the bone of his leg, first on one side of the bone where it was affected, then on the other side, after which they broke it off with a pair of forceps or pincers. They thus took away large pieces of the bone. When they broke off the first piece, Joseph screamed out so loudly, that I could not forbear running to him. On my entering his room, he cried out, "Oh, mother, go back, go back; I do not want you to come in—I will try to tough it out, if you will go away."

When the third piece was taken away, I burst into the room again—and oh, my God! what a spectacle for a mother's eye! The wound torn open, the blood still gushing from it, and the bed literally covered with blood. Joseph was as pale as a corpse, and large drops of sweat were rolling down his face, whilst upon every feature was depicted the utmost agony!

I was immediately forced from the room, and detained until the operation was completed; but when the act was accomplished, Joseph put upon a clean bed, the room cleared of every appearance of blood, and the instruments which were used in the operation removed, I was permitted again to enter.

Joseph immediately commenced getting better, and from this onward, continued to mend until he became strong and healthy. When he had so far recovered as to be able to travel, he went with his uncle,

Jesse Smith, to Salem, for the benefit of his health, hoping the sea-breezes would be of service to him, and in this he was not disappointed.

Having passed through about a year of sickness **[66]** and distress, health again returned to our family, and we most assuredly realized the blessing; and indeed, we felt to acknowledge the hand of God, more in preserving our lives through such a tremendous scene of affliction, than if we had, during this time, seen nothing but health and prosperity.

CHAPTER 17

JOSEPH SMITH, SENIOR, REMOVES TO NORWICH, THENCE TO PALMYRA—HIS DREAM OF THE IMAGES—OF THE JUDGMENT

WHEN health returned to us, as one would naturally suppose, it found us in quite low circumstances. We were compelled to strain every energy to provide for our present necessities, instead of making arrangements for the future, as we had previously contemplated.

Shortly after sickness left our family, we moved to Norwich, in the state of Vermont. In this place we established ourselves on a farm belonging to one Esquire Moredock. The first year our crops failed; yet, by selling fruit which grew on the place, we succeeded in obtaining bread for the family, and by making considerable exertion, we were enabled to sustain ourselves.

The crops the second year were as the year before—a perfect failure. Mr. Smith now determined to plant once more, and if he should meet with no better success than he had the two preceding years, he would then go to the state of New York, where wheat was raised in abundance.

The next year an untimely frost destroyed the crops, and being the third year in succession in which the crops had failed, it almost caused a famine. This was enough; my husband was now altogether decided upon going to New York. He **[67]** came in, one day, in quite a thoughtful mood, and sat down; after meditating some time, he observed that, could he so arrange his affairs, he would be glad to start soon for New York with a Mr. Howard, who was going to Palmyra. He further remarked, that he could not leave consistently, as the situation of the family would not admit of his absence; besides, he was owing some money that must first be paid.

I told him it was my opinion he might get both his creditors and debtors together, and arrange matters between them in such a way as to give satisfaction to all parties concerned; and, in relation to the family, I thought I could make every necessary preparation to follow as soon as he would be ready for us. He accordingly called upon all with whom he had any dealings, and settled up his accounts with them. There were, however, some who, in the time of settlement, neglected to bring forward their books, consequently they were not balanced, or there were no entries made in them to show the settlement; but in cases of this kind, he called witnesses, that there might be evidence of the fact.

Having thus arranged his business, Mr. Smith set out for Palmyra, in company with Mr. Howard. After his departure, I and those of the family who were of much size, toiled faithfully, until we considered ourselves fully prepared to leave at a moment's warning. We shortly received a communication from Mr. Smith, requesting us to make ourselves ready to take up a journey for Palmyra. In a short time after this, a team came for us. As we were about starting on this journey, several of those gentlemen who had withheld their books in the time of settlement now brought them forth, and claimed the accounts which had been settled, and which they had, in the presence of witnesses, agreed to erase. We were all ready for the journey, and the teams were waiting on expense. Under these circumstances I concluded it would be more to our advantage to pay their unjust claims than to hazard a lawsuit. Therefore, by making considerable [68] exertion, I raised the required sum, which was one hundred and fifty dollars, and liquidated the demand.

A gentleman by the name of Flog, a wealthy settler, living in the town of Hanover, also a Mr. Howard, who resided in Norwich, were both acquainted with the circumstance mentioned above. They were very indignant at it, and requested me to give them a sufficient time to get the witnesses together, and they would endeavour to recover that which had been taken from me by fraud. I told them I could not do so, for my husband had sent teams for me, which were on expense; moreover, there was an uncertainty in getting the money back again, and in case of failure, I should not be able to raise the means necessary to take the family where we contemplated moving.

They then proposed raising some money by subscription, saying, "We know the people feel as we do concerning this matter, and if you will receive it we will make you a handsome present." This I utterly refused. The idea of receiving assistance in such a way as this was indeed very repulsive to my feelings, and I rejected their offer.

My aged mother, who had lived with us some time, assisted in preparing for the journey. She came with us to Royalton, where she resided until she died, which was two years afterwards, in consequence of an injury which she received by getting upset in a waggon while travelling with us.

On arriving at Royalton I had a scene to pass through, and it was truly a severe one—one to which I shall ever look back with peculiar feelings. Here I was to take leave of my affectionate mother. The parting hour came; my mother wept over me, long and bitterly. She told me that it was not probable she should ever behold my face again; "But, my dear child," said she, "I have lived long—my days are nearly numbered—I must soon exchange the things of this world for those which pertain to another state of existence, where I hope to [69] enjoy the society of the blessed; and now, as my last admonition, I beseech you to continue faithful in the service of God to the end of your days, that I may have the pleasure of embracing you in another and fairer world above."

This parting scene was at one Willard Pierce's, a tavern keeper. From his house my mother went to Daniel Mack's, with whom she afterwards lived until her decease.

Having travelled a short distance, I discovered that Mr. Howard, our teamster, was an unprincipled and unfeeling wretch, by the way in which he handled both our goods and money, as well as by his treatment of my children, especially Joseph. He would compel him to travel miles at a time on foot, notwithstanding he was still lame. We bore patiently with his abuse, until we got about twenty miles west of Utica, when one morning, as we were getting ready to continue our journey, my oldest son came to me and said, "Mother, Mr. Howard has thrown the goods out of the waggon, and is about starting off with the team." Upon hearing this, I told him to call the man in. I met him in the bar-room, in the presence of a large company of travellers, both male and female, and I demanded his reason for the course which he was taking. He told me the money which I had given him was all expended, and he could go no further.

I then turned to those present and said, "Gentlemen and ladies, please give your attention for a moment. Now, as sure as there is a God in heaven, that team, as well as the goods, belong to my husband, and this man intends to take them from me, or at least the team, leaving me with eight children, without the means of proceeding on my journey." Then turning to Mr. Howard, I said, "Sir, I now forbid you touching the team, or driving it one step further. You can go about your own business; I have no use for you. I shall take charge of the team myself, and hereafter attend to my own affairs." I accordingly did so, and, proceeding on our journey, [70] we in a short time arrived at Palmyra, with a small portion of our effects, and barely two cents in cash.

When I again met my husband at Palmyra, we were much reduced—not from indolence, but on account of many reverses of fortune, with which our lives had been rather singularly marked.

Notwithstanding our misfortunes, and the embarassments with which we were surrounded, I was quite happy in once more having the society of my husband, and in throwing myself and children upon the care and affection of a tender companion and father.

We all now sat down, and counselled together relative to the course which was best for us to adopt in our destitute circumstances, and we came to the conclusion to unite our strength in endeavouring to obtain a piece of land. Having done considerable at painting oil-cloth coverings for tables, stands, &c., I set up the business, and did extremely well. I furnished all the provisions for the family, and, besides this, began to replenish our household furniture, in a very short time, by my own exertions.

My husband and his sons, Alvin and Hyrum, set themselves to work to pay for one hundred acres of land, which Mr. Smith contracted for with a land agent. In a year, we made nearly all of the first payment, erected a log house, and commenced clearing. I believe something like thirty acres of land were got ready for cultivation the first year.

I shall now deviate a little from my subject, in order to relate another very singular dream which my husband had about this time, being as follows: —

"I dreamed," said he, "that I was travelling on foot, and I was very sick, and so lame I could hardly walk. My guide, as usual, attended me. Travelling some time together, I became so lame that I thought I could go no further. I informed my guide of this, and asked him what I should do. He told me to travel on till I came to a certain garden. So I arose and started for this garden. While on my way thither, I asked my guide how I should know the place. He said, 'Proceed until you come to a [71] very large gate; open this, and you will see a garden, blooming with the most beautiful flowers that your eyes ever beheld, and there you shall be healed. By limping along with great difficulty, I finally reached the gate; and, on entering it, I saw the before-mentioned garden, which was beautiful beyond description, being filled with the most delicate flowers of every kind and colour. In the garden were walks about three and a half feet wide, which were set on both sides with marble stones. One of the walks ran from the gate through the centre of the garden; and on each side of this was a very richly-carved seat, and on each seat were placed six wooden images, each of which was the size of a very large man. When I came to the first image on the right side, it arose and bowed to me with much deference. I then turned to the one which sat opposite me, on the left side, and it arose and bowed to me in the same manner as the first. I continued turning, first to the right and then to the left, until the whole twelve had made their obeisance, after which I was entirely healed. I then asked my guide the meaning of all this, but I awoke before I received an answer."

I will now return to the subject of the farm. When the time for making the second payment drew nigh, Alvin went from home to get work, in order to raise the money, and after much hardship and fatigue, returned with the required amount. This payment being made, we felt relieved, as this was the only thing that troubled us; for we had a snug log-house, neatly furnished, and the means of living comfortably. It was now only two years since we entered Palmyra, almost destitute of money, property, or acquaintance. The hand of friendship was extended on every side, and we blessed God, with our whole heart, for his "mercy, which endureth for ever." And not only temporal blessings were bestowed upon us, but also spiritual were administered. The Scripture, which saith, "Your old men shall dream dreams," was fulfilled in the case of my husband, for, about this time, he had another vision, which I shall here relate; this, with one more, is all of his that I shall obtrude upon [72] the attention of my readers. He received two more visions, which would probably be somewhat interesting, but I cannot remember them distinctly enough to rehearse them in full. The following, which was the sixth, ran thus: —

"I thought I was walking alone; I was much fatigued, nevertheless I, continued travelling. It seemed to me that I was going to meeting, that it was the day of judgment, and that I was going to be judged.

"When I came in sight of the meeting-house, I saw multitudes of people coming from every direction, and pressing with great anxiety towards the door of this great building; but I thought I should get there in time, hence there was no need of being in a hurry. But, on arriving at the door, I found it shut; I knocked for admission, and was informed by the porter that I had come too late. I felt exceedingly troubled, and prayed earnestly for admittance. Presently I found that my flesh was perishing. I continued to pray, still my flesh withered upon my bones. I was almost in a state of total despair, when the porter asked me if I had done all that was necessary in order to receive admission. I replied, that I had done all that was in my power to do. 'Then,' observed the porter, 'justice must be satisfied; after this, mercy hath her claims.'

"It then occurred to me to call upon God, in the name of his son Jesus; and I cried out, in the agony of my soul, 'Oh, Lord God, I beseech thee, in the name of Jesus Christ, to forgive my sins.' After which I felt considerably strengthened, and I began to amend. The porter or angel then remarked, that it was necessary to plead the merits of Jesus, for he was the advocate with the Father, and a mediator between God and man.

"I was now made quite whole, and the door was opened, but, on entering, I awoke."

The following spring we commenced making preparations for building another house, one that would be more comfortable for persons in advanced life. **[73]**

CHAPTER 18

HISTORY OF JOSEPH THE PROPHET COMMENCES—SEVENTH VISION OF JOSEPH SMITH, SENIOR

I NOW come to the history of Joseph. By reference to the table (chap, 9.), you will find the date and place of his birth; beside which, except what has already been said, I shall say nothing respecting him until he arrived at the age of fourteen. However, in this I am aware that some of my readers will be disappointed, for I suppose, from questions which are frequently asked me, that it is thought by some that I shall be likely to tell many very remarkable incidents which attended his childhood; but, as nothing occurred during his early life, except those trivial circumstances which are common to that state of human existence, I pass them in silence.

At the age of fourteen, an incident occurred which alarmed us much, as we knew not the cause of it. Joseph being a remarkably quiet, well disposed child, we did not suspect that any one had aught against him. He was out one evening on an errand, and, on returning home, as he was passing through the door yard, a gun was fired across his pathway, with the evident intention of shooting him. He sprang to the door much frightened. We immediately went in search of the assassin, but could find no trace of him that evening. The next morning we found his tracks under a waggon, where he lay when he fired; and the following day we found the balls, which were discharged from the gun, lodged in the head and neck of a cow that was standing opposite the waggon, in a dark corner. We have not as yet discovered the man who made this attempt at murder, neither can we discover the cause thereof.

I shall here insert the seventh and last vision that **[74]** my husband had, which vision was received in the year 1819. It was as follows:—

> "I dreamed," said he, "that a man with a pedlar's budget on his back, came in, and thus addressed me: 'Sir, will you trade with me to-day? I have now called upon you seven times, I have traded with you each time, and have always found you strictly honest in all your dealings. Your measures are always heaped, and your weights overbalance; and I have now come to tell you that this is the last time I shall ever call on you, and that there is but one thing which you lack, in order to secure your salvation.' As I earnestly desired to know what it was that I still lacked, I requested him to write the same upon paper. He said he would do so. I then sprang to get some paper, but, in my excitement, I awoke."

Shortly after my husband received the foregoing vision, there was a great revival in religion, which extended to all the denominations of Christians in the surrounding country in which we resided. Many of the world's people, becoming concerned about the salvation of their souls, came forward and presented themselves as seekers after religion. Most of them were desirous of uniting with some church, but were not decided as to the particular faith which they would adopt. When the numerous meetings were about breaking up, and the candidates and the various leading church members began to consult upon the subject of adopting the candidates into some church or churches, as the case might be, a dispute arose, and there was a great contention among them.

While these things were going forward, Joseph's mind became considerably troubled with regard to religion; and the following extract from his history will show, more clearly than I can express, the state of his feelings, and the result of his reflections on this occasion:—

"I was at this time in my fifteenth year. My father's family was proselyted to the Presbyterian faith, and four of them joined that church, namely, my mother Lucy, my brothers Hyrum and Samuel Harrison, and my sister Sophronia. [75]

"During this time of great excitement my mind was called up to serious reflection and great uneasiness; but though my feelings were deep, and often pungent, still I kept myself aloof from all those parties, though I attended their several meetings as often as occasion would permit. But in process of time my mind became somewhat partial to the Methodist sect, and I felt some desire to be united with them, but so great was the confusion and strife among the different denominations, that it was impossible for a person, young as I was, and so unacquainted with men and things, to come to any certain conclusion who was right and who was wrong. My mind at different times was greatly excited, the cry and tumult were so great and incessant. The Presbyterians were most decided against the Baptists and Methodists, and used all their powers of either reason or sophistry to prove their errors, or at least to make the people think they were in error. On the other hand, the Baptists and Methodists, in their turn, were equally zealous to establish their own tenets and disprove all others.

"In the midst of this war of words, and tumult of opinions, I often said to myself, What is to be done? Who, of all these parties, are right? or, are they all wrong together? If any one of them be right, which is it? and how shall I know it?

"While I was labouring under the extreme difficulties caused by the contests of these parties of religionists, I was one day reading the epistle of James, first chapter and fifth verse, which reads, 'If any of you lack wisdom, let him ask of God, that giveth unto all men liberally, and upbraideth not, and it shall be given him.' Never did any passage of Scripture come with more power to the heart of man than this did at this time to mine. It seemed to enter with great force into every feeling of my heart. I reflected on it again and again, knowing that if any person needed wisdom from God, I did, for how to act I did not know, and, unless I could get more wisdom than I then had, would never know; for the teachers of religion of the different sects understood the same passage so differently, as to destroy all confidence in settling the question by an appeal to the Bible. At length I came to the conclusion, that I must either remain in darkness and confusion, or else I must do as James directs, that is, ask of God. I at length came to the determination to ask [76] of God, concluding that if he gave wisdom to them that lacked wisdom, and would give liberally, and not upbraid, I might venture. So, in accordance with this my determination to ask of God, I retired to the woods to make the attempt. It was on the morning of a beautiful clear day, early in the spring of 1820. It was the first time in my life that I had made such an attempt; for amidst all my anxieties I had never as yet made the attempt to pray vocally. After I had retired into the place where I had previously designed to go, having looked around me, and finding myself alone, I kneeled down and began to offer up the desires of my heart to God. I had scarcely done so, when immediately I was seized upon by some power which entirely overcame me, and had such astonishing influence over me as to bind my tongue, so that I could not speak. Thick darkness gathered around me, and it seemed to me for a time as if I were doomed to sudden destruction. But exerting all my powers to call upon God, to deliver me out of the power of this enemy which had seized upon me, and at the very moment when I was ready to sink into despair, and abandon myself to destruction—not to an imaginary ruin, but to the power of some actual being from the unseen world, who had such a marvellous power as I had never before felt in any being; just at this moment of great alarm, I saw a pillar of light exactly over my head, above the brightness of the sun, which descended gradually until it fell upon me. It no sooner appeared, than I found myself delivered from the enemy which held me bound. When the light rested upon me, I saw two personages, whose brightness and glory defy all description, standing above me in the air. One of them spake unto me, calling me by name, and said, pointing to the other, 'This is my beloved Son; hear him!'

"My object in going to enquire of the Lord, was to know which of all these sects was right, that I might know which to join. No sooner, therefore, did I get possession of myself, so as to be able to speak, than I asked the personages who stood above me in the light, which of all the sects was right—for at this time it had never entered into my heart that all were wrong—and which I should join. I was answered that I should join none of them, for they were all wrong; and the personage who addressed me said that all their creeds were an abomination in his sight; that those professors were all corrupt. [77] 'They draw near me with their lips, but their hearts are far from me; they teach for doctrine the commandments of men, having a form of godliness, but they deny the power thereof.' He again forbade me to join any of them; and many other things did he say unto me which I cannot write at this time. When I came to myself again, I found myself lying on my back, looking up into heaven. Some few days after I had this vision, I happened to be in company with one of the Methodist preachers who was very active in the before-mentioned religious excitement, and conversing with him upon the subject of religion, I took occasion to give him an account of the vision which I had had. I was greatly surprised at his behaviour: he treated my communication not only lightly, but with great contempt, saying it was all of the devil; that there was no such thing as visions or revelations in these days; that all such things had ceased with the Apostles, and that there never would be any more of them. I soon found, however, that my telling the story had excited a great deal of prejudice against me among professors of religion, and was the cause of great persecution, which continued to increase; and though I was an obscure boy, only between fourteen and fifteen years of age, and my circumstances in life such as to make a boy of no consequence in the world, yet men of high standing would take notice sufficient to excite the public mind against me and create a hot persecution; and this was common among all the sects—all united to persecute me. It has often caused me serious reflection, both then and since, how very strange it was that an obscure boy, of a little over fourteen years of age—and one, too, who was doomed to the necessity of obtaining a scanty maintenance by his daily labour, should be thought a character of sufficient importance to attract the attention of the great ones of the most popular sects of the day, so as to create in them a spirit of the hottest persecution and reviling. But strange or not, so it was, and was often cause of great sorrow to myself. However, it was, nevertheless, a fact that I had had a vision. I have thought since, that I felt much like Paul when he made his defence before King Agrippa, and related the account of the vision he had when he 'saw a light and heard a voice;' but still there were but few who believed him. Some said he was dishonest, others said he was mad, and he was ridiculed and reviled; but all this did [78] not destroy the reality of his vision. He had seen a vision—he knew he had—and all the persecution under heaven could not make it otherwise; and though they should persecute him unto death, yet he knew, and would know unto his latest breath, that he had both seen a light and heard a voice speaking to him, and all the world could not make him think or believe otherwise. So it was with me. I had actually seen a light, and in the midst of that light I saw two personages, and they did in reality speak unto me, or one of them did; and though I was hated and persecuted for saying that I had seen a vision, yet it was true; and while they were persecuting me, reviling me, and speaking all manner of evil against me falsely, for so saying, I was led to say in my heart, Why persecute for telling the truth? I have actually seen a vision; and who am I that I can withstand God? or why does the world think to make me deny what I have actually seen? for I had seen a vision. I knew it, and I knew that

God knew it; and I could not deny it, neither dare I do it—at least, I knew that by so doing I would offend God, and come under condemnation." — *Times and Seasons*, vol. 3, p. 727. *Supp.* to *Mil. Star*, vol. 14, p. 2.

From this time until the twenty-first of September, 1823, Joseph continued, as usual, to labour with his father, and nothing during this interval occurred of very great importance—though he suffered, as one would naturally suppose, every kind of opposition and persecution from the different orders of religionists.

On the evening of the twenty-first of September, he retired to his bed in quite a serious and contemplative state of mind. He shortly betook himself to prayer and supplication to Almighty God, for a manifestation of his standing before him, and while thus engaged he received the following vision:—

"While I was thus in the act of calling upon God, I discovered a light appearing in the room, which continued to increase until the room was lighter than at noon-day, when immediately a personage appeared at my bed-side, standing in the air, for his feet did not touch the floor. He had on a loose robe of most exquisite whiteness. It was a whiteness beyond anything earthly I had ever seen, nor do I believe that any earthly thing could be made to appear so exceedingly white and brilliant. His hands were naked, and his arms also, a little above the wrist; [79] so also were his feet naked, as were his legs a little above the ankles. His head and neck were also bare. I could discover that he had no other clothing on but this robe, as it was open, so that I could see into his bosom. Not only was his robe exceedingly white, but his whole person was glorious beyond description, and his countenance truly like lightning. The room was exceedingly light, but not so very bright as immediately around his person When I first looked upon him I was afraid, but the fear soon left me. He called me by name, and said unto me that he was a messenger sent from the presence of God to me, and that his name was Nephi;[1] that God had a work for me to do, and that my name should be had for good and evil among all nations, kindreds, and tongues; or that it should be both good and evil spoken of among all people. He said there was a book deposited, written upon gold plates, giving an account of the former inhabitants of this continent, and the source from whence they sprang. He also said that the fulness of the everlasting Gospel was contained in it, as delivered by the Saviour to the ancient inhabitants. Also, that there were two stones in silver bows, and these stones fastened to a breastplate, constituted what is called the Urim and Thummim, deposited with the plates; and the possession and use of these stones were what constituted Seers in ancient or former

---

[1] Moroni, see *Doc. & Cov.* sec. 50, par. 2; *Elders' Journal*, vol. 1, pp. 28 and 129; *History of Joseph Smith* under year 1838; *Deseret News*, No. 10, vol. 3.—Orson Pratt.

times; and that God had prepared them for the purpose of translating the book. After telling me these things, he commenced quoting the prophecies of the Old Testament. He first quoted part of the third chapter of Malachi; and he quoted also the fourth or last chapter of the same prophecy, though with a little variation from the way it reads in our Bible. Instead of quoting the first verse as it reads in our books, he quoted it thus: 'For behold the day cometh that shall burn as an oven; and all the proud, yea, and all that do wickedly, shall burn as stubble, for they that come shall burn them, saith the Lord of Hosts, that it shall leave them neither root nor branch.' And again he quoted the fifth verse thus: 'Behold, I will reveal unto you the Priesthood by the hand of Elijah the prophet, before the coming of the great and dreadful day of the Lord.' He also quoted the next verse differently: [80] 'And he shall plant in the hearts of the children the promises made to the fathers, and the hearts of the children shall turn to their fathers; if it were not so, the whole earth would be utterly wasted at its coming.' In addition to these, he quoted the eleventh chapter of Isaiah, saying that it was about to be fulfilled. He quoted also the third chapter of Acts, twenty-second and twenty-third verses, precisely as they stand in our New Testament. He said that that Prophet was Christ, but the day had not yet come 'when they who would not hear his voice should be cut off from among the people,' but soon would come. He also quoted the second chapter of Joel, from the twenty-eighth verse to the last. He also said that this was not yet fulfilled, but was soon to be. And he further stated the fulness of the Gentiles was soon to come in. He quoted many other passages of Scripture, and offered many explanations which cannot be mentioned here. Again, he told me that when I got those plates of which he had spoken, (for the time that they should be obtained was not then fulfilled,) I should not show them to any person, neither the breast-plate, with the Urim and Thummim, only to those to whom I should be commanded to show them: if I did I should be destroyed. While he was conversing with me about the plates, the vision was opened to my mind that I could see the place where the plates were deposited, and that so clearly and distinctly, that I knew the place again when I visited it.

"After this communication, I saw the light in the room begin to gather immediately around the person of him who had been speaking to me, and it continued to do so until the room was again left dark, except just around him; when instantly I saw, as it were, a conduit open right up into heaven, and he ascended up till he entirely disappeared, and the room was left as it had been before this heavenly light made its appearance.

"I lay musing on the singularity of the scene, and marvelling greatly at what had been told me by this extraordinary messenger, when, in the midst of my meditation, I suddenly discovered that my room was again beginning to get lighted, and, in an instant, as it were, the same heavenly messenger was again by my bed-side. He commenced, and again related the very same things which he had done at his first visit, without the least variation, which having done, he informed me of great [81] judgments which were coming upon the earth, with great desolations by famine, sword, and pestilence: and that these grievous judgments would come on the earth in this generation. Having related these things, he again ascended as he had done before." — *Times and Seasons,* vol. 3, p. 729. *Supp. to Mil. Star,* vol. 14, p. 4.

When the angel ascended the second time, he left Joseph overwhelmed with astonishment, yet gave him but a short time to contemplate the things which he had told him before he made his reappearance, and rehearsed the same things over, adding a few words of caution and instruction, thus: that he must beware of covetousness, and he must not suppose the Record was to be brought forth with the view of getting gain, for this was not the case, but that it was to bring forth light and intelligence, which had for a long time been lost to the world; and that when he went to get the plates, he must be on his guard, or his mind would be filled with darkness. The angel then told him to tell his father all which he had both seen and heard.

CHAPTER 19

THE ANGEL VISITS JOSEPH AGAIN—JOSEPH TELLS HIS FATHER WHAT HE HAS SEEN AND HEARD—HE IS PERMITTED TO BEHOLD THE PLATES—RECEIVES FURTHER INSTRUCTIONS—COMMUNICATES THE SAME TO THE FAMILY—TAKES THE PLATES INTO HIS HANDS—THEY ARE TAKEN FROM HIM, AND HE IS REPROVED—HIS DISAPPOINTMENT

THE next day, my husband, Alvin, and Joseph, were reaping together in the field, and as they were reaping Joseph stopped quite suddenly, and seemed to be in a very deep study. Alvin, observing it, hurried him, saying, "We must not slacken our hands or we will not be able to complete our task." Upon this Joseph went to work again, and after labouring a short time, he stopped just as he had done before. This being quite unusual and strange, it attracted the attention of his father, upon which he dis[82]covered that Joseph was very pale. My husband, supposing that he was sick, told him to go to the house, and have his mother doctor him. He accordingly ceased his work, and started, but on coming to a beautiful green, under an apple-tree, he stopped and lay down, for he was so weak he could proceed no further. He was here but a short time, when the messenger whom he saw the previous night, visited him again, and the first thing he said was, "Why did you not tell your father that which I commanded you to tell him?" Joseph replied, "I was afraid my father would not believe me." The angel rejoined, "He will believe every word you say to him."

Joseph then promised the angel that he would do as he had been commanded. Upon this, the messenger departed, and Joseph returned to the field, where he had left my husband and Alvin; but when he got there, his father had just gone to the house, as he was somewhat unwell. Joseph then desired Alvin to go straightway and see his father, and inform him that he had something of great importance to communicate to him, and that he wanted him to come out into the field where they were at work. Alvin did as he was requested, and when my husband got there, Joseph related to him all that had passed between him and the angel the previous night and that morning. Having heard this account, his father charged him not to fail in attending strictly to the instruction which he had received from this heavenly messenger.

Soon after Joseph had this conversation with his father, he repaired to the place where the plates were deposited, which place he describes as follows:—

> "Convenient to the village of Manchester, Ontario co., New York, stands a hill of considerable size, and the most elevated of any in the neighbourhood. On the west side of this hill, not far from the top, under a stone of considerable size, lay the plates, deposited in a stone box. This stone was thick and rounding in the middle, on the upper side, and thinner towards the edges, so that the [83] middle part of it was visible above the ground; but the edges all round were covered with earth.
>
> "Having removed the earth, and obtained a lever, which I got fixed under the edge of the stone, with a little exertion I raised it up. I looked, and there, indeed, did I behold the plates! the Urim and Thummim, and the breast-plate, as stated by the messenger." —(*Times and Seasons*, vol. 3, p. 729. *Supp. to Mil. Star*, vol. 14, p. 6.)

While Joseph remained here, the angel showed him, by contrast, the difference between good and evil, and likewise the consequences of both obedience and disobedience to the commandments of God, in such a striking manner, that the impression was always vivid in his memory until the very end of his days; and in giving a relation of this circumstance, not long prior to his death, he remarked, that "ever afterwards he was willing to keep the commandments of God."

Furthermore, the angel told him, at the interview mentioned last, that the time had not yet come for the plates to be brought forth to the world; that he could not take them from the place wherein they were deposited until he had learned to keep the commandments of God—not only till he was willing, but able, to do it. The angel bade Joseph come to this place every year, at the same time of the year, and he would meet him there and give him further instructions.

The ensuing evening, when the family were all together, Joseph made known to them all that he had communicated to his father in the field, and also of his finding the Record, as well as what passed between him and the angel while he was at the place where the plates were deposited.

Sitting up late that evening, in order to converse upon these things, together with over-exertion of mind, had much fatigued Joseph; and when Alvin observed it, he said, "Now, brother, let us go to bed, and rise early in the morning, in order to finish our day's work at an hour before sunset, then, if mother will get our suppers early, we will have a fine long evening, and we will all sit down for the [84] purpose of listening to you while you tell us the great things which God has revealed to you."

Accordingly, by sunset the next day we were all seated, and Joseph commenced telling us the great and glorious things which God had manifested to him; but, before proceeding, he charged us not to mention out of the family that which he was about to say to us, as the world was so wicked that when they came to a knowledge of these things they would try to take our lives; and that when we should obtain the plates, our names would be cast out as evil by all people. Hence the necessity of suppressing these things as much as possible, until the time should come for them to go forth to the world.

After giving us this charge, he proceeded to relate further particulars concerning the work which he was appointed to do, and we received them joyfully, never mentioning them except among ourselves, agreeable to the instructions which we had received from him.

From this time forth, Joseph continued to receive instructions from the Lord, and we continued to get the children together every evening, for the purpose of listening while he gave us a relation of the same. I presume our family presented an aspect as singular as any that ever lived upon the face of the earth—all seated in a circle, father, mother, sons, and daughters, and giving the most profound attention to a boy, eighteen years of age, who had never read the Bible through in his life: he seemed much less inclined to the perusal of books than any of the rest of our children, but far more given to meditation and deep study.

We were now confirmed in the opinion that God was about to bring to light something upon which we could stay our minds, or that would give us a more perfect knowledge of the plan of salvation and the redemption of the human family. This caused us greatly to rejoice, the sweetest union and happiness pervaded our house, and tranquillity reigned in our midst. [85]

During our evening conversations, Joseph would occasionally give us some of the most amusing recitals that could be imagined. He would describe the ancient inhabitants of this continent, their dress, mode of travelling, and the animals upon which they rode; their cities, their buildings, with every particular; their mode of warfare; and also their religious worship. This he would do with as much ease, seemingly, as if he had spent his whole life with them.

On the twenty-second of September, 1824, Joseph again visited the place where he found the plates the year previous; and supposing at this time that the only thing required, in order to possess them until the time for their translation, was to be able to keep the commandments of God — and he firmly believed he could keep every commandment which had been given him — he fully expected to carry them home with him. Therefore, having arrived at the place, and uncovering the plates, he put forth his hand and took them up, but, as he was taking them hence, the unhappy thought darted through his mind that probably there was something else in the box besides the plates, which would be of some pecuniary advantage to him. So, in the moment of excitement, he laid them down very carefully, for the purpose of covering the box, lest some one might happen to pass that way and get whatever there might be remaining in it. After covering it, he turned round to take the Record again, but behold it was gone, and where he knew not, neither did he know the means by which it had been taken from him.

At this, as a natural consequence, he was much alarmed. He kneeled down and asked the Lord why the Record had been taken from him; upon which the angel of the Lord appeared to him, and told him that he had not done as he had been commanded, for in a former revelation he had been commanded not to lay the plates down, or put them for a moment out of his hands, until he got into the house and deposited them in a chest or trunk, hav[86]ing a good lock and key, and, contrary to this, he had laid them down with the view of securing some fancied or imaginary treasure that remained.

In the moment of excitement, Joseph was overcome by the powers of darkness, and forgot the injunction that was laid upon him.

Having some further conversation with the angel on this occasion, Joseph was permitted to raise the stone again, when he beheld the plates as he had done before. He immediately reached forth his hand to take them, but instead of getting them, as he anticipated, he was hurled back upon the ground with great violence. When he recovered, the angel was gone, and he arose and returned to the house, weeping for grief and disappointment.

As he was aware that we would expect him to bring the plates home with him, he was greatly troubled, fearing that we might doubt his having seen them. As soon as he entered the house, my husband asked him if he had obtained the plates. The answer was, "No, father, I could not get them."

His father then said, "Did you see them?"

"Yes," replied Joseph, "I saw them, but could not take them."

"I would have taken them," rejoined his father, with much earnestness, "if I had been in your place."

"Why," returned Joseph, in quite a subdued tone, "you do not know what you say. I could not get them, for the angel of the Lord would not let me."

Joseph then related the circumstance in full, which gave us much uneasiness, as we were afraid that he might utterly fail of obtaining the Record through some neglect on his part. We, therefore, doubled our diligence in prayer and supplication to God, in order that he might be more fully instructed in his duty, and be preserved from all the wiles and machinations of him "who lieth in wait to deceive."

We were still making arrangements to build us a comfortable house, the management and control of which devolved chiefly upon Alvin. And when [87] Nov. 1822 arrived, the frame was raised, and all the materials necessary for its speedy completion were procured. This opened to Alvin's mind the pleasing prospect of seeing his father and mother once more comfortable and happy. He would say, "I am going to have a nice pleasant room for father and mother to sit in, and everything arranged for their comfort, and they shall not work any more as they have done."

CHAPTER 20

ALVIN'S SICKNESS AND DEATH

ON the fifteenth of Nov. 1824, about ten o'clock in the morning, Alvin was taken very sick with the bilious colic. He came to the house in much distress, and requested his father to go immediately for a physician. He accordingly went, and got one by the name of Greenwood, who, on arriving, immediately administered to the patient a heavy dose of calomel. I will here notice, that this Dr. Greenwood was not the physician commonly employed by the family; he was brought in consequence of the family physician's absence. And on this account, as I suppose, Alvin at first refused to take the medicine, but by much persuasion he was prevailed on to do so.

This dose of calomel lodged in his stomach, and all the medicine which was freely administered by four very skilful physicians could not remove it.

On the third day of his sickness, Dr. M'Intyre, whose services were usually employed by the family, as he was considered very skillful, was brought, and with him four other eminent physicians. But it was all in vain, their exertions proved unavailing, just as Alvin had said would be the case—he told them the [88] calomel was still lodged in the same place, after some exertion had been made to carry it off, and that it must take his life.

On coming to this conclusion, he called Hyrum to him, and said, "Hyrum, I must die. Now I want to say a few things, which I wish to have you remember, I have done all I could to make our dear parents comfortable. I want you to go on and finish the house, and take care of them in their old age, and do not any more let them work hard, as they are now in old age."

He then called Sophronia to him, and said to her, "Sophronia, you must be a good girl, and do all you can for father and mother—never forsake them; they have worked hard, and they are now getting old. Be kind to them, and remember what they have done for us."

In the latter part of the fourth night he called for all the children, and exhorted them separately in the same strain as above. But when he came to Joseph, he said, "I am now going to die, the distress which I suffer, and the feelings that I have, tell me my time is very short. I want you to be a good boy, and do everything that lies in your power to obtain the Record. Be faithful in receiving instruction, and in keeping every commandment that is given you. Your brother Alvin must leave you; but remember the example which he has set for you; and set the same example for the children that are younger than yourself, and always be kind to father and mother."

He then asked me to take my little daughter Lucy up, and bring her to him, for he wished to see her. He was always very fond of her, and was in the habit of taking her up and caressing her, which naturally formed a very strong attachment on her part for him. I went to her, and said, "Lucy, Alvin wants to see you." At this, she started from her sleep, and screamed out, "Amby, Amby; (she could not yet talk plain, being very young). We took her to him, and when she got within reach of him, she sprang from my arms and caught him round the neck, and [89] cried out, "Oh! my Amby," and kissed him again and again.

"Lucy," said he, "you must be the best girl in the world, and take care of mother; you can't have your Amby any more. Amby is going away; he must leave little Lucy." He then kissed her, and said, "take her away, I think my breath offends her." We took hold of her to take her away; but she clinched him with such a strong grasp, that it was with difficulty we succeeded in disengaging her hands.

As I turned with the child to leave him, he said, "father, mother, brothers, and sisters, farewell! I can now breathe out my life as calmly as a clock." Saying this, he immediately closed his eyes in death.

The child still cried to go back to Alvin. One present observed to the child, "Alvin is gone; an angel has taken his spirit to heaven." Hearing this, the child renewed her cries, and, as I bent over his corpse with her in my arms, she again threw her arms around him, and kissed him repeatedly. And until the body was taken from the house she continued to cry, and to manifest such mingled feelings of both terror and affection at the scene before her, as are seldom witnessed.

Alvin was a youth of singular goodness of disposition—kind and amiable, so that lamentation and mourning filled the whole neighbourhood in which he resided.

By the request of the principal physician, Alvin was cut open, in order to discover, if it were possible, the cause of his death. On doing so, they found the calomel lodged in the upper bowels, untouched by anything which he had taken to remove it, and as near as possible in its natural state, surrounded as it was with gangrene.

A vast concourse of people attended his obsequies, who seemed very anxious to show their sympathy for us in our bereavement.

Alvin manifested, if such could be the case, greater zeal and anxiety in regard to the Record that [90] had been shown to Joseph, than any of the rest of the family; inconsequence of which we could not bear to hear anything said upon the subject. Whenever Joseph spoke of the Record, it would immediately bring Alvin to our minds, with all his zeal, and with all his kindness; and, when we looked to his place, and realized that he was gone from it, to return no more in this life, we all with one accord wept over our irretrievable loss, and we could "not be comforted, because he was not."

CHAPTER 21

RELIGIOUS EXCITEMENT—JOSEPH'S PROPHECY—HE WORKS FOR MR. STOAL—BECOMES ACQUAINTED WITH EMMA HALE

SHORTLY after the death of Alvin, a man commenced labouring in the neigbourhood, to effect a union of the different churches, in order that all might be agreed, and thus worship God with one heart and with one mind.

This seemed about right to me, and I felt much inclined to join in with them; in fact, the most of the family appeared quite disposed to unite with their numbers; but Joseph, from the first, utterly refused even to attend their meetings, saying, "Mother, I do not wish to prevent your going to meeting, or any of the rest of the family's; or your joining any church you please; but, do not ask me to join them. I can take my Bible, and go into the woods, and learn more in two hours, than you can learn at meeting in two years, if you should go all the time."

To gratify me, my husband attended some two or three meetings, but peremptorily refused going any more, either for my gratification, or any other person's. [91]

During this excitement, Joseph would say, it would do us no injury to join them, that if we did, we should not continue with them long, for we were mistaken in them, and did not know the wickedness of their hearts. One day he said, that he would give us an example, and that we might set it down as a prophecy; viz: —

"You look at Deacon Jessup," said he, "and you hear him talk very piously. Well, you think he is a very good man. Now suppose that one of his poor neighbours should owe him the value of a cow, and that this poor man had eight little children; moreover, that he should be taken sick and die, leaving his wife with one cow, but destitute of every other means of supporting herself and family—now I tell you, that Deacon Jessup, religious as he is, would not scruple to take the last cow from the poor widow and orphans, in order to secure the debt, notwithstanding he himself has an abundance of every thing."

At that time this seemed impossible to us, yet one year had scarcely expired when we saw Joseph's supposition literally fulfilled.

The shock occasioned by Alvin's death, in a short time passed off, and we resumed our usual avocations with considerable interest. The first move towards business, was to complete the house before mentioned. This we did as speedily as possible, and, when it was finished, Mr. Stoddard, the principal workman, offered for it the sum of fifteen hundred dollars; but my husband refused his offer, as he was unwilling to leave the scene of our labour, where we had fondly anticipated spending the remainder of our days.

A short time before the house was completed, a man, by the name of Josiah Stoal, came from Chenango county, New York, with the view of getting Joseph to assist him in digging for a silver mine.[1] He came for Joseph on account of having heard that he [92] possessed certain keys, by which he could discern things invisible to the natural eye.

Joseph endeavoured to divert him from his vain pursuit, but he was inflexible in his purpose, and offered high wages to those who would dig

---

[1] This project of Stoal's was undertaken from this cause—an old document had fallen into his possession, in some way or other, containing information of silver mines being somewhere in the neighbourhood in which he resided.

for him, in search of said mine, and still insisted upon having Joseph to work for him. Accordingly, Joseph and several others, returned with him and commenced digging. After labouring for the old gentleman about a month, without success, Joseph prevailed upon him to cease his operations; and it was from this circumstance of having worked by the month, at digging for a silver mine, that the very prevalent story arose of Joseph's having been a money digger.

While Joseph was in the employ of Mr. Stoal, he boarded a short time with one Isaac Hale, and it was during this interval, that Joseph became acquainted with the daughter, Miss Emma Hale, to whom he immediately commenced paying his addresses, and was subsequently married.

When Mr. Stoal relinquished his project of digging for silver, Joseph returned to his father's house.

Soon after his return, we received intelligence of the arrival of a new agent for the Everson land, of which our farm was a portion. This reminded us of the last payment, which was still due, and which must be made before we could obtain a deed of the place.

Shortly after this, a couple of gentlemen, one of whom was the before-named Stoal, the other a Mr. Knight, came into the neighbourhood for the purpose of procuring a quantity of either wheat or flour; and we, having sown considerable wheat, made a contract with them, in which we agreed to deliver a certain quantity of flour to them the ensuing fall, for which we were to receive a sufficient amount of money to make the final payment on our farm. This being done, my husband sent Hyrum to Canandaigua to inform the new agent of the fact, namely, that the money should be forthcoming as soon as the twenty-fifth of December 1825. [93] This, the agent said, would answer the purpose, and he agreed to retain the land until that time. Having thus, as we supposed, made all secure pertaining to the land, we gave ourselves no further uneasiness in regard to the matter.

When the time had nearly arrived for the last payment to be made, and when my husband was about starting for Mr. Stoal's and Mr. Knight's, in order to get the money to make the same, Joseph called my husband and myself aside, and said, "I have been very lonely ever since Alvin died, and I have concluded to get married; and if you have no objections to my uniting myself in marriage with Miss Emma Hale, she would be my choice in preference to any other woman I have ever seen." We were pleased with his choice, and not only consented to his marrying her, but requested him to bring her home with him, and live with us. Accordingly he set out with his father for Pennsylvania.

CHAPTER 22

JOSEPH SMITH, SEN., LOSES HIS FARM—JOSEPH, JUN., IS MARRIED—
HAS ANOTHER INTERVIEW WITH THE ANGEL, BY WHOM HE IS
CHASTISED—RECEIVES FURTHER INSTRUCTIONS

A FEW days subsequent to my husband's departure, I set myself to work to put my house in order for the reception of my son's bride; and I felt all that pride and ambition in doing so, that is common to mothers upon such occasions.

My oldest son had, previous to this, formed a matrimonial relation with one of the most excellent of women, with whom I had seen much enjoyment, and I hoped for as much happiness with my second daughter-in-law, as I had received from the society [94] of the first, and there was no reason why I should expect anything to the contrary.

One afternoon, after having completed my arrangements, I fell into a very agreeable train of reflections. The day was exceedingly fine, and of itself calculated to produce fine feelings; besides this, every other circumstance seemed to be in unison, and to contribute to raise in the heart those soothing and grateful emotions which we all have seasons of enjoying when the mind is at rest. Thus, as I stood musing, among other things, upon the prospect of a quiet and comfortable old age, my attention was suddenly arrested by a trio of strangers who were just entering. Upon their near approach I found one of these gentlemen to be Mr. Stoddard, the principal carpenter in building the house in which we then lived.

When they entered the house, I seated them, and commenced common-place conversation. But shortly one of them began to ask questions which I considered rather impertinent—questions concerning our making the last payment on the place; and if we did not wish to sell the house; furthermore, where Mr. Smith and my son had gone, &c. &c.

"Sell the house!" I replied, "No, sir, we have no occasion for that, we have made every necessary arrangement to get the deed, and also have an understanding with the agent. So you see we are quite secure, in regard to this matter."

To this they made no answer, but went out to meet Hyrum, who was approaching the house. They asked him the same questions, and he answered them the same as I had done. When they had experimented in this way, to their satisfaction, they proceeded to inform my son, that he need put himself to no further trouble with regard to the farm; "for," said they, "we have bought the place, and paid for it, and we now forbid your touching anything on the farm; and we also warn you to leave

72

forthwith, and give possession to the lawful owners." **[95]**

This conversation passed within my hearing. When they re-entered the house, I said, Hyrum, is it a reality? or only a sham to startle us? But one collected look at the men convinced me of their fiendish determination—I was overcome, and fell back into my chair almost deprived of sensibility.

When I recovered, we (Hyrum and myself) talked to them some time, endeavoring to persuade them to change their vile course; but the only answer we could get from them was, "Well, we've got the place, and d—n you, help yourselves if you can."

Hyrum, in a short time, went to an old friend, Dr. Robinson, and related to him the grievous story. Whereupon, the old gentleman sat down, and wrote at some considerable length the character of the family—our industry, and faithful exertions to secure a home, with many commendations calculated to beget confidence in us with respect to business transactions. And, keeping this writing in his own hands, he went through the village, and in an hour procured sixty subscribers. He then sent the same, by the hand of Hyrum, to the land agent, who lived in Canandaigua.

On receiving this, the agent was highly enraged. He said the men had told him that Mr. Smith and his son Joseph had run away, and that Hyrum was cutting down the sugar orchard, hauling off the rails, burning them, and doing all manner of mischief to the farm. That, believing this statement, he was induced to sell the place, for which he had given a deed, and received the money.

Hyrum told him the circumstances under which his father and brother had left home; also the probability of their being detained on the road, to attend to some business. Upon this, the agent directed him to address a number of letters to my husband, and have them sent and deposited in public-houses on the road which he travelled, that, perchance some of them might meet his eye, and thus cause him to return more speedily than he would otherwise. He then despatched a mes[96]senger to those individuals to whom he had given a deed of the farm in question, with the view of making a compromise with them; but they refused to do anything respecting the matter. The agent sent a message to them, stating that if they did not make their appearance forthwith, he would fetch them with a warrant. To this they gave heed, and they came without delay.

The agent strove to convince them of the disgraceful and impolitic course which they were pursuing, and endeavoured to persuade them to retract, and let the land go back into Mr. Smith's hands again.

For some time they said but little, except in a sneering and taunting way, about as follows: — "We've got the land, sir, and we've got the deed, so just let Smith help himself. Oh, no matter about Smith, he has gold plates, gold bibles, he is rich—he don't want anything." But finally, they agreed, if Hyrum could raise them one thousand dollars, by Saturday at ten o'clock in the evening, they would give up the deed.

It was now Thursday about noon, and Hyrum was at Canandaigua, which was nine miles distant from home, and hither he must ride before he could make the first move towards raising the required amount. He came home with a heavy heart. When he arrived, he found his father, who had returned a short time before him. His father had fortunately found, within fifty miles of home, one of those letters which Hyrum had written.

The following day, by the request of my husband, I went to see an old Quaker, a gentleman with whom we had been quite intimate since our commencement on the farm, and who had always seemed to admire the neat arrangement of the same. We hoped that he would be both able and willing to purchase the place, that we might at least have the benefit of the crops that were upon the ground, as he was a friend and would be disposed to show us favour. But we were disappointed, not in his will or [97] disposition, but in his ability. He had just paid out to the land agent all the money he could spare, to redeem a piece of land belonging to a friend in his immediate neighborhood. If I had arrived at his house thirty minutes sooner, I would have found him with fifteen-hundred dollars in his pocket.

When I rehearsed to him what had taken place, he was much distressed for us, and very much regretted his inability to relieve our necessity. He said, however, "If I have no money, I will try to do something for you, and you may say to your husband, that I will see him as soon as I can, and let him know what the prospect is."

It was nearly night—the country was new, and my road lay through a dense forest. The distance that I had to travel was ten miles, and that alone, yet I hastened to inform my husband of the disappointment that I had met with.

The old gentleman, as soon as I left, started in search of some one that could afford us assistance, and hearing of a Mr. Durfee, who lived four miles distant, he came the same night, and directed us to go and see what he could devise for our benefit.

Accordingly, my husband started without delay for Mr. Durfee's, and arrived at his house before daylight in the morning. He sent my husband three miles further, to one of his sons, who was High Sheriff, instructing him to say to the young man that his father wished to see him as soon as possible. Mr. Durfee, the younger, was obedient to the call.

Immediately after he arrived at his father's, the three proceeded together to see the farm, and arrived about ten o'clock A.M. They tarried a short time, then rode on to see the agent and those villains who held the deed of our place.

The anxiety of mind that I suffered that day can more easily be imagined than described. I now looked upon the proceeds of our industry, which smiled around us on every hand, with a kind of yearning attachment that I never before had ex[98]perienced; and our early losses I did not feel so keenly, for I then realized that we were young, and by making some exertions we might improve our circumstances; besides, I had not felt the inconveniences of poverty as I had since.

My husband, and the Messrs. Durfee, arrived in Canandaigua at half-past nine o'clock in the evening. The agent sent immediately for Mr. Stoddard and his friends, and they came without delay; but in order to make difficulty, they contended that it was after ten o'clock; however, not being able to sustain themselves upon this ground, they handed over the deed to Mr. Durfee, the High Sheriff, who now became the possessor of the farm.

I stated before, that at the time Mr. Smith started to see Knight and Stoal, Joseph accompanied him. When he returned, Joseph also returned with him, and remained with us, until the difficulty about the farm came to an issue; he then took leave for Pennsylvania, on the same business as before mentioned, and the next January returned with his wife, in good health and fine spirits.

Not long subsequent to his return, my husband had occasion to send him to Manchester, on business. As he set off early in the day, we expected him home at most by six o'clock in the evening, but when six o'clock came, he did not arrive. We always had a peculiar anxiety about him whenever he was absent, for it seemed as though something was always taking place to jeopardize his life. But to return. He did not get home till the night was far spent. On coming in, he threw himself into a chair, apparently much exhausted. My husband did not observe his appearance, and immediately exclaimed, "Joseph, why are you so late? has anything happened to you? we have been much distressed about you these three hours." As Joseph made no answer, he continued his interrogations, until, finally, I said, "Now, father, let him rest a moment—don't trouble him now—you see he is home safe, and he is very tired, so pray wait a little." [99]

The fact was, I had learned to be a little cautious about matters with regard to Joseph, for I was accustomed to see him look as he did on that occasion, and I could not easily mistake the cause thereof.

Presently he smiled, and said in a calm tone, "I have taken the severest chastisement that I have ever had in my life."

My husband, supposing that it was from some of the neighbours, was quite angry, and observed, "I would like to know what business anybody has to find fault with you!"

"Stop, father, stop," said Joseph, "it was the angel of the Lord: as I passed by the hill of Cumorah, where the plates are, the angel met me, and said that I had not been engaged enough in the work of the Lord; that the time had come for the Record to be brought forth; and that I must be up and doing, and set myself about the things which God had commanded me to do. But, father, give yourself no uneasiness concerning the reprimand which I have received, for I now know the course that I am to pursue, so all will be well."

It was also made known to him, at this interview, that he should make another effort to obtain the plates, on the twenty-second of the following Sept., but this he did not mention to us at that time.

CHAPTER 23

JOSEPH OBTAINS THE PLATES

ON the twentieth of September, Mr. Knight and his friend Stoal, came to see how we were managing matters with Stoddard and Co.; and they tarried with us until the twenty-second. On the night of the twenty-first, I sat up very late, as my work rather pressed upon my hands. I did not retire until **[100]** after twelve o'clock at night. About twelve o'clock, Joseph came to me, and asked me if I had a chest with a lock and key. I knew in an instant what he wanted it for, and not having one, I was greatly alarmed, as I thought it might be a matter of considerable moment. But Joseph, discovering my anxiety, said, "Never mind, I can do very well for the present without it—be calm—all is right."

Shortly after this, Joseph's wife passed through the room with her bonnet and riding dress; and in a few minutes they left together, taking Mr. Knight's horse and waggon. I spent the night in prayer and supplication to God, for the anxiety of my mind would not permit me to sleep. At the usual hour, I commenced preparing breakfast. My heart fluttered at every footstep, as I now expected Joseph and Emma momentarily, and feared lest Joseph might meet with a second disappointment.

When the male portion of the family were seated at the breakfast table, Mr. Smith enquired for Joseph, for he was not aware that he had left home. I requested my husband not to call him, for I would like to have him take breakfast with his wife that morning.

"No, no;" said my husband, "I must have Joseph sit down here and eat with me."

"Well, now, Mr. Smith," continued I, "*do* let him eat with his wife *this* morning; he almost always takes breakfast with you."

His father finally consented, and eat without him, and no further inquiries were made concerning his absence, but in a few minutes Mr. Knight came in quite disturbed.

"Why, Mr. Smith," exclaimed he, "my horse is gone, and I can't find him on the premises, and I wish to start for home in half an hour."

"Never mind the horse," said I. "Mr. Knight does not know all the nooks and corners in the pastures; I will call William, he will bring the horse immediately."

This satisfied him for the time being; but he soon [101] made another discovery. His waggon also was gone. He then concluded, that a rogue had stolen them both.

"Mr. Knight," said I, "do be quiet; I would be ashamed to have you go about, waiting upon yourself—just go out and talk with Mr. Smith until William comes, and if you really must go home, your horse shall be brought, and you shall be waited upon like a gentleman. He accordingly went out, and while he was absent Joseph returned.

I trembled so with fear, lest all might be lost in consequence of some failure in keeping the commandments of God, that I was under the necessity of leaving the room in order to conceal my feelings. Joseph saw this, and said, "Do not be uneasy mother, all is right—see here, I have got a key."

I knew not what he meant, but took the article of which he spoke into my hands, and, upon examination, found that it consisted of two smooth three-cornered diamonds set in glass, and the glasses were set in silver bows, which were connected with each other in much the same way as old fashioned spectacles. He took them again and left me, but said nothing respecting the Record.

In a short time he returned, and inquired of me in regard to getting a chest made. I told him to go to a certain cabinet-maker, who had made some furniture for my oldest daughter, and tell him that we would pay him for making a chest, as we did for the other work which he had done for us, namely, one half in cash and the other in produce.

Joseph remarked that he would do so, but that he did not know where the money would come from, for there was not a shilling in the house.

The following day one Mr. Warner came to him, and told him that a widow by the name of Wells, who was living in Macedon, wanted some labour done in a well, for which she would pay the money, and that she was anxious to have him (Joseph) do this labour for her. As this afforded us an opportunity to pay the cabinet maker for the chest, Joseph went [102] immediately to the house of Mrs. Wells, and commenced work.

The next day after he left home, one of the neighbours asked Mr. Smith many questions concerning the plates. I will here observe, that no one ever heard anything from us respecting them, except a confidential friend, whom my husband had spoken to about them some two or three years previous. It appeared that Satan had now stirred up the hearts of those who had gotten a hint of the matter from our friend, to search into it, and make every possible move towards thwarting the purposes of the Almighty.

My husband soon learned that ten or twelve men were clubbed together, with one Willard Chase, a Methodist class leader, at their head; and what was still more ridiculous, they had sent sixty or seventy miles for a certain conjuror, to come and divine the place where the plates were secreted.

We supposed that Joseph had taken the plates, and hid them somewhere, and we were apprehensive that our enemies might discover their place of deposit. Accordingly, the next morning, after hearing of their plans, my husband concluded to go among the neighbours to see what he could learn with regard to the plans of the adverse party. The first house he came to, he found the conjuror and Willard Chase, together with the rest of the clan. Making an errand, he went in and sat down near the door, leaving it a little ajar, in order to overhear their conversation. They stood in the yard near the door, and were devising plans to find "Joe Smith's gold bible," as they expressed themselves. The conjuror seemed much animated, although he had travelled sixty miles the day and night previous.

Presently, the woman of the house, becoming uneasy at the exposures they were making, stepped through a back door into the yard, and called to her husband, in a suppressed tone, but loud enough to be heard distinctly by Mr. Smith, "Sam, Sam, you are cutting your own throat." At this the conjuror [103] bawled out at the top of his voice, "I am not afraid of any body—we will have them plates in spite of Joe Smith or all the devils in hell."

When the woman came in again, Mr. Smith laid aside a newspaper which he had been holding in his hand, and remarked, "I believe I have not time to finish reading the paper now." He then left the house, and returned home.

Mr. Smith, on returning home, asked Emma, if she knew whether

Joseph had taken the plates from their place of deposit, or if she was able to tell him where they were. She said, she could not tell where they were, or whether they were removed from their place. My husband then related what he had both seen and heard.

Upon this Emma said, that she did not know what to do, but she supposed if Joseph was to get the Record, he *would* get it, and, that they would not be able to prevent him.

"Yes," replied Mr. Smith, "he will, if he is watchful and obedient; but remember, that for a small thing, Esau lost his birthright and his blessing. It may be so with Joseph."

"Well," said Emma, "if I had a horse I would go and see him."

Mr. Smith then said, "you shall have one in fifteen minutes, for although my team is gone, there is a stray on the place, and I will send William to bring him immediately."

In a few minutes William brought up the horse with a large hickory withe round his neck (for it was according to law, to put a withe round the neck of a stray before turning it into an enclosure;) and Emma was soon under way for Macedon.

Joseph kept the Urim and Thummim constantly about his person, by the use of which he could in a moment tell whether the plates were in any danger. Just before Emma rode up to Mrs. Wells, Joseph, from an impression that he had had, came up out of the well in which he was labouring, and met her not far from the house. Emma immediately in[104]formed him of what had transpired, whereupon he looked in the Urim and Thummim, and saw that the Record was as yet safe; nevertheless, he concluded to return with his wife, as something might take place that would render it necessary for him to be at home where he could take care of it.

He then told Mrs. Wells that business at home rendered it necessary for him to return. To this she did not agree at first, but finally consented. She then sent a boy for a horse, which Joseph mounted in his linen frock, and with his wife by his side on her horse decorated as before with a hickory withe round his neck, he rode through the village of Palmyra, which was on the way home.

On arriving at home, he found, his father pacing the ground near his door in great anxiety of mind. Joseph spoke to him, saying, "Father, there is no danger—all is perfectly safe—there is no cause of alarm."

When he had taken a little refreshment, he sent Carlos, my youngest son, to his brother Hyrum's, to have him come up immediately, as he desired to see him. When he came, Joseph requested him to get a chest, having a good lock and key, and to have it there by the time he (Joseph) should return. And, after giving these instructions, Joseph started for the plates.

The plates were secreted about three miles from home, in the following manner. Finding an old birch log much decayed, excepting the bark, which was in a measure sound, he took his pocket knife and cut the bark with some care, then turned it back, and made a hole of sufficient size to receive the plates, and laying them in the cavity thus formed, he replaced the bark; after which he laid across the log, in several places, some old stuff that happened to lay near, in order to conceal, as much as possible, the place in which they were deposited.

Joseph, on coming to them, took them from their secret place, and, wrapping them in his linen frock, placed them under his arm and started for home. **[105]**

After proceeding a short distance, he thought it would be more safe to leave the road and go through the woods. Travelling some distance after he left the road, he came to a large windfall, and as he was jumping over a log, a man sprang up from behind it, and gave him a heavy blow with a gun. Joseph turned around and knocked him down, then ran at the top of his speed. About half a mile further he was attacked again in the same manner as before; he knocked this man down in like manner as the former, and ran on again; and before he reached home he was assaulted the third time. In striking the last one he dislocated his thumb, which, however, he did not notice until he came within light of the house, when he threw himself down in the corner of the fence in order to recover his breath. As soon as he was able, he arose and came to the house. He was still altogether speechless from fright and the fatigue of running.

After resting a few moments, he desired me to send Carlos for my husband, Mr. Knight, and his friend Stoal, and have them go immediately and see if they could find the men who had been pursuing him. And after Carlos had done this, he wished to have him sent to Hyrum's, to tell him to bring the chest.

I did as I was requested, and when Carlos arrived at Hyrum's, he found him at tea, with two of his wife's sisters. Just as Hyrum was raising a cup to his mouth, Carlos touched his shoulder. Without waiting to hear one word from the child, he dropped the cup, sprang from the table, caught the chest, turned it upside down, and emptying its contents on the floor, left the house instantly with the chest on his shoulder.

The young ladies were greatly astonished at his singular behaviour, and declared to his wife—who was then confined to her bed, her oldest daughter, Lovina, being but four days old—that he was certainly crazy.

His wife laughed heartily, and replied, "Oh, not **[106]** in the least, he has just thought of something which he has neglected, and it is just like him to fly off in a tangent when he thinks of anything in that way."

When the chest came, Joseph locked up the Record, then threw himself upon the bed, and after resting a little, so that he could converse freely, he arose and went into the kitchen, where he related his recent adventure to his father, Mr. Knight, and Mr. Stoal, besides many others, who had by this time collected, with the view of hearing something in regard to the strange circumstance which had taken place. He showed them his thumb, saying, "I must stop talking, father, and get you to put my thumb in place, for it is very painful."

I will here mention that my husband, Mr. Knight, and Mr. Stoal, went in pursuit of those villains who had attempted Joseph's life, but were not able to find them.

When Joseph first got the plates, the angel of the Lord stood by, and said: —

> "Now you have got the Record into your own hands, and you are but a man, therefore you will have to be watchful and faithful to your trust, or you will be overpowered by wicked men, for they will lay every plan and scheme that is possible to get it away from you, and if you do not take heed continually, they will succeed. While it was in my hands, I could keep it, and no man had power to take it away; but now I give it up to you. Beware, and look well to your ways, and you shall have power to retain it, until the time for it to be translated."

That of which I spoke, which Joseph termed a key, was indeed, nothing more nor less than the Urim and Thummim, and it was by this that the angel showed him many things which he saw in vision; by which he could also ascertain, at any time, the approach of danger, either to himself or the Record, and on account of which he always kept the Urim and Thummim about his person. **[107]**

CHAPTER 24

JOSEPH BRINGS HOME THE BREAST-PLATE—MARTIN HARRIS AND HIS WIFE INTRODUCED—THE TRANSLATION COMMENCES—MRS. HARRIS BEGINS TO OPPOSE THE WORK

AFTER bringing home the plates, Joseph commenced working with his father and brothers on the farm, in order to be as near as possible to the treasure which was confided to his care.

Soon after this, he came in from work, one afternoon, and after remaining a short time, he put on his great coat, and left the house. I was engaged at the time, in an upper room, in preparing some oil-cloths for painting. When he returned, he requested me to come down stairs. I told him, that I could not leave my work just then, yet, upon his urgent request, I finally concluded to go down, and see what he wanted, upon which he handed me the breastplate spoken of in his history.

It was wrapped in a thin muslin handkerchief, so thin that I could see the glistening metal, and ascertain its proportions without any difficulty.

It was concave on one side, and convex on the other, and extended from the neck downwards, as far as the centre of the stomach of a man of extraordinary size. It had four straps of the same material, for the purpose of fastening it to the breast, two of which ran back to go over the shoulders, and the other two were designed to fasten to the hips. They were just the width of two of my fingers, (for I measured them,) and they had holes in the end of them, to be convenient in fastening.

The whole plate was worth at least five hundred dollars: after I had examined it, Joseph placed it in the chest with the Urim and Thummim.

Shortly after this circumstance, Joseph came to the house in great haste, and inquired, if there [108] had been a company of men about. I told him, not a single individual had come to the house since he left. He then said, that a mob would be there that night, if they did not come before that time, to search for the Record, and that it must be removed immediately.

Soon afterwards, a man by the name of Braman came in from the village of Livonia, a man in whom we reposed much confidence, and who was well worthy of the same. Joseph told him his apprehensions of a mob being there that night, and that they must prepare themselves to drive them away; but, that the first thing to be attended to, was to secure the Record and breast-plate.

In view of this, it was determined that a portion of the hearth should be taken up, and that the Record and breast-plate should be buried under the same, and then the hearth be relaid, to prevent suspicion.

This was done as speedily as possible, but the hearth was scarcely relaid when a large company of men well armed came rushing up to the house. Joseph threw open the doors, and taking a hint from the stratagem of his grandfather Mack, hallooed as if he had a legion at hand, in the meanwhile, giving the word of command with great emphasis; while all the male portion of the family, from the father down to little Carlos, ran out of the house with such fury upon the mob, that it struck them with terror and dismay, and they fled before the little Spartan band into the woods, where they dispersed themselves to their several homes.

In a short time Joseph received another intimation of the approach of a mob, also of the necessity of removing the Record and breast-plate from the place wherein they were secreted, consequently he took them out of the box in which they were placed, and wrapping them in clothes, carried them across the road to a cooper's shop, and laid then in a quantity of flax which was stowed in the shop loft. After which he nailed up the box again, then tore up the floor of the shop, and put it under the same. [109]

As soon as night came, the mob came also, and commenced ransacking the place. They rummaged round the house, and all over the premises, but did not come into the house. After making satisfactory search they went away.

The next morning we found the floor of the cooper's shop torn up, and the box which was laid under it shivered in pieces.

In a few days afterwards we learned the cause of this last move—why their curiosity led them in the direction of the cooper's shop. A young woman by the name of Chase, sister to Willard Chase, found a green glass, through which she could see many very wonderful things, and among her great discoveries she said that she saw the precise place where "Joe Smith kept his gold bible hid," and obedient to her directions, the mob gathered their forces and laid siege to the cooper's shop.

Notwithstanding their disappointment in not finding the plates in the shop, their confidence was not in the least shaken in Miss Chase, for they still went from place to place by her direction, determined to get, if possible, the much desired object of their search.

Not long after the circumstance of the mob's going into the cooper's shop, and splitting in pieces the box, Joseph began to make arrangements to accomplish the translation of the Record. The first step that he was instructed to take in regard to this work, was to make a *fac-simile* of some of the characters, which were called reformed Egyptian, and to send them to some of the most learned men of this generation, and ask them for the translation thereof.

The reader will here observe, that on a preceding, page of this volume, I spoke of a confidential friend to whom my husband merely mentioned the existence of the plates, some two or three years prior to their coming forth. This was no other than Martin Harris, one of the witnesses to the book subsequent to its being translated. [110]

With the view of commencing the work of translation, and carrying it forward as speedily as circumstances would permit, Joseph came to me one afternoon and requested me to go to this Mr. Harris, and inform him that he had got the plates, and that he desired to see Mr. Harris concerning the matter. This, indeed, was an errand which I much disliked, as Mr. Harris's wife was a very peculiar woman, one that was naturally of a very jealous disposition; besides this, she was rather dull of hearing, and when anything was said that she did not hear distinctly, she suspected that it was some secret, which was designedly kept from her. So I told Joseph that I would rather not go, unless I could have the privilege of speaking to her first upon the subject. To this he consented, and I went according to his request.

On arriving at Mr. Harris's, I cautiously detailed the particulars with regard to Joseph's finding the plates, so far as wisdom dictated and necessity demanded, in order to satisfy Mrs. Harris's curiosity. However, she did not wait for me to get through with my story, before she commenced urging upon me a considerable amount of money, that she had at her command. Her husband always allowed her to keep a private purse, in order to satisfy her singular disposition, and it was this private money that she wished me to receive. She also had a sister living with her who desired me to receive an amount of money, I think some seventy-five dollars, to assist in getting the Record translated.

I told her that I came on no such business, that I did not want her money, and that Joseph would attend to his own affairs; but, that I would like to talk with Mr. Harris a moment, and then return home, as my family would soon be expecting me. Yet, notwithstanding all this, she was determined to assist in the business, for she said she knew that we should want money, and she could spare two hundred dollars as well as not.

After detaining me a few minutes, she went with **[111]** me to her husband, and told him that I wished to speak to him. He replied, that he was not going to stop his work, for he was just laying the last brick in his hearth.

"You see," said he, "this is the last work I have to do on the house, and it is the last work I shall do about the house, or on the farm, in one year. And when this is done, I am going to hire a hand to work a year for me, as I shall travel that length of time before I shall settle myself at home again."

After completing the work in which he was engaged, he left the house, but was absent only a short time. On returning, he came to me and said, "Now I am a free man — my hands are altogether untied — I can come and go and do as I please."

I related, in short, the errand on which I had come. He said, that he would see Joseph in the course of a few days. At this his wife exclaimed, "Yes, and I am coming to see him too, and I will be there on Tuesday afternoon, and will stop over night."

Accordingly, when Tuesday afternoon arrived, Mrs. Harris made her appearance, and as soon as she was well seated, she began to importune my son relative to the truth of what he had said concerning the Record, declaring that if he really had any plates, she *would* see them, and that she was determined to help him publish them.

He told her she was mistaken—that she could not see them, for he was not permitted to exhibit them to any one, except those whom the Lord should appoint to testify of them. "And, in relation to assistance," he observed, "I always prefer dealing with men, rather than their wives."

This highly displeased Mrs. Harris, for she considered herself altogether superior to her husband, and she continued her importunities. She would say, "Now, Joseph, are you not telling me a lie? Can you look full in my eye, and say before God, that you have in reality found a Record, as you pretend?" [112]

To this, Joseph replied, rather indifferently, "Why, yes, Mrs. Harris, I would as soon look you in the face, and say so as not, if that will be any gratification to you."

Then, said she, "Joseph, I will tell you what I will do, if I can get a witness that you speak the truth, I will believe all you say about the matter, and I shall want to do something about the translation—I mean to help you any way."

This closed the evening's conversation. The next morning, soon after she arose, she related a very remarkable dream which she said she had had during the night. It ran about as follows. She said that a personage appeared to her, who told her, that as she had disputed the servant of the Lord, and said his word was not to be believed, and had also asked him many improper questions, she had done that which was not right in the sight of God. After which he said to her, "Behold, here are the plates, look upon them, and believe."

After giving us an account of her dream, she described the Record very minutely, then told us that she had made up her mind in relation to the course which she intended to pursue, namely that she had in her possession twenty-eight dollars which she received from her mother just before she died, while she was on her death bed, and that Joseph should accept of it. If he *would* he might give his note, but he should certainly take it upon some terms.

The last proposal Joseph accepted, in order to get rid of further importunity upon the subject.

Soon afterwards, Alva Hale, Joseph's brother-in-law, came to our house, from Pennsylvania, for the purpose of moving Joseph to his father-in-law's, as word had been sent to them, that Joseph desired to move there as soon as he could settle up his business. During the short interval of Alva's stay with us, he and Joseph were one day in Palmyra, at a public-house, transacting some business. As they were thus engaged, Mr. Harris came in: he stepped immediately up to my son, and taking him by the [113] hand, said, "How do you do, Mr. Smith." After which, he took a bag of silver from his pocket, and said again, "Here, Mr. Smith, is fifty dollars; I give this to you to do the Lord's work with; no, I give it to the Lord for his own work."

"No," said Joseph, "We will give you a note, Mr. Hale, I presume, will sign it with me."

"Yes," said Alva, "I will sign it."

Mr. Harris, however, insisted that he would give the money to the Lord, and called those present to witness the fact that he gave it freely, and did not demand any compensation, that it was for the purpose of helping Mr. Smith to do the Lord's work. And as I have been informed, many were present on that occasion, who witnessed the same circumstance.

Joseph, in a short time, arranged his affairs, and was ready for the journey. The Record and breast-plate for security, he nailed up in a box and then put them into a strong cask; and after filling the cask with beans, headed it up again.

When it became generally known that Joseph was about moving to Pennsylvania, a mob of fifty men collected themselves together, and they went to one Dr. Mc. Intyre, and requested him to take the command of the company, stating, that they were resolved on following "Joe Smith," and taking his "gold bible" from him. The doctor's ideas and feelings did not altogether harmonize with theirs, and he told them they were a pack of devilish fools, and to go home and mind their own business; that, if Joseph Smith had any business of that sort to attend to, he was capable of doing it, and that it would be better for them to busy themselves about that which more concerned them.

After this, a quarrel arose among them respecting who should be captain, and it ran so high that it broke up the expedition.

When Joseph had had a sufficient time to accomplish the journey, and transcribe some of the Egyptian characters, it was agreed that Martin Harris should follow him—and that he (Martin) should take [114] the characters to the East, and, on his way, he was to call on all the professed linguists, in order to give them an opportunity to display their talents in giving a translation of the characters.

When Mrs. Harris heard of what her husband had in contemplation, she resolved to accompany him; but he, concluding that it would be better to go without her, left quite suddenly without her knowledge,

Mrs. Harris soon missed her husband, and came to me, for the purpose of ascertaining if I knew where he was. I told her what he had said concerning his leaving, suppressing, however, his remarks pertaining to herself.

On hearing this, she became highly exasperated, and charged me with planning the whole affair. I protested against it, asserting that I had nothing to do with the plan, nor the execution of it. Furthermore, that the business of a house, which was the natural cares of a woman, was all that I attempted to dictate, or interfere with, unless it was by my husband's or son's request.

Mrs. Harris then observed, that she had property, and knew how to take care of it, which she would convince me of.

"Now, stop," said I, "do you not know that we have never asked you for money or property? and that if we had been disposed to take advantage of your liberality, could we not have got, at least, two hundred and seventy dollars of your cash?" She answered in the affirmative, notwithstanding she went home in a great rage, determined to have satisfaction for the treatment which she had received.

In a short time Mr. Harris returned, and his wife's anger kindled afresh at his presence, insomuch that she prepared a separate bed and room for him, which room she refused to enter.

A young man by the name of Dikes, had been paying some attention to Miss Lucy, Martin Harris's oldest daughter. To this young man Mr. Harris was quite attached, and his daughter Lucy was by [115] no means opposed to him; but Mrs. Harris, of course, was decidedly upon the negative. However, just at this crisis, a scheme entered her brain which materially changed her deportment to Mr. Dikes. She told him, if he would manage to get the Egyptian characters from Mr. Harris's possession, and procure a room in Palmyra for the purpose of transcribing them, and then bring her the transcript, that she would consent to his marriage with her daughter Lucy.

To this, Mr. Dikes cheerfully consented, and suffice it to say, he succeeded to her satisfaction, and thus received the promised reward.

When Mr. Harris began to make preparations to start for Pennsylvania the second time, with the view of writing for Joseph, his wife told him that she had fully decreed in her heart to accompany him. Mr. Harris, having no particular objections, informed her that she might do so; that she might go and stay one or two weeks, and then he would bring her home again, after which he would return, and resume his writing for Joseph. To this she cheerfully agreed. But Mr. Harris little suspected what he had to encounter by this move. The first time he exhibited the characters before named, she took out of her pocket an exact copy of the same; and told those present, that "Joe Smith" was not the only one who was in possession of this great curiosity, that she had the same characters, and, they were quite as genuine as those shown by Mr. Harris. This course she continued to pursue, until they arrived at Joseph's.

As soon as she arrived there, she informed him that her object in coming, was to see the plates, and that she would never leave until she had accomplished it. Accordingly, without delay, she commenced ransacking every nook and corner about the house—chests, trunks, cupboards, &c.; consequently, Joseph was under the necessity of removing both the breast-plate and the Record from the house, and secreting them elsewhere. Not finding them in the [116] house, she concluded that Joseph had buried them, and the next day she commenced searching out of doors, which she continued to do until about two o'clock P.M. She then came in rather ill-natured; after warming herself a little, she asked Joseph's wife if there were snakes in that country in the winter. She replied in the negative. Mrs. Harris then said, "I have been walking round in the woods to look at the situation of your place, and as I turned round to come home, a tremendous black snake stuck up his head before me, and commenced hissing at me."

The woman was so perplexed and disappointed in all her undertakings, that she left the house and took lodgings during her stay in Pennsylvania with a near neighbour, to whom she stated that the day previous she had been hunting for the plates, and that, after a tedious search, she at length came to a spot where she judged, from the appearance of things, they must be buried; but upon stooping down to scrape away the snow and leaves, in order to ascertain the fact, she encountered a horrible black snake, which gave her a terrible fright, and she ran with all possible speed to the house.

While this woman remained in the neighbourhood, she did all that lay in her power to injure Joseph in the estimation of his neighbours—telling them that he was a grand impostor, and, that by his specious pretensions, he had seduced her husband into the belief that he (Joseph Smith) was some great one, merely through a design upon her husband's property.

When she returned home, being about two weeks after her arrival in Harmony, the place where Joseph resided, she endeavoured to dissuade her husband from taking any further part in the publication of the Record; however, Mr. Harris paid no attention to her, but returned and continued writing.

Immediately after Martin Harris left home for Pennsylvania, his wife went from place to place, and from house to house, telling her grievances, and [117] declaring that Joseph Smith was practising a deception upon the people, which was about to strip her of all that she possessed, and that she was compelled to deposit a few things away from home in order to secure them. So she carried away her furniture, linen, and bedding; also other moveable articles, until she nearly stripped the premises of every thing that could conduce either to comfort or convenience, depositing them with those of her friends and acquaintances, in whom she reposed sufficient confidence to assure her of their future safety.

CHAPTER 25

MARTIN HARRIS IS PERMITTED TO TAKE THE MANUSCRIPT HOME WITH HIM — HE LOSES IT — THE SEASON OF MOURNING WHICH ENSUED

MARTIN HARRIS, having written some one hundred and sixteen pages for Joseph, asked permission of my son to carry the manuscript home with him, in order to let his wife read it, as he hoped it might have a salutary effect upon her feelings.

Joseph was willing to gratify his friend as far as he could consistently, and he inquired of the Lord to know if he might do as Martin Harris had requested, but was refused. With this, Mr. Harris was not altogether satisfied, and, at his urgent request, Joseph inquired again, but received a second refusal. Still, Martin Harris persisted as before, and Joseph applied again, but the last answer was not like the two former ones. In this the Lord permitted Martin Harris to take the manuscript home with him, on condition that he would exhibit it to none, save five individuals whom he had mentioned, and who belonged to his own family. **[118]**

Mr. Harris was delighted with this, and bound himself in a written covenant of the most solemn nature, that he would strictly comply with the injunctions which he had received. Which being done, he took the manuscript and went home.

Joseph did not suspect but that his friend would keep his faith, consequently, he gave himself no uneasiness with regard to the matter.

Shortly after Mr. Harris left, Joseph's wife became the mother of a son, which, however, remained with her but a short time before it was snatched from her arms by the hand of death. And the mother seemed, for some time, more like sinking with her infant into the mansion of the dead, than remaining with her husband among the living. Her situation was such for two weeks, that Joseph slept not an hour in undisturbed quiet. At the expiration of this time she began to recover, but as Joseph's anxiety about her began to subside, another cause of trouble forced itself upon his mind. Mr. Harris had been absent nearly three weeks, and Joseph had received no intelligence whatever from him, which was altogether aside of the arrangement when they separated. But Joseph kept his feelings from his wife, fearing that if she became acquainted with them it might agitate her too much.

In a few days, however, she mentioned the subject herself, and desired her husband to go and get her mother to stay with her, while he should repair to Palmyra, for the purpose of learning the cause of Mr. Harris's absence as well as silence. At first Joseph objected, but seeing her so cheerful, and so willing to have him leave home, he finally consented.

He set out in the first stage that passed for Palmyra, and, when he was left to himself, he began to contemplate the course which Martin had taken, and the risk which he (Joseph) had run in letting the manuscript go out of his own hands—for it could not be obtained again, in case Martin had lost it through transgression, except by the power of God, which **[119]** was something Joseph could hardly hope for—and that, by persisting in his entreaties to the Lord, he had perhaps fallen into transgression, and thereby lost the manuscript. When, I say, he began to contemplate these things, they troubled his spirit, and his soul was moved with fearful apprehensions. And, although he was now nearly worn out, sleep fled from his eyes, neither had he any desire for food, for he felt that he had done wrong, and how great his condemnation was he did not know.

Only one passenger was in the stage besides himself: this man, observing Joseph's gloomy appearance, inquired the cause of his affliction, and offered to assist him if his services would be acceptable. Joseph thanked him for his kindness, and mentioned that he had been watching some-time with a sick wife and child, that the child had died, and that his wife was still very low; but refrained from giving any further explanation. Nothing more passed between them upon this subject, until Joseph was about leaving the stage; at which time he remarked, that he still had twenty miles further to travel on foot that night, it being then about ten o'clock. To this the stranger objected, saying, "I have watched you since you first entered the stage, and I know that you have neither slept nor eat since that time, and you shall not go on foot twenty miles alone this night; for, if you must go, I will be your company. Now tell me what can be the trouble that makes you thus dispirited?"

Joseph replied, about as before—that he had left his wife in so low a state of health, that he feared he should not find her alive when he returned; besides, he had buried his first and only child but a few days previous. This was true, though there was another trouble lying at his heart, which he dared not to mention.

The stranger then observed, "I feel to sympathize with you, and I fear that your constitution, which is evidently not strong, will be inadequate to support you. You will be in danger of falling asleep **[120]** in the forest, and of meeting with some awful disaster."

Joseph again thanked the gentleman for his kindness, and, leaving the stage, they proceeded together. When they reached our house it was nearly daylight. The stranger said he was under the necessity of leading Joseph the last four miles by the arm; for nature was too much exhausted to support him any longer, and he would fall asleep as he was walking along, every few minutes, towards the last of this distance.

On entering our house, the stranger remarked that he had brought our son through the forest, because he had insisted on coming, that he was sick, and needed rest, as well as refreshment, and that he ought to have some pepper tea to warm his stomach. After thus directing us, relative to our son, he said, that when we had attended to Joseph he would thank us for a little breakfast for himself, as he was in haste to be on his journey again.

When Joseph had taken a little nourishment, according to the directions of the stranger, he requested us to send immediately for Mr. Harris! This we did without delay. And when we had given the stranger his breakfast, we commenced preparing breakfast for the family; and we supposed that Mr. Harris would be there, as soon as it was ready, to eat with us, for he generally came in such haste when he was sent for. At eight o'clock we set the victuals on the table, as we were expecting him every moment. We waited till nine, and he came not—till ten, and he was not there—till eleven, still he did not make his appearance. But at half-past twelve we saw him walking with a slow and measured tread towards the house, his eyes fixed thoughtfully upon the ground. On coming to the gate, he stopped, instead of passing through, and got upon the fence, and sat there some time with his hat drawn over his eyes. At length he entered the house. Soon after which we sat down to the table, Mr. Harris with the rest. He took up his knife and **[121]** fork as if he were going to use them, but immediately dropped them. Hyrum, observing this, said "Martin, why do you not eat; are you sick?" Upon which, Mr. Harris pressed his hands upon his temples, and cried out, in a tone of deep anguish, "Oh, I have lost my soul! I have lost my soul!"

Joseph, who had not expressed his fears till now, sprang from the table, exclaiming, "Martin, have you lost that manuscript? have you broken your oath, and brought down condemnation upon my head, as well as your own?"

"Yes, it is gone," replied Martin, "and I know not where."

"Oh, my God!" said Joseph, clinching his hands. "All is lost! all is lost! What shall I do? I have sinned—it is I who tempted the wrath of God. I should have been satisfied with the first answer which I received from the Lord; for he told me that it was not safe to let the writing go out of my possession." He wept and groaned, and walked the floor continually.

At length he told Martin to go back and search again.

"No," said Martin, "it is all in vain; for I have ripped open beds and pillows; and I know it is not there."

"Then must I," said Joseph, "return to my wife with such a tale as this? I dare not do it, lest I should kill her at once. And how shall I appear before the Lord? Of what rebuke am I not worthy from the angel of the Most High?"

I besought him not to mourn so, for perhaps the Lord would forgive him, after a short season of humiliation and repentance. But what could I say to comfort him, when he saw all the family in the same situation of mind as himself; for sobs and groans, and the most bitter lamentations filled the house. However, Joseph was more distressed than the rest, as he better understood the consequences of disobedience. And he continued, pacing back and forth, meantime weeping and grieving, until [122] about sunset, when, by persuasion, he took a little nourishment.

The next morning we set out for home. We parted with heavy hearts, for it now appeared that all which we had so fondly anticipated, and which had been the source of so much secret gratification, had in a moment fled, and fled for ever.

CHAPTER 26

MARTIN HARRIS'S PERFIDY

I WILL now give a sketch of the proceedings of Martin Harris during the time he was absent from Joseph.

After leaving Joseph he arrived at home with the manuscript in safety. Soon after he exhibited the manuscript to his wife and family. His wife was so pleased with it, that she gave him the privilege of locking it up in her own set of drawers, which was a special favour, for she had never before this allowed him even the privilege of looking into them. After he had shown the manuscript to those who had a right, according to his oath, to see it, he went with his wife to visit one of her relatives, who lived some ten or fifteen miles distant.

After remaining with them a short time, he returned home, but his wife declined accompanying him back. Soon after his return, a very particular friend of his made him a visit, to whom he related all that he knew concerning the Record. The man's curiosity was much excited, and, as might be expected, he earnestly desired to see the manuscript. Martin was so anxious to gratify his friend, that, although it was contrary to his obligation, he went to the drawer to get the manuscript, but the key [123] was gone. He sought for it some time, but could not find it. Resolved, however, to carry his purpose into execution, he picked the lock, and, in so doing, considerably injured his wife's bureau. He then took out the manuscript, and, after showing it to this friend, he removed it to his own set of drawers, where he could have it at his command. Passing by his oath, he showed it to any good friend that happened to call on him.

When Mrs. Harris returned, and discovered the marred state of her bureau, her irascible temper was excited to the utmost pitch, and an intolerable storm ensued, which descended with the greatest violence upon the devoted head of her husband.

Having once made a sacrifice of his conscience, Mr. Harris no longer regarded its scruples; so he continued to exhibit the writings, until a short time before Joseph arrived, to anyone whom he regarded as prudent enough to keep the secret, except our family, but *we* were not allowed to set our eyes upon them.

For a short time previous to Joseph's arrival, Mr. Harris had been otherwise engaged, and thought but little about the manuscript. When Joseph sent for him, he went immediately to the drawer where he had left it, but, behold it was gone! He asked his wife where it was. She solemnly averred that she did not know anything respecting it. He then made a faithful search throughout the house, as before related.

The manuscript has never been found; and there is no doubt but Mrs. Harris took it from the drawer, with the view of retaining it, until another translation should be given, then, to alter the original translation, for the purpose of showing a discrepancy between them, and thus make the whole appear to be a deception.

It seemed as though Martin Harris, for his transgression, suffered temporally as well as spiritually. The same day on which the foregoing circumstance took place, a dense fog spread itself over his fields, [124] and blighted his wheat while in the blow, so that he lost about two-thirds of his crop, whilst those fields which lay only on the opposite side of the road, received no injury whatever.

I well remember that day of darkness, both within and without. To us, at least, the heavens seemed clothed with blackness, and the earth shrouded with gloom. I have often said within myself, that if a continual punishment, as severe as that which we experienced on that occasion, were to be inflicted upon the most wicked characters who ever stood upon the footstool of the Almighty—if even their punishment were no greater than that, I should feel to pity their condition.

CHAPTER 27

THE URIM AND THUMMIM ARE TAKEN FROM JOSEPH—HE RECEIVES THEM AGAIN

FOR nearly two months after Joseph returned to his family, in Pennsylvania, we heard nothing from him, and becoming anxious about him, Mr. Smith and myself set off to make him a visit. When we came within three-quarters of a mile of the house, Joseph started to meet us, telling his wife, as he left, that father and mother were coming. When he met us, his countenance wore so pleasant an aspect, that I was convinced he had something agreeable to communicate with regard to the work in which he was engaged. When I entered, the first thing which attracted my attention was a red morocco trunk, lying on Emma's bureau, which Joseph shortly informed me contained the Urim and Thummim, and the plates. And, in the evening, he gave us the following relation of what had transpired since our separation:— **[125]**

"On leaving you," said Joseph, "I returned immediately home. Soon after my arrival, I commenced humbling myself in mighty prayer before the Lord, and, as I was pouring out my soul in supplication to God, that if possible, I might obtain mercy at his hands, and be forgiven of all that I had done contrary to his will, an angel stood before me, and answered me, saying, that I had sinned in delivering the manuscript into the hands of a wicked man, and, as I had ventured to become responsible for his faithfulness, I would of necessity have to suffer the consequences of his indiscretion, and I must now give up the Urim and Thummim into his (the angel's) hands."

"This I did as I was directed, and as I handed them to him, he remarked, 'If you are very humble and penitent, it may be you will receive them again; if so, it will be on the twenty-second of next September.'"

Joseph then related a revelation which he received soon after the angel visited him. A part of which is as follows:—

"Behold, you have been entrusted with these things, but how strict were your commandments, and remember, also, the promises which were made to you, if you did not transgress them; and behold how oft you have transgressed the commandments, and the laws of God, and have gone on in the persuasions of men. For behold, you should not have feared man more than God. Although men set at nought the counsels of God, and despise his words, yet you should have been faithful, and he would have extended his arm, and supported you against all the fiery darts of the adversary, and he would have been with you in every time of trouble.

"Behold, thou art Joseph, and thou wast chosen to do the work of the Lord; but because of transgression, if thou art not aware, thou wilt fall. But remember, God is merciful; therefore, repent of that which thou hast done, which is contrary to the commandment which I gave you, and thou art still chosen, and art again called to the work. Except thou do this, thou shalt be delivered up, and become as other men, and have no more gift.

"And when thou deliveredst up that which God had given thee sight and power to translate, thou deliveredst up that which was sacred, into the hands of a **[126]** wicked man, who has set at nought the counsels of God, and has broken the most sacred promises which were made before God, and has depended upon his own judgment, and boasted in his own wisdom; and this is the reason that thou hast lost thy privileges for a season, for thou hast suffered the counsel of thy director to be trampled upon from the beginning.

"Nevertheless, my work shall go forth, for inasmuch as the knowledge of a Saviour has come unto the world through the testimony of the Jews, even so shall the knowledge of a Saviour come unto my people."

For the sake of brevity, I have omitted part of this revelation, but the reader will find it in the *Doc. and Cov.*, sec. 30.

I will now return to Joseph's recital.

"After the angel left me," said he, "I continued my supplications to God, without cessation, and on the twenty-second of September, I had the joy and satisfaction of again receiving the Urim and Thummim, with which I have again commenced translating, and Emma writes for me, but the angel said that the Lord would send me a scribe, and I trust his promise will be verified. The angel seemed pleased with me when he gave me back the Urim and Thummim, and he told me that the Lord loved me, for my faithfulness and humility."

A few months after Joseph received them, he inquired of the Lord, and obtained the following revelation:—

"Now, behold I say unto you, that because you delivered up those writings which you had power given unto you to translate, by the means of the Urim and Thummim, into the hands of a wicked man, you have lost them, and you also lost your gift at the same time, and your mind became darkened; nevertheless, it is now restored unto you again;

therefore, see that you are faithful, and continue on unto the finishing of the remainder of the work of translation as you have begun. Do not run faster, or labor more than you have strength and means provided to enable you to translate, but be diligent unto the end, pray always, that you may come off conqueror, yea, that you may conquer Satan, and that you may escape the hands of the servants of Satan that do uphold his work. [127] Behold, they have sought to destroy you, yea, even the man in whom you have trusted, has sought to destroy you, and for this cause I said, that he is a wicked man, for he has sought to take away the things wherewith you have been entrusted, and he has also sought to destroy your gift; and because you have delivered the writings into his hands, behold wicked men have taken them from you. Therefore, you have delivered them up, yea, that which was sacred, unto wickedness. And behold, Satan has put it into their hearts to alter the words which you have caused to be written, or which you have translated, which have gone out of your hands; and behold, I say unto you, that because they have altered the words, they read contrary from that which you translated and caused to be written; and on this wise the devil has sought to lay a cunning plan, that he may destroy this work. For he has put it into their hearts to do this, that by lying, they may say they have caught you in the words." —*Doc. and Cov.*, sec. 36.

While on this visit we became acquainted with Emma's father, whose name was Isaac Hale; also his family, which consisted of his wife, Elizabeth, his sons, Jesse, David, Alva, Isaac Ward, and Reuben; and his daughters, Phebe, Elizabeth, and A——.

They were an intelligent and highly respectable family. They were pleasantly situated, and lived in good style, in the town of Harmony, on the Susquehannah river, within a short distance of the place where Joseph resided.

The time of our visit with them, we passed very agreeably, and returned home relieved of a burden which was almost insupportable, and our present joy far overbalanced all our former grief. [128]

CHAPTER 28

OLIVER COWDERY COMMENCES WRITING FOR JOSEPH—THEY ATTEND TO THE ORDINANCE OF BAPTISM

WHEN Mr. Smith and myself arrived at home, we found Samuel and Sophronia very sick, indeed, they were so low that Hyrum had left his own house, and quitted business, in order to take care of them during our absence. They continued sick a length of time—Samuel did not altogether recover for a number of months.

Soon after we returned from Harmony, a man by the name of Lyman Cowdery, came into the neighbourhood, and applied to Hyrum, (as he was one of the trustees,) for the district school. A meeting of the trustees was called, and Mr. Cowdery was employed. But the following day, this Mr. Cowdery brought his brother Oliver to the trustees, and requested them to receive him instead of himself, as circumstances had transpired which rendered it necessary for him to disappoint them, or which would not allow of his attending to the school himself; and he would warrant the good conduct of the school under his brother's supervision. All parties being satisfied, Oliver commenced his school, boarding for the time being at our house. He had been in the school but a short time, when he began to hear from all quarters concerning the plates, and as soon began to importune Mr. Smith upon the subject, but for a considerable length of time did not succeed in eliciting any information. At last, however, he gained my husband's confidence, so far as to obtain a sketch of the facts relative to the plates.

Shortly after receiving this information, he told Mr. Smith that he was highly delighted with what he had heard, that he had been in a deep study upon the subject all day, and that it was impressed [129] upon his mind, that he should yet have the privilege of writing for Joseph. Furthermore, that he had determined to pay him a visit at the close of the school, which he was then teaching.

On coming in on the following day, he said, "The subject upon which we were yesterday conversing seems working in my very bones, and I cannot, for a moment, get it out of my mind, finally, I have resolved on what I will do. Samuel, I understand, is going down to Pennsylvania to spend the spring with Joseph; I shall make my arrangements to be ready to accompany him thither, by the time he recovers his health; for I have made it a subject of prayer, and I firmly believe that it is the will of the Lord that I should go. If there is a work for me to do in this thing, I am determined to attend to it."

Mr. Smith told him, that he supposed it was his privilege to know whether this was the case, and advised him to seek for a testimony for himself, which he did, and received the witness spoken of in the Book of *Doc. and Cov.* sec. 8.

From this time, Oliver was so completely absorbed in the subject of the Record, that it seemed impossible for him to think or converse about anything else.

As the time for which we had agreed for the place was now drawing to a close, we began to make preparations to remove our family and effects to the house in which Hyrum resided. We now felt more keenly than ever the injustice of the measure which had placed a landlord over us on our own premises, and who was about to eject us from them.

This I thought would be a good occasion for bringing to Oliver's mind, the cause of all our present privations, as well as the misfortunes which he himself was liable to if he should turn his back upon the world, and set out in the service of God.

"Now, Oliver," said I, "see what a comfortable home we have had here, what pains each child we have has taken to provide for us every thing neces[130]sary to make old age comfortable, and long life desirable. Here, especially, I look upon the handy-work of my beloved Alvin, who even upon his death-bed, and in his last moments, charged his brothers to finish his work of preparing a place of earthly rest for us; that if it were possible, through the exertions of the children, our last days might be our best days. Indeed, there is scarcely anything which I here see, that has not passed through the hands of that faithful boy, and afterwards, by his brothers, been arranged precisely according to his plan, thus showing to me, their affectionate remembrance, both of their parents, and of the brother whom they loved. All these tender recollections render our present trial doubly severe, for these dear relics must now pass into the hands of wicked men, who fear not God, and regard not man. And upon what righteous principle has all this been brought about? Have they ever lifted a finger to earn any part of that which they now claim? I tell you they have not. Yet I now give up all this for the sake of Christ and salvation, and I pray God to help me to do so, without a murmur or a tear. In the strength of God, I say, that from this time forth, I will not cast one longing look upon anything which I now leave behind me. However, in consequence of these things, Oliver, we cannot make you comfortable any longer, and you will be under the necessity of taking boarding somewhere else."

"Mother," exclaimed the young man, "let me stay with you, for I can live in any log hut where you and father live, but I cannot leave you, so do not mention it."

In April, Samuel, and Mr. Cowdery set out for Pennsylvania. The weather, for some time previous, had been very wet and disagreeable—raining, freezing, and thawing alternately, which had rendered the roads almost impassable, particularly in the middle of the day. Notwithstanding, Mr. Cowdery was not to be detained, either by wind or [131] weather, and they persevered until they arrived at Joseph's.

Joseph had been so hurried with his secular affairs, that he could not proceed with his spiritual concerns so fast as was necessary for the speedy completion of the work; there was also another disadvantage under which he laboured, his wife had so much of her time taken up with the care of her house, that she could write for him but a small portion of the time. On account of these embarrassments, Joseph called upon the Lord, three days prior to the arrival of Samuel and Oliver, to send him a scribe, according to the promise of the angel; and he was informed that the same should be forthcoming in a few days. Accordingly, when Mr. Cowdery told him the business that he had come upon, Joseph was not at all surprised.

They sat down and conversed together till late. During the evening, Joseph told Oliver his history, as far as was necessary for his present information, in the things which mostly concerned him. And the next morning they commenced the work of translation, in which they were soon deeply engaged.

One morning they sat down to their work, as usual, and the first thing which presented itself through the Urim and Thummim, was a commandment for Joseph and Oliver to repair to the water, and attend to the ordinance of Baptism. They did so, and as they were returning to the house, they overheard Samuel engaged in secret prayer. Joseph said, that he considered this as a sufficient testimony of his being a fit subject for Baptism; and as they had now received authority to baptize, they spoke to Samuel upon the subject, and he went straightway to the water with them, and was baptized. After which, Joseph and Oliver proceeded with the work of translation as before. **[132]**

CHAPTER 29

MRS. HARRIS PROSECUTES JOSEPH

ABOUT the first of August, Samuel returned home, bringing us news of Joseph's success. This intelligence produced in Martin Harris a great desire to go down to Pennsylvania to see how they were prospering. This being made known to his wife, she resolved to prevent him from going, also to bring Joseph into difficulty, which would perhaps hinder him from ever accomplishing the work in which he was engaged.

To this end, she undertook to prove, that Joseph never had the Record which he professed to have, and that he pretended to have in his possession certain gold plates, for the express purpose of obtaining money. Accordingly, she mounted her horse, flew from house to house through the neighbourhood, like a dark spirit, making diligent inquiry wherever she had the least hopes of gleaning anything, and stirring up every malicious feeling which would tend to subserve her wicked purpose. Having ascertained the number and strength of her adherents, she entered a complaint against Joseph, before a certain magistrate of Lyons. She then sent word to Lyman Cowdery, requesting him to come thither, prepared to go post haste to Pennsylvania, (provided the decision should be given against Joseph,) to assist the officers in securing and confining him in prison. This call, Lyman Cowdery answered immediately, and all things seemed going on prosperously with Mrs. Harris. She made affidavit to many things herself, and directed the officers whom to subpoena. Among the number was her husband, who was a principal witness in the case.

When the day of trial came on, the neighbours came and informed us, that the witnesses had gone to Lyons with the declared intention to obtain a [133] verdict against Joseph, if it could be done by swearing. Immediately after our friends left, Hyrum came in, and I asked him what could be done.

"Why, mother," said he, "we can do nothing, except to look to the Lord: in him is all help and strength; he can deliver from every trouble."

I had never neglected this important duty, yet, seeing such confidence in my son, strengthened me in this hour of trial. Not being accustomed to lawsuits of this character, I trembled for the issue, for this was the first time a suit had ever been preferred before a court against any of my family. I retired to a secluded place, and poured out my whole soul in entreaties to God, for the safety of my son, and continued my supplication for some time; at length the spirit fell upon me so powerfully, that every foreboding of ill was entirely removed from my mind, and a voice spoke to me, saying, "not one hair of his head shall be harmed." I was satisfied. I arose, and repaired to the house. I had never before in my life experienced such happy moments. I sat down and began to read, but my feelings were too intense to allow me to do so. My daughter-in-law, Jerusha, came into the room soon after this, and when she turned her eyes upon me, she stopped short, and exclaimed, "why! mother! what is the matter? I never saw you look so strangely in my life."

I told her, that I had never felt so happy before in my life, that my heart was so light, and my mind so completely at rest, that it did not appear possible to me that I should ever have any more trouble while I should exist. I then informed her in relation to the witness which I had received from the Lord.

In the evening the proceedings of the court were rehearsed to us, which were as follows: —

The witnesses, being duly sworn, the first arose and testified, that Joseph Smith told him that the box which he had, contained nothing but sand; and [134] he, Joseph Smith, said it was gold, to deceive the people.

Second witness swore, that Joseph Smith had told him that it was nothing but a box of lead, and he was determined to use it as he saw fit.

Third witness declared, that he once inquired of Joseph Smith what he had in that box, and Joseph Smith told him that there was nothing at all in the box, saying, that he had made fools of the whole of them, and all he wanted was, to get Martin Harris's money away from him, and that he (witness) was knowing to the fact that Joseph Smith had, by his persuasion, already got two or three hundred dollars.

Next came Mrs. Harris's affidavit, in which she stated, that she believed the chief object which Joseph Smith had in view, was to defraud her husband out of all his property, and that she did not believe that Joseph Smith had ever been in possession of the gold plates which he talked so much about.

The magistrate then forbid the introduction of any more witnesses, until Martin Harris should be sworn. Martin being called upon, testified with boldness, decision, and energy, to a few simple facts. When he arose, he raised his hand to heaven, and said, "I can swear, that Joseph Smith never has got one dollar from me by persuasion, since God made me. I did once, of my own free will and accord, put fifty dollars into his hands, in the presence of many witnesses, for the purpose of doing the work of the Lord. This, I can pointedly prove; and I can tell you, furthermore, that I have never seen, in Joseph Smith, a disposition to take any man's money, without giving him a reasonable compensation for the same in return. And as to the plates which he professes to have, gentlemen, if you do not believe it, but continue to resist the truth, it will one day be the means of damning your souls."

After hearing this testimony the magistrate told [135] them they need not call any more witnesses, but ordered them to bring him what had been written of the testimony already given. This he tore in pieces before their eyes, and told them to go home about their business, and trouble him no more with such ridiculous folly. And they did go home, perfectly discomfited.

_____

CHAPTER 30

JOSEPH AND OLIVER REMOVE TO WATERLOO—THEY FINISH THE TRANSLATION

WE will now return to Pennsylvania, where we left Joseph and Oliver busily engaged in translating the Book of Mormon.

After Samuel left them, they still continued the work as before, until about the time of the trial that took place in New York. Near this time, as Joseph was translating by means of the Urim and Thummim, he received, instead of the words of the Book, a commandment to write a letter to a man by the name of David Whitmer, who lived in Waterloo, requesting him to come immediately with his team, and convey himself and Oliver to his own residence, as an evil-designing people were seeking to take away his (Joseph's) life, in order to prevent the work of God from going forth to the world. The letter was written and delivered, and was shown by Mr. Whitmer to his father, mother, brothers, and sisters, and their advice was asked in regard to the best course for him to take in relation to the matter.

His father reminded him that he had as much, wheat sown upon the ground as he could harrow in in two days, at least; besides this, he had a quantity of plaster of paris to spread, which must be done immediately, consequently he could not go, unless he [136] could get a witness from God that it was absolutely necessary.

This suggestion pleased David, and he asked the Lord for a testimony concerning his going for Joseph, and was told by the voice of the Spirit to go as soon as his wheat was harrowed in. The next morning, David went to the field, and found that he had two heavy days' work before him. He then said to himself that, if he should be enabled, by any means, to do this work sooner than the same had ever been done on the farm before, he would receive it as an evidence, that it was the will of God, that he should do all in his power to assist Joseph Smith in the work in which he was engaged. He then fastened his horses to the harrow, and instead of dividing the field into what is, by farmers, usually termed bands, he drove round the whole of it, continuing thus till noon, when, on stopping for dinner, he looked around, and discovered, to his surprise, that he had harrowed in full half the wheat. After dinner he went on as before, and by evening he finished the whole two days' work.

His father, on going into the field the same evening, saw what had been done, and he exclaimed, "There must be an overruling hand in this, and I think you had better go down to Pennsylvania as soon as your plaster of paris is spread."

The next morning, David took a wooden measure under his arm, and went out to spread the plaster, which he had left, two days previous, in heaps near his sister's house, but, on coming to the place, he discovered that it was gone! He then ran to his sister, and inquired of her if she knew what had become of it. Being surprised, she said, "Why do you ask me? was it not all spread yesterday?"

"Not to my knowledge," answered David.

"I am astonished at that," replied his sister; "for the children came to me in the forenoon, and begged of me to go out and see the men sow plaster in the field, saying, that they never saw anybody sow plaster so fast in their lives. I accordingly went, [137] and saw three men at work in the field, as the children said, but, supposing that you had hired some help, on account of your hurry, I went immediately into the house, and gave the subject no further attention."

David made considerable inquiry in regard to the matter, both among his relatives and neighbours, but was not able to learn who had done it. However, the family were convinced that there was an exertion of supernatural power connected with this strange occurrence.

David immediately set out for Pennsylvania, and arrived there in two days, without injuring his horses in the least, though the distance was one hundred and thirty-five miles. When he arrived, he was under the necessity of introducing himself to Joseph, as this was the first time that they had ever met.

I will observe, that the only acquaintance which existed between the Smith and Whitmer families, was that formed by Mr. Smith and myself, when on our way from Manchester to Pennsylvania to visit Joseph, at which time we stopped with David over night, and gave him a brief history of the Record.

When Joseph commenced making preparations for the journey, he inquired of the Lord to know in what manner he should carry the plates. The answer was, that he should commit them into the hands of an angel, for safety, and after arriving at Mr. Whitmer's, the angel would meet him in the garden, and deliver them up again into his hands.

Joseph and Oliver set out without delay, leaving Emma to take charge of affairs during her husband's absence. On arriving at Waterloo, Joseph received the Record according to promise. The next day, he and Oliver resumed the work of translation, which they continued without further interruption until the whole work was accomplished. [138]

CHAPTER 31

THE PLATES ARE SHOWN TO TWELVE WITNESSES—JOSEPH MAKES ARRANGEMENTS FOR PRINTING THE BOOK OF MORMON

As soon as the Book of Mormon was translated, Joseph despatched a messenger to Mr. Smith, bearing intelligence of the completion of the work, and a request that Mr. Smith and myself should come immediately to Waterloo.

The same evening, we conveyed this intelligence to Martin Harris, for we loved the man, although his weakness had cost us much trouble. Hearing this, he greatly rejoiced, and determined to go straightway to Waterloo to congratulate Joseph upon his success. Accordingly, the next morning, we all set off together, and before sunset met Joseph and Oliver at Mr. Whitmer's.

The evening was spent in reading the manuscript, and it would be superfluous for me to say, to one who has read the foregoing pages, that we rejoiced exceedingly. It then appeared to those of us who did not realize the magnitude of the work, as if the greatest difficulty was then surmounted; but Joseph better understood the nature of the dispensation of the Gospel which was committed unto him.

The next morning, after attending to the usual services, namely, reading, singing, and praying, Joseph arose from his knees, and approaching Martin Harris with a solemnity that thrills through my veins to this day, when it occurs to my recollection, said, "Martin Harris, you have got to humble yourself before your God this day, that you may obtain a forgiveness of your sins. If you do, it is the will of God that you should look upon the plates, in company with Oliver Cowdery and David Whitmer."

In a few minutes after this, Joseph, Martin, Oliver, and David, repaired to a grove, a short distance from the house, where they commenced calling upon [139] the Lord, and continued in earnest supplication, until he permitted an angel to come down from his presence, and declare to them, that all which Joseph had testified of concerning the plates was true.

When they returned to the house it was between three and four o'clock P.M. Mrs. Whitmer, Mr. Smith, and myself, were sitting in a bedroom at the time. On coming in, Joseph threw himself down beside me, and exclaimed, "Father, mother, you do not know how happy I am; the Lord has now caused the plates to be shown to three more besides myself. They have seen an angel, who has testified to them, and they will have to bear witness to the truth of what I have said, for now they know for themselves, that I do not go about to deceive the people, and I feel as if I was relieved of a burden which was almost too heavy for me to bear, and it rejoices my soul, that I am not any longer to be entirely alone in the world." Upon this, Martin Harris came in: he seemed almost overcome with joy, and testified boldly to what he had both seen and heard. And so did David and Oliver, adding, that no tongue could express the joy of their hearts, and the greatness of the things which they had both seen and heard.

Their written testimony, which is contained in the Book of Mormon, is as follows: —

THE TESTIMONY OF THREE WITNESSES

"Be it known unto all nations, kindreds, tongues, and people, unto whom this work shall come, that we, through the grace of God the Father, and our Lord Jesus Christ, have seen the plates which contain this Record, which is a Record of the people of Nephi, and also of the Lamanites, their brethren, and also of the people of Jared, who came from the tower, of which hath been spoken; and we also know that they have been translated by the gift and power of God, for his voice hath declared it unto us; wherefore we know of a surety that the work is true. And we also testify that we have seen the engravings which are upon the plates; and they have been shown unto us by the power of [140] God, and not of man. And we declare, with words of soberness, that an angel of God came down from heaven, and he brought and laid before our eyes, that we beheld and saw the plates, and the engravings thereon; and we know that it is by the grace of God the Father, and our Lord Jesus Christ, that we beheld and bear record that these things are true; and it is marvellous in our eyes, nevertheless, the voice of the Lord commanded us that we should bear record of it; wherefore, to be obedient unto the commandments of God, we bear testimony of these things. And we know that if we are faithful in Christ, we shall rid our garments of the blood of all men, and be found spotless before the judgment-seat of Christ, and shall dwell with him eternally in the heavens. And the honor be to the Father, and to the Son, and to the Holy Ghost, which is one God. Amen.

"OLIVER COWDERY,
"DAVID WHITMER,
"MARTIN HARRIS."

The following day, we returned, a cheerful, happy company. In a few days we were followed by Joseph, Oliver, and the Whitmers, who came to make us a visit, and make some arrangements about getting the book printed. Soon after they came, all the male part of the company, with my husband, Samuel, and Hyrum, retired to a place where the family were in the habit of offering up their secret devotions to God. They went to this place, because it had been revealed to Joseph that the plates would be carried thither by one of the ancient Nephites. Here it was, that those eight witnesses, whose names are recorded in the Book of Mormon, looked upon them and handled them. Of which they bear record in the following words:—

THE TESTIMONY OF EIGHT WITNESSES

"Be it known unto all nations, kindreds, tongues, and people, unto whom this work shall come, that Joseph Smith, Jr. the translator of this work, has shown unto us the plates of which hath been spoken, which have the appearance of gold; and as many of the leaves as the said [141] Smith has translated, we did handle with our hands; and we also saw the engravings thereon, all of which has the appearance of ancient work, and of curious workmanship. And this we bear record, with words of soberness, that the said Smith has shown unto us, for we have seen and hefted, and know of a surety, that the said Smith has got the plates of which we have spoken. And we give our names unto the world, to witnesses unto the world that which we have seen; and we lie not, God bearing witness of it.

"CHRISTIAN WHITMER,   "HIRAM PAGE,
"JACOB WHITMER,   "JOSEPH SMITH, SEN.,
"PETER WHITMER, JUN.,   "HYRUM SMITH,
"JOHN WHITMER,   "SAMUEL H. SMITH."

After these witnesses returned to the house, the angel again made his appearance to Joseph, at which time Joseph delivered up the plates into the angel's hands. The ensuing evening, we held a meeting, in which all the witnesses bore testimony to the facts, as stated above; and all of our family, even to Don Carlos, who was but fourteen years of age, testified of the truth of the Latter-day Dispensation—that it was then ushered in. In a few days, the whole company from Waterloo, went to Palmyra to make arrangements for getting the book printed; and they succeeded in making a contract with one E. B. Grandin, but did not draw the writings at that time. The next day, the company from Waterloo returned home, excepting Joseph, and Peter Whitmer, Joseph remaining to draw writings in regard to the printing of the manuscript, which was to be done on the day following.

When Joseph was about starting for Palmyra, where the writings were to be executed, Dr. M'Intyre came in and informed us, that forty men were collected in the capacity of a mob, with the view of waylaying Joseph on his way thither; that they requested him (Dr. M'Intyre) as they had done once before, to take command of the company, and, that upon his refusing to do so, one Mr. Huzzy, a hatter of Palmyra, proffered his services, and was chosen as their leader. [142]

On hearing this I besought Joseph not to go; but he smiled at my fears, saying, "never mind, mother, just put your trust in God, and nothing will hurt me to day." In a short time he set out for Palmyra. On his way thither, lay a heavy strip of timber, about half a mile in width, and, beyond it, on the right side of the road, lay a field belonging to David Jacaway. When he came to this field, he found the mob seated on the string of fence running along the road. Coming to Mr. Huzzy first, he took off his hat, and good-naturedly saying, "Good morning, Mr. Huzzy," passed on to the next, whom he saluted in like manner, and the next, and so on till he came to the last.

This struck them with confusion, and while they were pondering in amazement, he passed on, leaving them perched upon the fence, like so many roosting chickens, and arrived at Palmyra without being molested. Here he met Mr. Grandin, and writings were drawn up between them to this effect: That half of the price for printing was to be paid by Martin Harris, and the residue by my two sons, Joseph and Hyrum. These writings were afterwards signed by all the parties concerned.

When Joseph returned from Palmyra, he said, "Well, mother, the Lord has been on my side to-day, the devil has not overpowered me in any of my proceedings. Did I not tell you that I should be delivered from the hands of all my enemies! They thought they were going to perform great feats; they have done wonders to prevent me from getting the book printed; they mustered themselves together, and got upon the fence, made me a low bow, and went home, and I'll warrant you they wish they had stayed there in the first place. Mother, there is a God in heaven, and I know it."

Soon after this, Joseph secured the copyright; and before he returned to Pennsylvania, where he had left his wife, he received a commandment, which was, in substance, as follows: —

First, that Oliver Cowdery should transcribe the [143] whole manuscript. Second, that he should take but one copy at a time to the office, so that if one copy should get destroyed, there would still be a copy remaining. Third, that in going to and from the office, he should always have a guard to attend him, for the purpose of protecting the manuscript. Fourth, that a guard should be kept constantly on the watch, both night and day, about the house, to protect the manuscript from malicious persons, who would infest the house for the purpose of destroying the manuscript. All these things were strictly attended to, as the Lord commanded Joseph. After giving these instructions, Joseph returned to Pennsylvania.

CHAPTER 32

THE PRINTING IS BEGUN — A MEETING OF THE CITIZENS HELD IN REFERENCE TO THE BOOK

OLIVER COWDERY commenced the work immediately after Joseph left, and the printing went on very well for a season, but the clouds of persecution again began to gather. The rabble, and a party of restless religionists, began to counsel together, as to the most efficient means of putting a stop to our proceedings.

About the first council of this kind was held in a room adjoining that in which Oliver and a young man by the name of Robinson were printing. Mr. Robinson, being curious to know what they were doing in the next room, applied his ear to a hole in the partition wall, and by this means overheard several persons expressing their fears in reference to the **[144]** Book of Mormon. One said, "it was destined to break down every thing before it, if not put a stop to," and, "that it was likely to injure the prospects of their ministers," and then inquired, whether they should endure it. "No, no," was the unanimous reply. It was then asked, "how shall we prevent the printing of this book?" Upon which it was resolved by the meeting, that three of their company should be appointed to go to the house of Mr. Smith, on the following Tuesday or Wednesday, while the men were gone to their work, and request Mrs. Smith to read the manuscript to them; that, after she had done reading it, two of the company should endeavour to divert her attention from it to some other object, while the third, seizing the opportunity, should snatch it from the drawer, or wherever it should be kept, and commit it immediately to the flames.

"Again," said the speaker, "suppose we fail in this, and the book is printed in defiance of all that we can do to the contrary, what means shall we then adopt? Shall we buy their books and allow our families to read them?" They all responded, "No." They then entered into a solemn covenant, never to purchase even a single copy of the work, or permit one member of their families to buy or read one, that they might thus avert the awful calamity which threatened them.

Oliver Cowdery came home that evening, and, after relating the whole affair with much solemnity, he said, "Mother, what shall I do with the manuscript? where shall I put it to keep it away from them?"

"Oliver," said I, "I do not think the matter so serious after all, for there is a watch kept constantly about the house, and I need not take out the manuscript to read it to them unless I choose, and for its present safety I can have it deposited in a chest, under the head of my bed, in such a way that it never will be disturbed." I then placed it in a chest, which was so high, that when placed under **[145]** the bed, the whole weight of the bedstead rested upon the lid. Having made this arrangement, we felt quite at rest, and, that night, the family retired to rest at the usual hour, all save Peter Whitmer, who spent the night on guard. But as for myself, soon after I went to bed I fell into a train of reflections which occupied my mind, and which caused sleep to forsake my eyelids till the day dawned, for, when I meditated upon the days of toil, and nights of anxiety, through which we had all passed for years previous, in order to obtain the treasure that then lay beneath my head; when I thought upon the hours of fearful apprehensions which we had all suffered on the same account, and that the object was at last accomplished, I could truly say that my soul did magnify the Lord, and my spirit rejoiced in God my Saviour. I felt that the heavens were moved in our behalf, and that the angels who had power to put down the mighty from their seats, and to exalt them who were of low degree, were watching over us; that those would be filled who hungered and thirsted after righteousness, when the rich would be sent empty away; that God had helped his servant Israel in remembrance of his promised mercy, and in bringing forth a Record, by which is made known the seed of Abraham, our father. Therefore we could safely put our trust in him, as he was able to help in every time of need.

On the fourth day subsequent to the afore-mentioned council, soon after my husband left the house to go to his work, those three delegates appointed by the council, came to accomplish the work assigned them. Soon after they entered, one of them began thus:—

"Mrs. Smith, we hear that you have a gold bible; we have come to see if you will be so kind as to show it to us?"

"No, gentlemen," said I, "we have no gold bible, but we have a translation of some gold plates, which have been brought forth for the purpose of making known to the world the plainness of the Gospel, and also to give a history of the people which formerly inhabited [146] this continent." I then proceeded to relate the substance of what is contained in the Book of Mormon, dwelling particularly upon the principles of religion therein contained. I endeavoured to show them the similarity between these principles, and the simplicity of the Gospel taught by Jesus Christ in the New Testament. "Notwithstanding all this," said I, "the different denominations are very much opposed to us. The Universalists are alarmed lest their religion should suffer loss, the Presbyterians tremble for their salaries, the Methodists also come, and they rage, for they worship a God without body or parts, and they know that our faith comes in contact with this principle."

After hearing me through, the gentlemen said, "can we see the manuscript, then?"

"No, sir," replied I, "you cannot see it. I have told you what it contains, and that must suffice."

He made no reply to this, but said, "Mrs. Smith, you and the most of your children have belonged to our church for some length of time, and we respect you very highly. You say a great deal about the Book of Mormon, which your son has found, and you believe much of what he tells you, yet we cannot bear the thoughts of losing you, and they do wish—I wish, that if you do believe those things, you would not say anything more upon the subject—I do wish you would not."

"Deacon Beckwith," said I, "if you should stick my flesh full of faggots, and even burn me at the stake, I would declare, as long as God should give me breath, that Joseph has got that Record, and that I know it to be true."

At this, he observed to his companions, "You see it is of no use to say anything more to her, for we cannot change her mind." Then, turning to me, he said, "Mrs. Smith, I see that it is not possible to persuade you out of your belief, therefore I deem it unnecessary to say anything more upon the subject."

"No, sir," said I, "it is not worth your while."

He then bid me farewell, and went out to see **[147]** Hyrum, when the following conversation took place between them.

Deacon Beckwith. "Mr. Smith, do you not think that you may be deceived about that Record, which your brother pretends to have found?"

Hyrum. "No, sir, I do not."

Deacon Beckwith. "Well, now, Mr. Smith, if you find that you are deceived, and that he has not got the Record, will you confess the fact to me?"

Hyrum. "Will you, Deacon Beckwith, take one of the books, when they are printed, and read it, asking God to give you an evidence that you may know whether it is true?"

Deacon Beckwith. "I think it beneath me to take so much trouble, however, if you will promise that you will confess to me that Joseph never had the plates, I will ask for a witness whether the book is true."

Hyrum. "I will tell you what I will do, Mr. Beckwith, if you do get a testimony from God, that the book is not true, I will confess to you that it is not true."

Upon this they parted, and the Deacon next went to Samuel, who quoted to him, Isaiah, 56: 9-11: "All ye beasts of the field, come to devour; yea, all ye beasts in the forest. His watchman are blind: they are all ignorant, they are all dumb dogs, they cannot bark; sleeping, lying down, loving to slumber; yea, they are greedy dogs, which can never have enough, and they are shepherds that cannot understand: they all look to their own way, every one for his gain, from his quarter."

Here Samuel ended the quotation, and the three gentlemen left without ceremony. **[148]**

––––––––––

CHAPTER 33

THE work of printing still continued with little or no interruption, until one Sunday afternoon, when Hyrum became very uneasy as to the security of the work left at the printing office, and requested Oliver to accompany him thither, to see if all was right. Oliver hesitated for a moment, as to the propriety of going on Sunday, but finally consented, and they set off together.

On arriving at the printing establishment, they found it occupied by an individual by the name of Cole, an ex-justice of the peace, who was busily employed in printing a newspaper. Hyrum was much surprised at finding him there, and remarked, "How is it, Mr. Cole, that you are so hard at work on Sunday?"

Mr. Cole replied, that he could not have the press, in the day time during the week, and was obliged to do his printing at night, and on Sundays.

Upon reading the prospectus of his paper, they found that he had agreed with his subscribers to publish one form of "Joe Smith's Gold Bible" each week, and thereby furnish them with the principal portion of the book in such a way that they would not be obliged to pay the Smiths for it. His paper was entitled, DOGBERRY PAPER ON WINTER HILL. In this, he had thrown together a parcel of the most vulgar, disgusting prose, and the meanest, and most low-lived doggrel, in juxtaposition with a portion of the Book of Mormon, which he had pilfered. At this perversion of common sense and moral feeling, Hyrum was shocked, as well as indignant at the dishonest course which Mr. Cole had taken, in order to possess himself of the work. **[149]**

"Mr. Cole," said he, "what right have you to print the Book of Mormon in this manner? Do you not know that we have secured the copyright?"

"It is none of your business," answered Cole, "I have hired the press, and will print what I please, so help yourself."

"Mr. Cole," rejoined Hyrum, "that manuscript is sacred, and I forbid your printing any more of it."

"Smith," exclaimed Cole, in a tone of anger, "I don't care a d—n for you: that d—d gold bible is going into my paper, in spite of all you can do."

Hyrum endeavoured to dissuade him from his purpose, but finding him inexorable, left him to issue his paper, as he had hitherto done; for when they found him at work, he had already issued six or eight numbers, and by taking them ten or twenty miles into the country, had managed to keep them out of our sight.

On returning from the office, they asked my husband what course was best for them to pursue, relative to Mr. Cole. He told them that he considered it a matter with which Joseph ought to be made acquainted. Accordingly, he set out himself for Pennsylvania, and returned with Joseph the ensuing Sunday. The weather was so extremely cold, that they came near perishing before they arrived at home, nevertheless, as soon as Joseph made himself partially comfortable, he went to the printing office, where he found Cole employed, as on the Sunday previous. "How do you do, Mr. Cole," said Joseph, "You seem hard at work."

"How do you do, Mr. Smith," answered Cole, dryly.

Joseph examined his DOGBERRY PAPER, and then said firmly, "Mr. Cole, that book, [the Book of Mormon] and the right of publishing it, belongs to me, and I forbid you meddling with it any further."

At this Mr. Cole threw off his coat, rolled up his sleeves, and came towards Joseph, smacking his fists together with vengeance, and roaring out, "do you want to fight, sir? do you want to fight? I will pub[150]lish just what I please. Now, if you want to fight, just come on."

Joseph could not help smiling at his grotesque appearance, for his behaviour was too ridiculous to excite indignation. "Now, Mr. Cole," said he, "you had better keep your coat on—it is cold, and I am not going to fight you, nevertheless, I assure you, sir, that you have got to stop printing my book, for I know my rights, and shall maintain them."

"Sir," bawled out the wrathy gentleman, "if you think you are the best man, just pull off your coat and try it."

"Mr. Cole," said Joseph, in a low, significant tone, "there is law, and you will find that out, if you do not understand it, but I shall not fight you, sir."

At this, the ex-justice began to cool off a little, and finally concluded to submit to an arbitration, which decided that he should stop his proceedings forthwith, so that he made us no further trouble.

Joseph, after disposing of this affair, returned to Pennsylvania, but not long to remain there, for when the inhabitants of the surrounding country perceived that the work still progressed, they became uneasy, and again called a large meeting. At this time, they gathered their forces together, far and near, and organizing themselves into a committee of the whole, they resolved, as before, never to purchase one of our books, when they should be printed. They then appointed a committee to wait upon E. B. Grandin, and inform him of the resolutions which they had passed, and also to explain to him the evil consequences which would result to him therefrom. The men who were appointed to do this errand, fulfilled their mission to the letter, and urged upon Mr. Grandin the necessity of his putting a stop to the printing, as the Smiths had lost all their property, and consequently would be unable to pay him for his work, except by the sale of the books. And this they would never be able to do, for the people would not purchase them. This information caused Mr. Grandin to stop printing, and we were again [151] compelled to send for Joseph. These trips, back and forth, exhausted nearly all our means, yet they seemed unavoidable.

When Joseph came, he went immediately with Martin Harris to Grandin, and succeeded in removing his fears, so that he went on with the work, until the books were printed, which was in the spring of eighteen hundred and thirty.

CHAPTER 34

THE CHURCH ORGANIZED

ABOUT the first of April of the same year in which the Book of Mormon was published, Joseph came again from Pennsylvania, and preached to us several times. On the morning of the sixth day of the same month, my husband and Martin Harris were baptized. When Mr. Smith came out of the water, Joseph stood upon the shore, and taking his father by the hand, he exclaimed, with tears of joy, "Oh, my God! have I lived to see my own father baptized into the true Church of Jesus Christ!" On the same day, April 6, 1830, the Church was organized.

Shortly after this, my sons were all ordained to the ministry, even Don Carlos, who was but fourteen years of age. Samuel was directed to take a number of the Books of Mormon, and go on a mission to Livonia, to preach, and make sale of the books, if possible. Whilst he was making preparations to go on this mission, Miss Almira Mack arrived in Manchester from Pontiac. This young woman was a daughter of my brother, Stephen Mack, whose history I have already given. She received the Gospel as soon as she heard it, and was baptized [152] immediately, and has ever since remained a faithful member of the Church.

On the thirtieth of June, Samuel started on the mission to which he had been set apart by Joseph, and in travelling twenty-five miles, which was his first day's journey, he stopped at a number of places in order to sell books, but was turned out of doors as soon as he declared his principles. When evening came on, he was faint and almost discouraged, but coming to an inn, which was surrounded with every appearance of plenty, he called to see if the landlord would buy one of his books. On going in, Samuel inquired of him, if he did not wish to purchase a history of the origin of the Indians.

"I do not know," replied the host, "how did you get hold of it?"

"It was translated," rejoined Samuel, "by my brother, from some gold plates that he found buried in the earth."

"You d—d liar!" cried the landlord, "get out of my house—you shan't stay one minute with your books."

Samuel was sick at heart, for this was the fifth time he had been turned out of doors that day. He left the house, and travelled a short distance, and washed his feet in a small brook, as a testimony against the man. He then proceeded five miles further on his journey, and seeing an apple tree a short distance from the road, he concluded to pass the night under it; and here he lay all night upon the cold, damp ground. In the morning, he arose from his comfortless bed, observing a small cottage at no great distance, he drew near, hoping to get a little refreshment. The only inmate was a widow, who seemed very poor. He asked her for food, relating the story of his former treatment. She prepared him some victuals, and, after eating, he explained to her the history of the Book of Mormon. She listened attentively, and believed all that he told her, but, in consequence of her poverty, she was unable to purchase one of the books. He presented her with one, [153] and proceeded to Bloomington, which was eight miles further. Here he stopped at the house of one John P. Green, who was a Methodist preacher, and was at that time about starting on a preaching mission. He, like the others, did not wish to make a purchase of what he considered at that time to be a nonsensical fable, however, he said that he would take a subscription paper, and if he found any one on his route who was disposed to purchase, he would take his name, and in two weeks, Samuel might call again, and he would let him know what the prospect was of selling. After making this arrangement, Samuel left one of his books with him, and returned home. At the time appointed, Samuel started again for the Rev. John P. Green's, in order to learn the success which this gentleman had met with in finding sale for the Book of Mormon. This time, Mr. Smith, and myself accompanied him, and it was our intention to have passed near the tavern, where Samuel was so abusively treated a fortnight previous, but just before we came to the house, a sign of small-pox intercepted us. We turned aside, and meeting a citizen of the place, we inquired of him, to what extent this disease prevailed. He answered, that the tavernkeeper and two of his family had died with it not long since, but he did not know that any one else had caught the distemper, and that it was brought into the neighbourhood by a traveller, who stopped at the tavern over night.

This is a specimen of the peculiar disposition of some individuals, who would purchase their death for a few shillings, but sacrifice their soul's salvation rather than give a Saint of God a meal of victuals. According to the Word of God, it shall be more tolerable for Sodom and Gomorrah, in the day of judgment, than for such persons.

We arrived at Esquire Beaman's, in Livonia, that night. The next morning Samuel took the road to Mr. Green's, and finding that he had made no sale of the books, we returned home the following day. **[154]**

CHAPTER 35

JOSEPH SMITH, SENIOR, AND DON CARLOS, VISIT STOCKHOLM

SOON after the Church was organized, my husband set out, with Don Carlos, to visit his father, Asael Smith. After a tedious journey, they arrived at the house of John Smith, my husband's brother. His wife Clarissa, had never before seen my husband, but as soon as he entered, she exclaimed, "There, Mr. Smith, is your brother Joseph." John, turning suddenly, cried out, "Joseph, is this you!

"It is I," said Joseph, "is my father yet alive? I have come to see him once more, before he dies."

For a particular account of this visit, I shall give my readers an extract from brother John Smith's journal. He writes as follows:—

"The next morning after brother Joseph arrived, we set out together for Stockholm to see our father, who was living at that place with our brother Silas. We arrived about dark at the house of my brother Jesse, who was absent with his wife. The children informed us, that their parents were with our father, who was supposed to be dying. We hastened without delay to the house of brother Silas, and upon arriving there were told, that father was just recovering from a severe fit, and, as it was not considered advisable to let him or mother know that Joseph was there, we went to spend the night with brother Jesse.

"As soon as we were settled, brothers Jesse and Joseph entered into conversation respecting their families. Joseph briefly related the history of his family, the death of Alvin, &c. He then began to speak of the discovery and translation of the Book of Mormon. At this, Jesse grew very angry, and exclaimed, 'If you say another word about that Book of Mormon, you shall not stay a minute longer in my house, and if I can't get you out any other way, I will hew you down with my broad axe.' **[155]**

"We had always been accustomed to being treated with much

harshness by our brother, but he had never carried it to so great an extent before. However, we spent the night with him, and the next morning visited our aged parents. They were overjoyed to see Joseph, for he had been absent from them so long, that they had been fearful of never beholding his face again in the flesh.

"After the usual salutations, enquiries, and explanations, the subject of the Book of Mormon was introduced. Father received with gladness, that which Joseph communicated; and remarked, that he had always expected that something would appear to make known the true Gospel.

"In a few minutes brother Jesse came in, and on hearing that the subject of our conversation was the Book of Mormon, his wrath rose as high as it did the night before. 'My father's mind,' said Jesse, 'is weak, and I will not have it corrupted with such blasphemous stuff, so just shut up your heads.' Brother Joseph reasoned mildly with him, but to no purpose. Brother Silas then said, 'Jesse, our brother has come to make us a visit, and I am glad to see him, and am willing he should talk as he pleases in my house.' Jesse replied in so insulting a manner, and continued to talk so abusively, that Silas was under the necessity of requesting him to leave the house.

"After this, brother Joseph proceeded in conversation, and father seemed to be pleased with every word which he said. But I must confess that I was too pious, at that time, to believe one word of it.

"I returned home the next day, leaving Joseph with my father. Soon after which, Jesse came to my house and informed me, that all my brothers were coming to make me a visit, 'and as true as you live,' said he, 'they all believe that cursed Mormon book, every word of it, and they are setting a trap for you, to make you believe it.'

"I thanked him for taking so much trouble upon himself, to inform me that my brothers were coming to see me, but told him, that I considered myself amply able to judge for myself in matters of religion. 'I know,' he replied, 'that you are a pretty good judge of such things, but I tell you, that they are as wary as the devil. And I want you to go with me and see our sisters, Susan and Fanny, and we will bar their minds against Joseph's influence." **[156]**

"We accordingly visited them, and conversed upon the subject as we thought proper, and requested them to be at my house the next day.

"My brothers arrived according to previous arrangement, and Jesse, who came also, was very careful to hear every word which passed among us, and would not allow one word to be said about the Book of Mormon. They agreed that night to visit our sisters the following day, and as we were about leaving, brother Asael took me aside and said, 'Now, John, I want you to have some conversation with Joseph, but if you do, you must cheat it out of Jesse. And if you wish, I can work the card for you.'

"I told him that I would be glad to talk with Joseph alone, if I could get an opportunity.

"'Well,' replied Asael, 'I will take a certain number in my carriage, and Silas will take the rest, and you may bring out a horse for Joseph to ride, but when we are out of sight, take the horse back to the stable again, and keep Joseph over night.'

"I did as Asael advised, and that evening Joseph explained to me the principles of 'Mormonism,' the truth of which I have never since denied.

"The next morning, we (Joseph and myself) went to our sisters, where we met our brothers, who censured me very sharply for keeping Joseph over night—Jesse, because he was really displeased; the others, to make a show of disappointment.

"In the evening, when we were about to separate, I agreed to take Joseph in my waggon twenty miles on his journey the next day. Jesse rode home with me that evening, leaving Joseph with our sisters. As Joseph did not expect to see Jesse again, when we were about starting, Joseph gave Jesse his hand in a pleasant, affectionate manner, and said, 'Farewell, brother Jesse!' 'Farewell, Jo, for ever,' replied Jesse, in a surly tone.

"'I am afraid,' returned Joseph in a kind, but solemn manner, 'it will be for ever, unless you repent.'

"This was too much for even Jesse's obdurate heart. He melted into tears; however, he made no reply, nor ever mentioned the circumstance afterwards.

"I took my brothers twenty miles on his journey the next day, as I had agreed. Before he left me, he requested me to promise him, that I would read a Book of Mormon, which he had given me, and even should I not [157] believe it, that I would not condemn it; 'for,' said he, 'if you do not condemn it, you shall have a testimony of its truth.' I fulfilled my promise, and thus proved his testimony to be true."

Just before my husband's return, as Joseph was about commencing a discourse one Sunday morning, Parley P. Pratt came in, very much fatigued. He had heard of us at some considerable distance, and had travelled very fast, in order to get there by meeting time, as he wished to hear what we had to say, that he might be prepared to show us our error. But when Joseph had finished his discourse, Mr. Pratt arose, and expressed his hearty concurrence in every sentiment advanced. The following day, he was baptized and ordained. In a few days he set off for Canaan, N. Y. where his brother Orson resided, whom he baptized on the nineteenth of September, 1830.

After Joseph ordained Parley, he went home again to Pennsylvania, for he was only in Manchester on business. About this time, his trouble commenced at Colesville with the mob, who served, a writ upon him, and dragged him from the desk as he was about taking his text to preach. But as a relation of this affair is given in his history,[1] I shall mention only one circumstance pertaining to it, for which I am dependant upon

---

[1] See *Times and Seasons*, vol. 4, pp. 40 and 61. *Supp. to Mil. Star*, vol. 14, p. 31.

Esquire Reid, Joseph's counsel in the case, and I shall relate it as near in his own words as my memory will admit: —

"I was so busy at that time, when Mr. Smith sent for me, that it was almost impossible for me to attend the case, and never having seen Mr. Smith, I determined to decline going. But soon after coming to this conclusion, I thought I heard some one say to me, 'You *must* go, and deliver the Lord's Anointed!' Supposing that it was the man who came after me, I replied, 'the Lord's Anointed? What do you mean by the Lord's Anointed?' He was surprised at being accosted in this manner, and replied, 'what do *you* mean, sir? I said nothing about the Lord's [158] Anointed.' I was convinced that he told the truth, for these few words filled my mind with peculiar feelings, such as I had never before experienced; and I immediately hastened to the place of trial. Whilst I was engaged in the case, these emotions increased, and when I came to speak upon it, I was inspired to an eloquence which was altogether new to me, and which was overpowering and irresistible. I succeeded, as I expected, in obtaining the prisoner's discharge. This the more enraged the adverse party, and I soon discovered that Mr. Smith was liable to abuse from them, should he not make his escape. The most of them being fond of liquor, I invited them into another room to drink, and thus succeeded in attracting their attention, until Mr. Smith was beyond their reach. I knew not where he went, but I was satisfied that he was out of their hands."

Since this circumstance occurred, until this day, Mr. Reid has been a faithful friend to Joseph, although he has never attached himself to the Church.

After escaping the hands of the mob, Joseph travelled till day-break the next morning, before he ventured to ask for victuals, although he had taken nothing, save a small crust of bread, for two days. About day-break he arrived at the house of one of his wife's sisters, where he found Emma, who had suffered great anxiety about him, since his first arrest. They returned home together, and immediately afterwards Joseph received a commandment by revelation, to move his family to Waterloo.

We had at this time just completed a house, which Joseph had built on a small farm, that he had purchased of his father-in-law; however, he locked up his house with his furniture in it, and repaired with Emma, immediately to Manchester. About the time of his arrival at our house, Hyrum had settled up his business, for the purpose of being at liberty to do whatever the Lord required of him: [159] and he requested Joseph to ask the Lord for a revelation concerning the matter. The answer given was, that he should take a bed, his family, and what clothing he needed for them, and go straightway to Colesville, for his enemies were combining in secret chambers to take away his life. At the same time, Mr.

Smith received a commandment to go forthwith to Waterloo, and prepare a place for our family, as our enemies also sought his destruction in the neighbourhood in which we then resided, but in Waterloo he should find favour in the eyes of the people. The next day, by ten o'clock, Hyrum was on his journey. Joseph and Emma left for Macedon, and William went away from home in another direction, on business. Samuel was absent on a third mission to Livonia, for which he had set out on the 1st of October, soon after the arrival of my husband and Don Carlos from their visit to father Smith. Catherine and Don Carlos were also away from home. Calvin Stodard and his wife, Sophronia, had moved several miles distant some time previous. This left no one but Mr. Smith, myself, and our little girl, Lucy, at home.

CHAPTER 36

JOSEPH SMITH, SENIOR, IMPRISONED—AN ATTEMPT TO TAKE HYRUM

ON the same day that Hyrum left for Colesville, which was Wednesday, the neighbours began to call, one after another, and inquire very particularly for Hyrum.

This gave me great anxiety, for I knew that they had no business with him. The same night, my husband was taken rather ill, and, continuing unwell the next day, he was unable to take breakfast with **[160]** me. About ten o'clock I commenced preparing him some milk porridge, but, before it was ready for him, a Quaker gentleman called to see him, and the following is the substance of their conversation:—

Quaker. "Friend Smith, I have a note against thee of fourteen dollars, which I have lately bought, and I have come to see if thou hast the money for me."

Mr. Smith. "Why, sir, did you purchase that note? You certainly was in no want of the money?"

Quaker. "That is business of my own; I want the money, and must have it."

Mr. Smith. "I can pay you six dollars now,—the rest you will have to wait for, as I cannot get it for you."

Quaker. "No, I will not wait one hour; and if thou dost not pay me immediately, thou shalt go forthwith to the jail, unless *(running to the fire place, and making violent gestures with his hands towards the fire)* thou wilt burn up those Books of Mormon; but if thou wilt burn them up, then I will forgive thee the whole debt."

Mr. Smith (decidedly). "That I shall not do."

Quaker. "Then, thou shalt go to jail."

"Sir," I interrupted *(taking my gold beads from my neck, and holding them towards him)*, "these beads are the full value of the remainder of the debt. I beseech you to take them, and give up the note."

Quaker. "No, I will not. Thou must pay the money, or thy husband shall go straightway to jail."

"Now, here, sir," I replied, "just look at yourself as you are. Because God has raised up my son to bring forth a book, which was written for the salvation of the souls of men, for the salvation of your soul as well as mine, you have come here to distress me, by taking my husband to jail; and you think, by this, that you will compel us to deny the work of God, and destroy a book which was translated by [161] the gift and power of God. But, sir, we shall not burn the Book of Mormon, nor deny the inspiration of the Almighty."

The Quaker then stepped to the door, and called a constable, who was waiting there for the signal. The constable came forward, and, laying his hand on Mr. Smith's shoulder, said, "You are my prisoner."

I entreated the officer to allow me time to get some one to become my husband's security, but he refused. I then requested that he might be permitted to eat the porridge which I had been preparing, as he had taken no nourishment since the night before. This was also denied, and the Quaker ordered my husband to get immediately into a waggon which stood waiting to convey him to prison.

After they had taken him to the waggon, the Quaker stood over him as guard, and the officer came back and eat up the food which I had prepared for my husband, who sat in the burning sun, faint and sick.

I shall make no remarks in regard to my feelings on this occasion. Any human heart can imagine how I felt. But verily, verily, those men will have their reward.

They drove off with my husband, leaving me alone with my little girl. The next morning, I went on foot several miles to see a friend by the name of Abner Lackey, who, I hoped, would assist me. I was not disappointed. He went without delay to the magistrate's office, and had my papers prepared, so that I could get my husband out of the prison cell, although he would still be confined in the jail yard.

Shortly after I returned home, a pert young gentleman came in, and asked if Mr. Hyrum Smith was at home. I told him, as I had others, that he was in Colesville. The young man said that Hyrum was owing a small debt to Dr. M'Intyre, and that he had come to collect it by the doctor's orders, as he (M'Intyre) was from home. I told the young man [162] that this debt was to be paid in corn and beans, which should be sent to him the next day. I then hired a man to take the produce the following day to the doctor's house, which was accordingly done, and, when the man returned, he informed me that the clerk agreed to erase the account. It was now too late in the day to set out for Canandaigua, where my husband was confined in prison, and I concluded to defer going, till the next morning, in hopes that some of my sons would return during the interval. The night came on, but neither of my sons made their appearance. When the night closed in, the darkness was hideous, scarcely any object was discernible. I sat down and began to contemplate the situation of myself and family. My husband, an affectionate companion and tender father, as ever blessed the confidence of a family, was an imprisoned debtor, torn from his family and immured in a dungeon, where he had already lain two dismal nights, and now another must be added to the number, before I could reach him to render him any assistance. And where were his children? Alvin was murdered by a quack physician; but still he lay at peace. Hyrum was flying from his home, and why I knew not; the secret combinations of his enemies were not yet fully developed. Joseph had but recently escaped from his persecutors, who sought to accomplish his destruction. Samuel was gone, without purse or scrip, to preach the Gospel, for which he was as much despised and hated as were the ancient disciples. William was also gone, and, I had not, unlike Naomi, even my daughters-in-law to comfort my heart in this the hour of my affliction. While I was thus meditating, a heavy rap at the door brought me suddenly to my feet. I bid the stranger enter. He asked me, in a hurried manner, where Hyrum was. I answered the question, as usual. Just then a second person came in, and the first observed to a second, "Mrs. Smith says her son is not at home." The person addressed looked suspiciously around, and remarked, "he is [163] at home, for your neighbours have seen him here today." "Then, sir," I replied, "they have seen what I have not." "We have a search warrant," rejoined he, "and, if you do not give him up, we shall be under the necessity of taking whatever we find that belongs to him." Finding some corn, stored in the chamber above the room where Hyrum had lived, they declared their intention of taking it, but I forbade their meddling with it. At this instant, a third stranger entered, and then a fourth. The last observed, "I do not know, but you will think strange of so many of us coming in, but my candle was out, and I came in to re-light it by your fire." I told him I did not know what to think, I had but little reason to consider myself safe either day or night, and that I would like to know what their business was, and for what cause they were seizing upon our property. The foremost replied that it was wanted to settle a debt which Hyrum was owing to Dr. M'Intyre. I told him that it was paid. He disputed my word, and ordered his men to take the corn.

As they were going up stairs, I looked out of the window, and one glance almost turned my head giddy. As far as I could see by the light of two candles and a pair of carriage lamps, the heads of men appeared in every direction, some on foot, some on horseback, and the rest in waggons. I saw that there was no way but for me to sit quietly down, and see my house pillaged by a banditti of blacklegs, religious bigots, and cut-throats, who were united in one purpose, namely, that of destroying us from the face of the earth. However, there was one resource, and to that I applied. I went aside and kneeled before the Lord, and begged that he would not let my children fall into their hands, and that they might be satisfied with plunder without taking life.

Just at this instant, William bounded into the house. "Mother," he cried, "in the name of God, what is this host of men doing here? Are they robbing or murdering? What are they about?" **[164]**

I told him, in short, that they had taken his father to prison, and had now come after Hyrum, but, not finding him, they were plundering the house. Hereupon William seized a large handspike, sprang up stairs, and, in one instant, cleared the scoundrels out of the chamber. They scampered down stairs; he flew after them, and, bounding into the very midst of the crowd, he brandished his handspike in every direction, exclaiming, "Away from here, you cut-throats, instantly, or I will be the death of every one of you."

The lights were immediately extinguished, yet he continued to harangue them boisterously until he discovered that his audience had left him. They seemed to believe what he said, and fled in every direction, leaving us again to ourselves.

Between twelve and one o'clock, Calvin Stodard and his wife, Sophronia, arrived at our house. Calvin said he had been troubled about us all the afternoon, and, finally, about the setting of the sun, he told Sophronia that he would even then start for her father's if she felt inclined to go with him.

Within an hour after their arrival, Samuel came. He was much fatigued, for he had travelled twenty-one miles after sunset. I told him our situation, and that I wished him to go early the next morning to Canandaigua, and procure his father's release from the dungeon. "Well, mother," said he, "I am sick; fix me a bed, that I may lie down and rest myself, or I shall not be able to go, for I have taken a heavy cold, and my bones ache dreadfully."

However, by a little nursing and some rest, he was able to set off by sunrise, and arrived in Canandaigua at ten o'clock. After informing the jailor of his business, he requested that his father might be immediately liberated from the cell. The jailor refused, because it was Sunday, but permitted Samuel to go into the cell, where he found my husband confined in the same dungeon with a man committed for murder. Upon Samuel inquiring what his treatment had been, Mr. Smith replied as follows:— **[165]**

> "Immediately after I left your mother, the men by whom I was taken commenced using every possible argument to induce me to renounce the Book of Mormon, saying, 'how much better it would be for you to deny that silly thing, than to be disgraced and imprisoned, when you might not only escape this, but also have the note back, as well as the money which you have paid on it.' To this I made no reply. They still went on in the same manner till we arrived at the jail, when they hurried me into this dismal dungeon. I shuddered when I first heard these heavy doors creaking upon their hinges; but then, I thought to myself, I was not the first man who had been imprisoned for the truth's sake; and when I should meet Paul in the Paradise of God, I could tell him that I, too, had been in bonds for the Gospel which he had preached. And this has been my only consolation.
>
> "From the time that I entered until now, and this is the fourth day, I have had nothing to eat, save a pint basin full of very weak broth; and there *(pointing to the opposite side of the cell)* lies the basin yet."

Samuel was very much wounded by this, and, having obtained permission of the jailor, he immediately went out and brought his father some comfortable food. After which he remained with him until the next morning, when the business was attended to, and Mr. Smith went out into the jail yard to a cooper's shop, where he obtained employment at coopering, and followed the same until he was released, which was thirty days. He preached during his confinement here every Sunday, and when he was released he baptized two persons whom he had thus converted. **[166]**

CHAPTER 37

THE FAMILY OF JOSEPH SMITH, SENIOR, REMOVE TO WATERLOO

SAMUEL returned from Canandaigua the same day that my husband was liberated from the cell. After relating to us the success he had met with at Canandaigua, he gave us an account of his third mission to Livonia:—

> "When I arrived at Mr. Green's," said he, "Mrs. Green informed me that her husband was absent from home, that there was no prospect of selling my books, and even the one which I had left with them, she expected I would have to take away, as Mr. Green had no disposition to purchase it, although she had read it herself, and was much pleased with it. I then talked with her a short time, and, binding my knapsack

upon my shoulders, rose to depart; but, as I bade her farewell, it was impressed upon my mind to leave the book with her. I made her a present of it, and told her that the Spirit forbade my taking it away. She burst into tears, and requested me to pray with her. I did so, and afterwards explained to her the most profitable manner of reading the book which I had left with her; which was, to ask God, when she read it, for a testimony of the truth of what she had read, and she would receive the Spirit of God, which would enable her to discern the things of God. I then left her, and returned home."

I shall now turn aside from my narrative, and give a history of the above book. When Mr. Green returned home, his wife requested him to read it, informing him very particularly, with regard to what Samuel had said to her, relative to obtaining a testimony of the truth of it. This, he, for a while, refused to do, but finally yielded to her persuasions, and took the book, and commenced perusing the same, calling upon God for the testimony of his Spirit. The result of which was, that he and Mrs. Green were in a short time baptized. They gave [167] the book to Phineas Young, Mrs. Green's brother, who read it, and commenced preaching it forthwith. It was next handed to Brigham Young, and from him to Mrs. Murray, his sister, who is also the mother of Heber C. Kimball's wife. They all received the work without hesitancy, and rejoiced in the truth thereof. Joseph Young was at this time in Canada, preaching the Methodist doctrine; but, as soon as Brigham became convinced of the truth of the Gospel, as contained in the Book of Mormon, he went straightway to his brother Joseph, and persuaded him to cease preaching Methodism, and embrace the truth, as set forth in the Book of Mormon, which he carried with him.

Thus was this book the means of convincing this whole family, and bringing them into the Church, where they have continued faithful members from the commencement of their career until now. And, through their faithfulness and zeal, some of them have become as great and honorable men as ever stood upon the earth.

I shall now resume my subject. The first business which Samuel set himself about after he returned home, was preparing to move the family to Waterloo, according to the revelation given to Joseph. And after much fatigue and perplexities of various kinds, he succeeded in getting us there. We moved into a house belonging to an individual by the name of Kellog. Shortly after arriving there, we were made to realize that the hearts of the people were in the hands of the Lord; for we had scarcely unpacked our goods, when one of our new neighbours, a Mr. Osgood, came in and invited us to drive our stock and teams to his barn-yard, and feed them from his barn, free of cost, until we could make further arrangements. Many of our neighbours came in, and welcomed us to

Waterloo. Among whom was Mr. Hooper, a tavern-keeper, whose wife came with him, and brought us a present of some delicate eatables. Such manifestations of kindness as these were shown us from day to day, during our con[168]tinuance in the place. And they were duly appreciated, for we had experienced the opposite so severely, that the least show of good feeling gave rise to the liveliest sensations of gratitude.

Having settled ourselves in this place, we established the practice of spending the evenings in singing and praying. The neighbours soon became aware of this, and it caused our house to become a place of evening resort, for some dozen or twenty persons. One evening, soon after we commenced singing, a couple of little boys came in, and one of them, stepping softly up to Samuel, whispered, "Mr. Smith, won't you pray pretty soon? Our mother said, we must be home by eight o'clock, and we would like to hear you pray before we go."

Samuel told them, that prayer should be attended to immediately. Accordingly, when we had finished the hymn, which we were then singing, we closed the evening services with prayer, in order that the little boys might be gratified. After this, they were never absent during our evening devotions, while we remained in the neighbourhood.

CHAPTER 38

THE FIRST WESTERN MISSION—JOSEPH SMITH, JUNIOR, MOVES TO KIRTLAND

I MENTIONED, in a foregoing chapter, that when Joseph and Emma left Manchester, they went to Macedon. Here, he commenced his ministerial labors, and continued, for some time, to preach successively, in this place, Colesville, Waterloo, Palmyra, and Manchester, till, finally, he sent to Pennsylvania [169] for his goods, and settled himself in Waterloo. Soon after which, a revelation was given, commanding Parley P. Pratt, Ziba Peterson, Peter Whitmer, and Oliver Cowdery, to take a mission to Missouri, preaching by the way. As soon as this revelation was received, Emma Smith, and several other sisters, began to make arrangements to furnish those who were set apart for this mission, with the necessary clothing, which was no easy task, as the most of it had to be manufactured out of the raw material.

Emma's health at this time was quite delicate, yet she did not favor herself on this account, but whatever her hands found to do, she did with her might, until she went so far beyond her strength, that she brought upon herself a heavy fit of sickness, which lasted four weeks. And, although her strength was exhausted, still her spirits were the same, which, in fact, was always the case with her, even under the most trying circumstances. I have never seen a woman in my life, who would endure every species of fatigue and hardship, from month to month, and from year to year, with that unflinching courage, zeal, and patience, which she has ever done; for I know that which she has had to endure—she has been tossed upon the ocean of uncertainty—she has breasted the storms of persecution, and buffeted the rage of men and devils, which would have borne down almost any other woman. It may be, that many may yet have to encounter the same—I pray God, that this may not be the case; but, should it be, may they have grace given them according to their day, even as has been the case with her.

As soon as those men designated in the Revelation, were prepared to leave home, they started on their mission, preaching and baptizing on their way, wherever an opportunity afforded. On their route they passed through Kirtland, where they preached a short time, and raised up a branch of twenty or thirty members. Before leaving this place, they addressed a letter to Joseph, desiring him to send [170] an Elder to preside over the branch which they had raised up. Accordingly, Joseph despatched John Whitmer to take the presidency of the Church at Kirtland; and when he arrived there, those appointed to go to Missouri, proceeded on their mission, preaching and baptizing as before.

In December of the same year, Joseph appointed a meeting at our house. While he was preaching, Sidney Rigdon and Edward Partridge came in, and seated themselves in the congregation. When Joseph had finished his discourse, he gave all who had any remarks to make, the privilege of speaking. Upon this, Mr. Partridge arose, and stated that he had been to Manchester, with the view of obtaining further information respecting the doctrine which we preached; but, not finding us, he had made some inquiry of our neighbours concerning our characters, which they stated had been unimpeachable, until Joseph deceived us relative to the Book of Mormon. He also said, that he had walked over our farm, and observed the good order and industry which it exhibited; and, having seen what we had sacrificed for the sake of our faith, and having heard that our veracity was not questioned upon any other point than that of our religion, he believed our testimony, and was ready to be baptized, "if," said he,"brother Joseph will baptize me."

"You are now," replied Joseph, "much fatigued, brother Partridge, and you had better rest to-day, and be baptized to-morrow."

"Just as brother Joseph thinks best," replied Mr. Partridge, "I am ready at any time."

He was accordingly baptized the next day. Before he left, my husband returned home from prison, bringing along with him considerable clothing, which he had earned at coopering in the jail yard.

The latter part of the same month, Joseph received a letter from John Whitmer, desiring his immediate assistance at Kirtland in regulating the affairs of the Church there. Joseph inquired of the Lord, and received a commandment to go straightway to [171] Kirtland with his family and effects; also to send a message to Hyrum to have him take that branch of the Church, over which he presided, and start immediately for the same place. And my husband was commanded, in the same revelation, to meet Hyrum at the most convenient point, and accompany him to Kirtland. Samuel was sent on a mission, into the same region of country, while I, and my two sons, William and Carlos, were to be left till the ensuing spring, when we were to take the remainder of the branch at Waterloo, and move also to Kirtland.

It was but a short time till Joseph and Emma were on their way, accompanied by Sidney Rigdon, Edward Partridge, Ezra Thayre, and Newel Knight. When they were about starting, they preached at our house on Seneca River; and, on their way, they preached at the house of Calvin Stodard, and likewise at the house of Preserved Harris. At each of these places, they baptized several individuals into the Church.

On Joseph's arrival at Kirtland, he found a Church consisting of nearly one hundred members, who were, in general, good brethren, though a few of them had imbibed some very erroneous ideas, being greatly deceived by a singular power, which manifested itself among them in strange contortions of the visage, and sudden unnatural exertions of the body. This they supposed to be a display of the power of God. Shortly after Joseph arrived, he called the Church together, in order to show them the difference between the Spirit of God, and the spirit of the devil. He said, if a man arose in meeting to speak, and was seized with a kind of paroxysm, that drew his face and limbs, in a violent and unnatural manner, which made him appear to be in pain; and if he gave utterance to strange sounds, which were incomprehensible to his audience, they might rely upon it, that he had the spirit of the devil. But, on the contrary, when a man speaks by the Spirit of God, he speaks from the abundance of [172] his heart—his mind is filled with intelligence, and even should he be excited, it does not cause him to do anything ridiculous or unseemly. He then called upon one of the brethren to speak, who arose and made the attempt, but was immediately seized with a kind of spasm, which drew his face, arms, and fingers in a most astonishing manner.

Hyrum, by Joseph's request, laid hands on the man, whereupon he sunk back in a state of complete exhaustion. Joseph then called upon another man to speak, who stood leaning in an open window. This man also attempted to speak, but was thrown forward into the house, prostrate, unable to utter a syllable. He was administered to, and the same effects followed as in the first instance.

These, together with a few other examples of the same kind, convinced the brethren of the mistake under which they had been labouring; and they all rejoiced in the goodness of God, in once more condescending to lead the children of men by revelation, and the gift of the Holy Ghost.

CHAPTER 39

THE DIFFERENT BRANCHES OF THE CHURCH REMOVE TO KIRTLAND—MIRACLE AT BUFFALO

SOON after my husband and Joseph left for Kirtland, William, being one of the teachers, visited the Church; and calling upon each family, he remained with them until each individual belonging to the house had prayed in his hearing.

When the brethren considered the spring sufficiently open for travelling on the water, we all began to prepare for our removal to Kirtland. We hired a boat of a certain Methodist preacher, and [173] appointed a time to meet at our house, for the purpose of setting off together; and when we were thus collected, we numbered eighty souls. The people of the surrounding country came and bade us farewell, invoking the blessing of heaven upon our heads.

A few minutes before we started, an old brother by the name of Humphry, arrived from Potsdam. This man was brought into the Church by Don Carlos, at the time that he visited his grandfather in company with my husband. At this time, brother Humphry was the oldest Elder in the Church, and Don Carlos the youngest.

On account of brother Humphry's age, I wished him to take charge of the company, but he refused, saying, that every thing should be done, just as mother Smith said; and to this the whole company responded, "yes." At that instant, one Esquire Chamberlain came on board, and asked me, if I had what money I wanted to make my family comfortable. I replied, that I had an abundance for myself and children, but he might, perhaps, find some on board, who stood in need of assistance. "Well," said he, "here is a little money, and you can deal it out as you like," and, handing me seventeen dollars, he left the boat. Soon after this we were pushed off and under fine headway.

I then called the brethren and sisters together, and reminded them that we were travelling by the commandment of the Lord, as much as father Lehi was, when he left Jerusalem; and, if faithful, we had the same reason to expect the blessings of God. I then desired them to be solemn, and to lift their hearts to God continually in prayer, that we might be prospered. We then seated ourselves and sang a hymn. The captain was so delighted with the music, that he called to the mate, saying, "Do, for God' sake, come here, and steer the boat; for I must hear that singing." He afterwards expressed his pleasure and surprise at seeing such an appearance of devotion among us, stating that his wife had refused to [174] accompany him, on account of her prejudice against us, which he very much regretted.

At the approach of sunset, we seated ourselves, and sang another hymn. The music sounded beautifully upon the water, and had a salutary effect upon every heart, filling our souls with love and gratitude to God, for his manifold goodness towards us.

The services of the evening being ended, I inquired of the brethren concerning the amount of provisions which they had on hands for the journey; and, to my surprise, I ascertained that we had on board, besides twenty grown persons, thirty children, who were almost destitute of food. This was unaccountable to me at first, but I afterwards learned that they had converted their substance into clothing, expecting that those who were in better circumstances would support them, as well as defray their travelling expenses; those, however, from whom they expected the most assistance, disappointed them, consequently, the burthen was thrown entirely upon my shoulders. From this time forward, I furnished the whole fifty persons with food from day to day.

I soon discovered among the mothers, a kind of carelessness with regard to their children, even when their lives were in danger. So I called them together, and endeavoured to impress upon their minds the importance of doing their duty to their children; that in such a place as this, especially, they ought to keep them constantly by their side; that they should consider, that children were given to them for a blessing, and if they did not treat them as such, they would be taken from them. Still they were negligent, and excused themselves by saying, that their children were disobedient. I told the sisters, that I could manage their children, and if they were not better controlled by their mothers, I should take the control of them.

I then called the children around me, and said to them, "Now, children, mark what I say to you. When I come up stairs, and raise my hand, you [175] must, every one of you, run to me as fast as you can. Will you do as I tell you?"

"Yes," they replied, with one unanimous voice. And they strictly kept their faith to the end of the journey.

On getting about half way to Buffalo, the canal broke. This gave rise to much murmuring and discontentment, which was expressed in terms like the following: —

"Well, the canal is broke now, and here we are, and here we are likely to be, for we can go no further. We have left our homes, and here we have no means of getting a living, consequently we shall have to starve."

"No, no," said I, "you will not starve, brethren, nor anything of that sort; only do be patient and stop your murmuring. I have no doubt but the hand of the Lord is over us for good; perhaps it is best for us to be here a short time. It is quite probable that the boats cannot leave Buffalo harbour on account of the ice; if so, the town must inevitably be crowded with families, in which case it would be next to impossible for us to get into a comfortable house. Are we not in far better circumstances in our present situation?"

"Well, well," returned the sisters, "I suppose you know best; but it does seem as if it would have been better for us to have staid where we were, for there we could sit in our rocking chairs, and take as much comfort as we pleased, but here we are tired out, and have no place to rest ourselves."

Whilst this was passing, a citizen of the place came on board, and after inquiring what denomination we belonged to, he requested that, if there were any preachers on board, a meeting might be appointed in the neighbourhood. I introduced him to Elders Humphry and Page, who appointed a meeting for the next day, which was held on a beautiful green, bordering on the canal, and of sufficient size to accommodate a hundred persons. They listened with attention, and requested that another [176] meeting might be appointed for the succeeding day, but, as the canal was repaired by eleven o'clock, we proceeded on our journey, and arrived at Buffalo on the fifth day after leaving Waterloo.

Here we found the brethren from Colesville, who informed us that they had been detained one week in this place, waiting for the navigation to open. Also, that Mr. Smith and Hyrum had gone through to Kirtland by land, in order to be there by the first of April.

I asked them if they confessed to the people that they were "Mormons." "No, indeed," they replied, "neither must you mention a word about your religion, for if you do you will never be able to get a house, or a boat either."

I told them I should tell the people precisely who I was; "and," continued I, "if you are ashamed of Christ, you must not expect to be prospered; and I shall wonder if we do not get to Kirtland before you."

While we were talking with the Colesville brethren, another boat landed, having on board about thirty brethren, among whom was Thomas B. Marsh, who immediately joined us, and, like the Colesville brethren, he was decidedly opposed to our attending to prayer, or making known that we were professors of religion. He said that if our company persisted in singing and praying, as we had hitherto done, we should be mobbed before the next morning,

"Mob it is, then," said I, "we shall attend to prayer before sunset, mob or no mob." Mr. Marsh, at this, left considerably irritated. I then requested brothers Humphry and Page to go around among the boatmen, and inquire for one Captain Blake, who was formerly captain of a boat belonging to my brother, General Mack, and who, upon my brother's decease, purchased the boat, and still commanded the same. They went in search of the man, and soon found him, and learned from him that his boat was already laden with the usual amount of passengers and freight. He said, however, that he thought he could [177] make room for us if we would take a deck passage. As this was our only opportunity, we moved our goods on board the next day, and by the time that we had fairly settled ourselves, it began to rain. This rendered our situation very uncomfortable, and some of the sisters complained bitterly because we had not hired a house till the boat was ready to start. In fact, their case was rather a trying one, for some of them had sick children; in consequence of which, brother Page went out for the purpose of getting a room for the women and sick children, but returned unsuccessful. At this the sisters renewed their complaints, and declared that they would have a house, let the consequences be what they might. In order to satisfy them, I set out myself, with my son William, although it was still raining very fast, to see if it were possible to procure a shelter for them and their children.

I stopped at the first tavern, and inquired of the landlord if he could let me have a room for some women and children who were sick. The landlord replied that he could easily make room for them. At this, a woman, who was present, turned upon him very sharply, saying, "I have put up here myself, and I am not a-going to have anybody's things in my way. I'll warrant the children have got the whooping cough or measles, or some other contagious disease, and, if *they* come, I will go somewhere else."

"Why, madam," said the landlord, "that is not necessary, you can still have one large room."

"I don't care," said she, "I want 'em both, and if I cant have 'em, I won't stay — that's it."

"Never mind," said I, "it is no matter; I suppose I can get a room somewhere else, just as well."

"No, you can't though," rejoined the lady, "for we hunted all over the town, and we could not find one single one till we got here."

I left immediately, and went on my way. Pre[178]sently I came to a long row of rooms, one of which appeared to be almost vacant. I inquired if it could be rented for a few days. The owner of the buildings, I found to be a cheerful old lady, near seventy years of age. I mentioned the circumstances to her, as I before had done to the landlord.

"Well, I don't know," said she; "where be you going?"

"To Kirtland," I replied.

"What be you"" said she. "Be you Baptists?"

I told her that we were "Mormons."

"Mormons!" ejaculated she, in a quick, good natured tone. "What be they? I never heard of them before."

"I told you that we were 'Mormons,'" I replied, "because that is what the world call us, but the only name we acknowledge is Latter-Day Saints."

"Latter-Day Saints!" rejoined she, "I never heard of them either."

I then informed her that this Church was brought forth through the instrumentality of a Prophet, and that I was the mother of this Prophet.

"What!" said she, "a Prophet in these days! I never heard of the like in my life; and if you will come and sit with me, you shall have a room for your sisters and their children, but you yourself must come and stay with me, and tell me all about it."

This I promised to do, and then returned to the boat, and had the sisters, and their sick children, removed to the old lady's house; and after making them comfortable, I went into her room. We soon fell into conversation, in which I explained to her, as clearly as I could, the principles of the Gospel. On speaking of the laying on of hands for the reception of the Holy Ghost, she was as much surprised as those disciples were whom Paul found at Ephesus, and she asked me, "What do you mean by the Holy Ghost?" I continued my explanations until after two o'clock the next morning, when we removed to the boat again. On arriving there, Captain Blake **[179]** requested the passengers to remain on board, as he wished, from that time, to be ready to start at a moment's warning; at the same time he sent out a man to measure the depth of the ice, who, when he returned, reported that it was piled up to the height of twenty feet, and that it was his opinion that we would remain in the harbour at least two weeks longer.

At this, Porter Rockwell started on shore to see his uncle. His mother endeavoured, to prevent him, but he paid no attention to her, and she then appealed to me, saying, "Mother Smith, do get Porter back, for he won't mind any body but you." I told him that, if he went, we should leave him on shore, but he could do as he liked. He left the boat, and several others were about following him; but when I spoke to them, they replied, "We will do just as you say, Mother Smith," and returned immediately.

Just then, William whispered in my ear, "Mother, do see the confusion yonder; won't you go and put a stop to it!"

I went to that part of the boat where the principal portion of our company were. There I found several of the brethren and sisters engaged in a warm debate, others murmuring and grumbling, and a number of young ladies were flirting, giggling, and laughing with gentlemen passengers, who were entire strangers to them, whilst hundreds of people on shore and on other boats were witnessing this scene of clamour and vanity among our brethren with great interest. I stepped into their midst. "Brethren and sisters," said I, "we call ourselves Saints, and profess to have come out from the world for the purpose of serving God at the expense of all earthly things; and will you, at the very onset, subject the cause of Christ to ridicule by your own unwise and improper conduct? You profess to put your trust in God, then how can you feel to murmur and complain as you do! You are even more unreasonable than the children of Israel were; for [180] here are my sisters pining for their rocking chairs, and brethren from whom I expected firmness and energy, declare that they positively believe they shall starve to death before they get to the end of their journey. And why is it so? Have any of you lacked? Have not I set food before you every day, and made you, who had not provided for yourselves, as welcome as my own children? Where is your faith? Where is your confidence in God? Can you not realize that all things were made by him, and that he rules over the works of his own hands? And suppose that all the Saints here should lift their hearts in prayer to God, that the way might be opened before us, how easy it would be for him to cause the ice to break away, so that in a moment we could be on our journey!"

Just then a man on shore cried, "Is the Book of Mormon true?"

"That book," replied I, "was brought forth by the power of God, and translated by the gift of the Holy Ghost; and, if I could make my voice sound as loud as the trumpet of Michael, the Archangel, I would declare the truth from land to land, and from sea to sea, and the echo should reach to every isle, until every member of the family of Adam should be left without excuse. For I do testify that God has revealed himself to man again in these last days, and set his hand to gather his people upon a goodly land, and, if they obey his commandments, it shall be unto them for an inheritance; whereas, if they rebel against his law, his hand will

be against them to scatter them abroad, and cut them off from the face
of the earth; and that he has commenced a work which will prove a
savour of life unto life, or of death unto death, to every one that stands
here this day—of life unto life, if you will receive it, or of death unto
death, if you reject the counsel of God, for every man shall have the
desires of his heart; if he desires the truth, he may hear and live, but if he
tramples upon the simplicity of the word of God, he will shut the gate of
heaven against himself." Then, **[181]** turning to our own company, I said,
"Now, brethren and sisters, if you will all of you raise your desires to
heaven, that the ice may be broken up, and we be set at liberty, as sure
as the Lord lives it will be done." At that instant a noise was heard, like
bursting thunder. The captain cried, "Every man to his post." The ice
parted, leaving barely a passage for the boat, and so narrow, that as the
boat passed through, the buckets of the waterwheel were torn off with
a crash, which, joined to the word of command from the captain, the
hoarse answering of the sailors, the noise of the ice, and the cries and
confusion of the spectators, presented a scene truly terrible. We had
barely passed through the avenue, when the ice closed together again,
and the Colesville brethren were left in Buffalo, unable to follow us.

As we were leaving the harbour, one of the bystanders exclaimed,
"There goes the Mormon company! That boat is sunk in the water nine
inches deeper than ever it was before, and, mark it, she will sink—there
is nothing surer." In fact, they were so sure of it, that they went straight
to the office and had it published that we were sunk, so that when we
arrived at Fairport, we read in the papers the news of our own death.

After our miraculous escape from the wharf at Buffalo, we called our
company together, and had a prayer meeting, in which we offered up
our thanks to God for his mercy, which he had manifested towards us in
our deliverance; but before our meeting was broken up, the captain's
mate came to me and said, "Mrs. Smith, do, for God's sake, have your
children stop praying, or we shall all go to hell together; we cannot keep
one single man to his post, if we should go to the devil, for they are so
taken up with your praying." Therefore our meeting was broken up.

Soon after leaving Buffalo, some of our company began to feel the
effects of the motion of the boat, and were overcome with sea-sickness.
I went to **[182]** the cook, and, handing him twenty-five cents, asked him
if he could let me have some hot water for the sick folks. He complied
with my request, and I was thus furnished with the means of making
them comfortable.

Upon further acquaintance with the captain, I made myself known
to him as the sister of General Mack. He seemed highly pleased to find
in me a relative of his old friend; and I was treated with great attention

and respect, both by himself and crew, while I remained on the boat.

A short time before I arrived at Fairport, brother Humphry and myself went on shore to do some trading for the company. While on shore, this brother told me that I was making a slave of myself unnecessarily; that those sisters whose families I had the care of could as well wait upon their own husbands and children, as for me to do it; that, as for himself, he was not going to stay on board much longer. I thanked him for his kindness, but told him that I thought I could get along with the work, without injuring myself. Nothing further passed between us upon the subject. At the next landing, he left, and whither he went I did not know.

On drawing near Fairport, where we were to land, the captain, passengers, and crew, bade me farewell in tears. After landing, our company were more disheartened than ever, and the brethren came around me and requested that I should set their wives to sewing blankets together, and making tents of them, that the men might camp by their goods and watch them, for they had no hopes of getting any further.

I told them I should do nothing of the kind. As for the sisters, some of them were crying, some pouting, and a few of them were attending to the care of their families. As I passed among them, my attention was attracted by a stranger, who sat a short distance from us on the shore of the lake. I inquired of him the distance to Kirtland. He, starting up, exclaimed, "Is it possible that this is [183] mother Smith? I have sat here looking for you these three days."

Replying to his question in the affirmative, I asked him if it would be possible to procure teams to take our goods to Kirtland. He told me to give myself no uneasiness about the matter, that Joseph was expected every hour, and in less than twenty-four hours there would be teams sufficient to take all our company to houses that were waiting to receive them. When he mentioned Joseph's name, I started, for I just began to realize that I was so soon to see both my husband and my sons. I turned from the stranger, and met Samuel, who was coming towards me, closely followed by Joseph. I extended my right hand to Samuel and my left to Joseph. They wept for joy upon seeing me—Samuel, because he had been warned of God in a dream to meet the company from Waterloo, and feared that some disaster had befallen me; and Joseph, because of the information which he had received from brother Humphry, who had arrived at Kirtland a short time before this, he having informed Joseph that he apprehended, from the fatigue I was undergoing, that my life was in danger.

After they informed me of these things, Joseph said he should take me from the company. As the sisters begged to go with me, he took them as far as Painsville, where we stopped at the house of brother Partridge. Here we found a fine supper prepared for the whole company.

Soon after partaking of this refreshment, I was taken to Brother Kingsbury's, in his own carriage, where I was treated with great kindness and respect. From this place I went with Joseph to Kirtland. The first house that I entered was brother Morley's. Here I met my beloved husband, and great was our joy. Many of my readers may know my present situation. These can imagine with what feelings I recite such scenes as that which followed the re-union of our family; but let it pass—imagination must supply the ellipsis. Were I to [184] indulge my feelings upon such occasions as this, my strength would not support me to the end of my narrative.

Soon after arriving at Kirtland, a pair of twins were brought to Emma, which were given to her to fill the place of a pair of her own that had died.

CHAPTER 40

SAMUEL SMITH'S FIRST MISSION TO MISSOURI

WE remained two weeks at Mr. Morley's, then removed our family to a farm which had been purchased by Joseph for the Church. On this farm my family were all established with this arrangement, that we were to cultivate the farm, and, from the fruits of our labour, we were to receive our support; but all over and above this was to be used for the comfort of strangers or brethren, who were travelling through the place.

About this time Joseph was requested by Parley P. Pratt and his company, who were then in Missouri, to send some Elders to assist them. He inquired of the Lord, and received the revelation contained in the *Times and Seasons,* vol. 5, p. 416, in which Samuel H. Smith and Reynolds Cahoon were appointed to go together to Missouri. They departed immediately on their mission. Before they had proceeded far, they called at a town, the name of which I do not remember, where they found William E. Mc Lellin, who was employed as a clerk in a store. After making a little inquiry, they found that Mr. Mc Lellin was anxious to hear [185] them preach, and that he was willing to make some exertion to obtain a house and congregation for them, for the name of Latter-Day Saint was new to him, and he felt curious to hear what the principles of our faith were. So, by his interposition, they soon had a large congregation seated in a comfortable room. They preached that evening, and the next morning they pursued their journey.

Shortly after they left, Mr. Mc Lellin became very uneasy respecting his new acquaintances; he felt that it was his duty to have gone with them and assisted them on their journey. This feeling worked so strongly in his breast, as to deprive him of rest all the ensuing night; and, before morning, he concluded to set out for Missouri, at the hazard of business, character, and everything else. Accordingly, after settling with his employer, he started in pursuit of Samuel, and brother Cahoon. He passed them on their way, and got to Missouri, and was baptized before they arrived there.

On their route, Samuel and brother Cahoon suffered great privations, such as want of rest and food. At the time that they started for Missouri, near fifty others also set out for the same place, all taking different routes. When they arrived, they dedicated the spot for the Temple. About this time, or soon after, a number of revelations were received which the reader will find by following the History of Joseph in the *Times and Seasons,* vol. 5, from p. 448 to 466. A clause in one of these reads as follows:— "Let my servant Reynolds Cahoon, and my servant Samuel H. Smith, with whom I am well pleased, be not separated until they return to their homes, and this for a wise purpose in me." p. 465. And, here, let me say, that Samuel was never censured by revelation, to my knowledge, for he always performed his missions faithfully, and his work was well approved. **[186]**

CHAPTER 41

LUCY SMITH VISITS DETROIT

AS Hyrum, my eldest son, was directed to go to Missouri by the way of Detroit, I thought it would be a good opportunity to visit the family of my brother, General Mack. Accordingly, my niece, Almira Mack, Hyrum,—brothers Murdock, Lyman Wight, and Corril and I, set out together for Detroit. When we first went on board the vessel which took us across the lake, we concluded to keep perfectly still upon the subject of religion; but it was afterwards proposed by Hyrum, that mother Smith should say just what she pleased, and if she got into difficulty, the Elders should help her out of it. Shortly after this I was sitting at the door of the cabin, reading the book of Mormon, when a lady came up and inquired of me what book I was reading. "The Book of Mormon," I replied. But the title of the book was no advantage to her, for she had never before heard of there being such a work in existence. By her request I gave her a brief history of the discovery and translation of the book. This delighted her, and when I mentioned that it was a record of the origin of the Aborigines of America, she said, "how I *do wish* I could get one of your books to carry to my husband, for he is now a missionary among the Indians."

Just then, another lady, who was a doctor's wife, came near us, with the appearance of wishing to hear our conversation. She was gorgeously dressed, and carried herself very daintily, I assure you. She wore a splendid satin scarf, which, as she walked to and fro before us, she would occasionally let fall from the left shoulder, and expose a neck and bosom decorated with very brilliant jewels. Presently she stopped short, and said, "I do not want to hear any [187] more of that stuff, or anything more about Joe Smith either. They say that he is a Mormon Prophet; but it is nothing but deception and lies. There was one Mr. Murdock, who believed in Joe Smith's doctrines; and the Mormons all believe they can cure the sick and raise the dead; so when this Mr. Murdock's wife was sick, he refused to send for a doctor, although the poor woman wanted him to do so, and so by his neglect his wife died."

I told her I thought she must be a little mistaken, that I was acquainted with the family, and knew something in regard to the matter.

"I know all about it," said the lady.

"Well now, perhaps not," said I, "just stop a moment and I will explain it to you."

"No, I wont," returned the woman.

"Then" said I "I will introduce you to Mr. Murdock, and let him tell the story himself." I then turned to Mr. Murdock, who stood near, and gave her an introduction to him. Before this, however, the chambermaid went down stairs and complained to the doctor of his wife's unbecoming behaviour, and before she had heard a dozen words from our brother, her husband came bustling up stairs. "Here," said he, to his wife, "they tell me that you are abusing this old lady;" and taking her hand, he drew it within his arm, and marched her off without further ceremony.

This circumstance introduced the subject of "Mormonism" among the passengers, and it continued to be the topic of conversation until we arrived at Detroit. On landing in Detroit, we repaired immediately to a tavern, as my niece, Mrs. Cooper, was exceedingly nervous, and we deemed it imprudent to disturb her that evening. The next morning, Almira Mack and myself visited Mrs. Cooper, who was Almira's sister. Almira went into her room, and found her lying on the bed. After the usual salutations she informed Mrs. Cooper that aunt Lucy was in the parlor waiting to see her, and requested the privilege of inviting me into her [188] room; but it was some time before her nerves were sufficiently settled to see me. However, before I was admitted into her presence, she was further informed that her cousin Hyrum, as also several other Elders, had come to Detroit in company with me, and that I would expect them to be invited as well as myself. But this was refused, Mrs. Cooper, declaring that she could not endure the presence of so many visitors. She sent for me, but forbade her sisters inviting any one else.

I went to her, and after the compliments were over, I said, "Lovisa, I have with me four of my brethren, one of whom is your cousin Hyrum, if I stay they must be invited also."

"Oh! no, no; I never can consent to it," exclaimed she, — "Why, aunt, I am so nervous I am scarcely ever able to see any company."

"Now, Lovisa," I replied, "do you know what ails you? I can tell you exactly what it is: there is a good spirit and an evil one operating upon you, and the bad spirit has almost got possession of you; and when the good spirit is the least agitated, the evil one strives for the entire mastery, and sets the good spirit to fluttering, just ready to be gone, because it has so slight a foothold. But you have been so for a long time, and you may yet live many years. These men who are with me are clothed with the authority of the Priesthood, and through their administration you might receive a blessing; and even should you not be healed, do you not wish to know something about your Saviour before you meet him. Furthermore, if you refuse to receive my brethren into your house, I shall leave it myself."

It was finally concluded that a sumptuous dinner should be prepared, and that the brethren should all be invited. While they tarried with her they administered to her twice by the laying on of hands, in the name of the Lord. They stopped with her during the day, and in the evening left for Pontiac. When she learned that they were not expected back **[189]** again, she seemed greatly distressed, because she had not urged them to stay and preach.

The next morning, I and my niece set out for Pontiac, in the first stage, to visit sister Mack, my brother's widow, and her daughter, Mrs. Whitermore. Here we were treated with great attention and respect by Mr. Whitermore and his family. The subject of religion was introduced immediately after our arrival, and continued the theme of conversation until near tea-time, when sister Mack arose, saying, "sister Lucy, you must excuse me, for I find my nerves are so agitated I cannot bear conversation any longer; the subject is so entirely new, it confuses my mind." I requested her to stop a moment. I then repeated to her the same that I had done two days previous to Lovisa, adding, "suppose a company of fashionable people were to come in and begin to talk about balls, parties, and the latest style of making dresses, do you think that would agitate you so?" She smiled at this, and said, "I do not know that it would, sister Lucy; you know that those are more common things."

I then told her that I would excuse her, and that she might go where she pleased, concluding in my own mind never to mention the subject to her again, unless it should be by her own request. That night we slept in the same room. When I was about retiring to rest, she observed, "do not let my presence prevent you from attending to any duty which you have practised at home." And soon afterwards she again remarked, "the house is now still, and I would be glad to hear you talk, if you are not too much fatigued." I told her I would have no objections, provided the subject of religion would not make her nervous; and, as she did not think it would, we commenced conversation, the result of which was, she was convinced of the truth of the Gospel.

In a few days subsequent to this, we all set out to visit Mrs. Stanly, who was also my brother's daughter. Here Mr. Whitermore gave me an intro[190]duction to one Mr. Ruggles, the pastor of the Presbyterian church to which this Mr. Whitermore belonged.

"And you," said Mr. Ruggles, upon shaking hands with me, "are the mother of that poor, foolish, silly boy, Joe Smith, who pretended to translate the Book of Mormon."

I looked him steadily in the face, and replied, "I am, sir, the mother of Joseph Smith; but why do you apply to him such epithets as those?"

"Because," said his reverence, "that he should imagine he was going to break down all other churches with that simple Mormon book."

"Did you ever read that book?" I inquired.

"No," said he, "it is beneath my notice."

"But," rejoined I, "the Scriptures say, 'prove all things;' and, now sir, let me tell you boldly, that that book contains the everlasting Gospel, and it was written for the salvation of your soul, by the gift and power of the Holy Ghost."

"Pooh," said the minister, "nonsense—I am not afraid of any member of my church being led astray by such stuff; they have too much intelligence."

"Now, Mr. Ruggles," said I, and I spoke with emphasis, for the Spirit of God was upon me, "mark my words—as true as God lives, before three years we will have more than one-third of your church; and, sir, whether you believe it or not, we will take the very *Deacon too.*"

This produced a hearty laugh at the expense of the minister.

Not to be tedious, I will say that I remained in this section of country about four weeks, during which time I labored incessantly for the truth's sake, and succeeded in gaining the hearts of many, among whom were David Dort and his wife. Many desired me to use my influence to have an Elder sent into that region of country, which I agreed to do. As I was about starting home, Mr. Cooper observed that our ministers would have more influence if they dressed in broadcloth. **[191]**

"When I returned, I made known to Joseph the situation of things where I had been, so he despatched brother Jared Carter to that country. And in order that he might not lack influence, he was dressed in a suit of superfine broadcloth. He went immediately into the midst of Mr. Ruggles' church, and, in a short time, brought away seventy of his best members, among whom was the *Deacon*, just as I told the minister. This Deacon was brother Bent, who now presides over the High Council.

In less than a month after my arrival, Samuel returned home from Missouri, and remained until the succeeding October, at which time a revelation was given, commanding him and Wm. Mc Lellin to go to the town of Hiram, which was about thirty miles distant. Samuel commenced making preparations, but before he was ready to start, he heard a voice in the night, which said, "Samuel, arise immediately, and go forth on the mission which thou wast commanded to take to Hiram." He arose from his bed and took what clothing he had in readiness, and set off without further delay.

On arriving at the above-mentioned place, he found Wm. E. Mc Lellin there according to previous appointment. Here they commenced preaching together, and after labouring a while in this town, they went from place to place, bearing testimony of the truth in whatever city, town, or village they entered, until the twenty-seventh of December, at which time they arrived at Kirtland. Samuel was not long permitted to remain at home in quiet; on the first of January he was sent, with Orson Hyde, on a mission into the eastern country. They went and preached from city to city until they were called home to receive the ordinance of The Washing of Feet. **[192]**

CHAPTER 42

AN EXTRACT FROM THE HISTORY OF JOSEPH THE PROPHET—SIDNEY RIGDON'S TRANSGRESSION—TROUBLE IN JACKSON COUNTY

I SHALL now return to the month of September, 1831. Joseph, at this time, was engaged in translating the Bible, and Sidney Rigdon was writing for him. About the first of this month, Joseph came to the conclusion to remove himself and clerk, as well as their families, to the before-mentioned town of Hiram, in order to expedite the work. They moved to the house of Father Johnson, and lived with him in peace until the following March, when a circumstance occurred, which I shall relate in his own words: —

"On the twenty-fifth of March, (1832,) the twins before mentioned, which had been sick of the measles for some time, caused us to be broke of our rest in taking care of them, especially my wife. In the evening. I told her she had better retire to rest with one of the children, and I would watch with the sickest child. In the night, she told me I had better lie down on the trundle bed, and I did so, and was soon after awoke by her screaming *murder!* when I found myself going out of the door in the hands of about a dozen men; some of whose hands were in my hair, and some hold of my shirt, drawers, and limbs. The foot of the trundle bed was towards the door, leaving only room enough for the door to swing. My wife heard a gentle tapping on the windows, which she then took no particular notice of (but which was unquestionably designed for ascertaining whether we were all asleep), and, soon after, the mob burst open the door and surrounded the bed in an instant, and, as I said, the first I knew, I was going out of the door, in the hands of an infuriated mob. I made a desperate struggle, as I was forced out, to extricate myself, but only cleared one leg, with which I made a pass at one man, and he fell on the door steps. I was immediately confined again, and they **[193]** swore by God they would kill me if I did not be still, which quieted me. As they passed around the house with me, the fellow that I kicked, came to me and thrust his hand into my face all covered with blood, (for I hit him on the nose,) and with an exulting horse laugh, muttered 'ge, gee, *God d–mn ye, I'll fix ye.'*

"They then seized me by the throat, and held on till I lost my breath. After I came to, as they passed along with me, about thirty rods from the house, I saw Elder Rigdon stretched out on the ground, whither they had dragged him by the heels. I supposed he was dead.

"I began to plead with them, saying, you will have mercy and spare my life, I hope. To which they replied, '*God d–mn ye*, call on yer *God* for help, we'll show ye no mercy;' and the people began to show themselves in every direction: one coming from the orchard had a plank, and I expected they would kill me, and carry me off on a plank. They then turned to the right, and went on about thirty rods further — about sixty rods from the house, and about thirty from where I saw Elder Rigdon — into the meadow, where they stopped, and one said, 'Simonds, Simonds,' (meaning, I supposed, Simonds Rider,) 'pull up his drawers, pull up his drawers, he will take cold.' Another replied, '*A'nt ye going to kill 'im? A'nt ye going to kill 'im?*' when a group of mobbers collected a little way off, and said, 'Simonds, Simonds, come here;' and Simonds charged those who had hold of me to keep me from touching the ground (as they had done all the time), lest I should get a spring upon them. They went and held a council, and as I could occasionally overhear a word, I supposed it was to know whether it was best to kill me. They returned, after a while, when I learned that they had concluded not to kill me, but pound and scratch me well, tear off my shirt and drawers, and leave me naked: one cried, 'Simonds, Simonds, *where is the tar bucket?' 'I don't know,'* answered one, *'where 'tis, Eli's left it.'* They ran back and fetched the bucket of tar, when one exclaimed, *'God d–mn it, let us tar up his mouth;'* and they tried to force the tar paddle into my mouth; I twisted my head around, so that they could not; and they cried out, *'God d–mn ye, hold up your head and let us give ye some tar.'* They then tried to force a vial into my mouth, and broke it in my teeth. All my clothes wore torn off me, **[194]** except my shirt collar; and one man fell on me and scratched my body with his nails like a mad cat, and then muttered out, *'God d–mn ye, that's the way the Holy Ghost falls on folks.'*

"They then left me, and I attempted to rise, but fell again; I pulled the tar away from my lip's, &c., so that I could breathe more freely, and after a while I began to recover, and raised myself up, when I saw two lights. I made my way towards one of them, and found it was father Johnson's. When I had come to the door I was naked, and the tar made me look as though I was covered with blood; and when my wife saw me, she thought I was all mashed to pieces, and fainted. During the affray abroad, the sisters of the neighbourhood had collected at my room. I called for a blanket, they threw me one and shut the door; I wrapped it around me, and went in....

"My friends spent the night in scraping and removing the tar, and washing and cleansing my body; so that by morning I was ready to be clothed again. This being Sabbath morning, the people assembled for meeting at the usual hour of worship, and among those came also the mobbers, viz., Simonds Rider, a Campbellite preacher, and leader of the mob; one M'Clentic, son of a Campbellite minister; and Pelatiah Allen, Esq., who gave the mob a barrel of whiskey to raise their spirits; and many others. With my flesh all scarified and defaced, I preached to the congregation, as usual, and in the afternoon of the same day baptized three individuals." — *Times and Seasons*, vol. 5, p. 611. *Millennial Star*, vol. 14, p. 148.

Sidney Rigdon went immediately to Kirtland, but Joseph remained at father Johnson's to finish his preparations for a journey, which he contemplated making to Missouri. Immediately after Sidney's arrival at Kirtland, we met for the purpose of holding a prayer meeting, and, as Sidney had not been with us for some time, we hoped to hear from him upon this occcasion. We waited a long time before he made his appearance; at last he came in, seemingly much agitated. He did not go to the stand, but began to pace back and forth through the house. My husband said, "Brother Sidney, we **[195]** would like to hear a discourse from you to-day." Brother Rigdon replied, in a tone of excitement, "The keys of the kingdom are rent from the Church, and there shall not be a prayer put up in this house this day." "Oh! no," said Mr. Smith, "I hope not." "I tell you they are," rejoined Elder Rigdon, "and no man or woman shall put up a prayer in this place to-day."

This greatly disturbed the minds of many sisters, and some brethren. The brethren stared and turned pale, and the sisters cried. Sister Howe, in particular, was very much terrified: "Oh dear me!" said she, "what shall we do? what shall we do? The keys of the kingdom are taken from us, and what shall we do?" "I tell you again," said Sidney, with much feeling, "the keys of the kingdom are taken from you, and you never will have them again until you *build me a new house.*"

Hyrum was vexed at this frivolous nonsense, and, taking his hat, he went out of the house, saying, "I'll put a stop to this fuss, pretty quick; I'm going for Joseph."

"Oh don't," said sister Howe, "for pity's sake, don't go for him. Brother Sidney says the keys of the kingdom are taken from us, and where is the use of bringing Joseph here."

Hyrum took a horse, and went immediately to father Johnson's, for Joseph. He arrived there in the after-part of the night, and having aroused Joseph, he said, "You must go straight with me to Kirtland; we are having terrible times there, and I want you to come up and see to things." Joseph being informed of the precise situation of affairs, he got a horse of father Johnson, and started without delay, with Hyrum, for Kirtland. On his arrival there, the brethren were collected for meeting. Joseph went upon the stand, and informed the brethren that they were under a great mistake, that the Church had not transgressed; "and, as for the keys of the kingdom," said he, "I, myself, hold the keys of this Last Dispensation, and will for ever hold **[196]** them, both in time and in eternity; so set your hearts at rest upon that point, all is right."

He then went on and preached a comforting discourse, after which he appointed a council to sit the next day, by which Sidney was tried, for having lied in the name of the Lord. In this council Joseph told him, he must suffer for what he he had done, that he should be delivered over to the buffetings of Satan, who would handle him as one man handleth another, that the less Priesthood he had, the better it would be for him, and that it would be well for him to give up his license.

This counsel Sidney complied with, yet he had to suffer for his folly, for, according to his own account, he was dragged out of bed by the devil, three times in one night, by his heels. Whether this be true or not, one thing is certain, his contrition of soul was as great as a man could well live through.

After he had sufficiently humbled himself, he received another license; but the old one was retained, and is now in the bands of Bishop Whitney.

On the second of April, 1832, Joseph set off for Missouri,

accompanied by Newel K. Whitney, Peter Whitmer, and Jesse Gauze. They were taken by brother Pitkin to the town of Warren, where they were joined by brother Rigdon, and they all pursued their journey together.

During her husband's absence, Emma Smith lived with William Cahoon and brother Williams, occasionally spending a short time with us.

On the twenty-fourth of April, Joseph arrived at Independence. He made haste to attend to the business that lay before him, and on the sixth of May following, he, with brothers Whitney and Rigdon, left Independence for Kirtland. When they arrived at New Albany, brother Whitney had the misfortune to get his leg broken. This detained Joseph, who remained, in order to take care of him, four weeks at Mr. Porter's public-house in Greenville.[1] While they were at this place, Joseph had poison adminis[197]tered to him in his food, which operated very violently upon his system, but he soon recovered, and the next morning they pursued their journey again, and arrived in Kirtland some time in the month of June. When Joseph got home, he immediately procured a house for his wife; and after making his family comfortable, he went on a mission to the East, leaving his family in the care of Hyrum. Shortly after he left, Joseph Smith the third was born.

After Joseph returned from his mission to the East, he established a school for the Elders, and called them all home from the different parts of the country where they had been labouring. This was called the *School of the Prophets;* and was kept in an upper room of the house in which Joseph resided.

At this time my sons were all called home, and, shortly after they arrived, Joseph took all the male portion of our family into the before-named schoolroom, and administered to them the ordinance of Washing of Feet; after which the Spirit fell upon them, and they spake in tongues, and prophesied. The brethren gathered together to witness the manifestations of the power of God. At that time I was on the farm a short distance from the place where the meeting was held, and my children being anxious that I should enjoy the meeting, sent a messenger in great haste for me. I went without delay, and shared with the rest, the most glorious outpouring of the Spirit of God, that had ever before taken place in the Church. We felt that we had gained a decided victory over the adversary, and,

> "We could not believe,
> That we ever should grieve,

---

[1] See *Times and Seasons*, vol. 5, p 626. *Mil. Star*, vol. 14, p. 163.

Or ever should sorrow again."

But, alas! our joy was soon mingled with woe. It was not two months, before a messenger arrived from Missouri, with tidings of the difficulty in Jackson county; that brothers Partridge and Allen had been tarred and feathered, and put into prison; that some had been killed, and others shot; and among **[198]** the latter, was brother Dibble, who had been dangerously wounded.

Upon hearing this, Joseph was overwhelmed with grief. He burst into tears, and sobbed aloud. "Oh my brethren! my brethren;" he exclaimed, "would that I had been with you, to have shared your fate. Oh my God, what shall I do in such a trial as this."

After his grief had a little subsided, he called a council, and it was resolved, that the brethren from the surrounding country, as well as those in Kirtland, should go immediately to Missouri, and take with them money and clothing to relieve the brethren in their distress. Just before this, Jesse Smith, my husband's nephew, and Amos Fuller, arrived in Kirtland from Potsdam, and Jesse determined to go with the camp to Missouri. He was the son of Jesse Smith, my husband's oldest brother, of whose peculiar disposition I have spoken before. Knowing that his father would censure us, I endeavoured to dissuade him from going; but to no purpose, for he was determined upon being one of the company. After making the necessary collections, they set out for Missouri. The whole company amounted to two hundred in number.

CHAPTER 43

LUCY SMITH BUILDS A SCHOOL-HOUSE—JOSEPH AND HYRUM RETURN FROM MISSOURI—THEY REHEARSE THE HISTORY OF THEIR TROUBLE

PREVIOUS to taking leave for Missouri, the brethren commenced building a house, which was designed for both a meeting-house and a school. This was left in the hands of brother Reynolds Cahoon for completion; and was to be in readiness for use by the commencement of the ensuing winter. It is true we held meetings in it during the summer, but then it only served as a shelter from the sun. **[199]** We were now unusually anxious to meet together as often as possible, in order to unite our faith and prayers in behalf of our brethren; but, for a length of time after they left, almost every meeting was broken up by a storm. In consequence of this, together with the near approach of winter, we began to urge upon brother Cahoon the necessity of hurrying the building, but he said that he could do nothing about the matter, as he had neither time nor means. This made me very sorrowful. I studied upon it a long time. Finally, I told my husband, I believed that I could raise the means myself to finish the building, and, if he would give his consent, I would try and see what I could do. He said he would be glad if I could do anything towards forwarding the work, and that I might take any course I saw fit, in order to accomplish it. I then wrote a subscription paper, in which I agreed to refund all the money that should be given, in case it could not be appropriated to the purpose for which it should be subscribed. This article I first took to each member of my family who were at home, as also my boarders, then proceeded with it to father Bosley's. Here I received considerable assistance, and, as I was leaving the house, I met brother Cahoon, and informed him of what I was doing. He seemed pleased, and told me to go on and prosper. And it was even so, I did prosper; so that in two weeks I had everything in fine order for commencing the work. I employed a man by the name of Bar to make and case the doors, and also to case the windows and make the sashes. All this was to be done at a very reduced price. Mr. Bar went immediately to the house, and began to take the measurement of the windows; but, in consequence of some misunderstanding, brother Cahoon forbade him touching the work. Mr. Bar came to my husband for an explanation of the affair. A council was called, and, after three hours sitting, it was voted that mother Smith should go on, and finish the house as she thought proper. Accordingly, I con[200]tinued to collect means and employ hands, until the house was thoroughly completed, even to the fastenings of the doors; and when this was accomplished, there was but six dollars remaining unpaid. And this debt my husband afterwards discharged by the sale of produce.

Late in the fall, Joseph and Hyrum returned. They were overjoyed to meet us again in health, more especially on account of the perils which they had passed through during their absence. Joseph and Hyrum sat down beside me, each holding one of my hands in his, while they related the following story: —

"When we started on our journey, we made arrangements to have every one made as comfortable as possible; but the sufferings which are incident to such an excursion made some of the brethren discontented, and they began to murmur against us, saying, 'the Lord never required them to take such a tiresome journey,' and that it was folly for them to suffer such fatigue and inconvenience just to gratify us. We warned them, in the name of the Lord, to stop their murmuring; for, if they did not, the displeasure of the Almighty would be manifested in judgments in their midst. But the majority of them paid no attention to what we said, until one morning when they went out to harness up their horses, and found them all so lame as to be unable to travel. We then told them that this was a curse which had come upon them because of transgression; but, if they would repent, it might be removed—if not, a greater curse would come upon them. They believed what we said, and repented of their folly. The consequence was, we were soon on our journey again. It was not long, however, till the spirit of dissension arose again, and was not quelled, so as to produce any degree of good feeling, until we arrived at Missouri.

"Soon after arriving at the point of destination, the cholera broke out in our midst; the brethren were so violently attacked that it seemed impossible to render them any assistance. They immediately sent for us to lay hands on them, but we soon discovered that this also, was a judgment from the Almighty; for, when we laid our hands upon them, in the name of the Lord, the dis[201]ease immediately fastened itself upon us, and in a few minutes we were in awful agony. We made signals to each other and left the house, in order to join in prayer to God that he would deliver us from this dreadful influence; but, before we could get to a sufficient distance from the house to be secure from interruption, we were hardly able to stand upon our feet, and we feared that we should die in that western wilderness without the privilege of blessing our children, or giving them one word of parting counsel. We succeeded in getting a few steps further, and then fell upon our knees and cried unto the Lord that he would deliver us from this awful calamity, but we arose worse than before. We kneeled down the second time, and when we commenced praying the cramp seized us, gathering the cords in our arms and legs in bunches, and operating equally severe throughout our system. We still besought the Lord, with all our strength, to have mercy upon us, but all in vain. It seemed as though the heavens were sealed against us, and that every power that could render us any assistance was shut within its gates. We then kneeled down the third time, concluding never to rise to our feet again, until one or the other should get a testimony that we should be healed; and that the one who should get the first intimation of the same from the Spirit, should make it known to the others."

They stated further, that after praying some time the cramp began to release its hold; and, in a short time, Hyrum sprang to his feet and exclaimed, "Joseph, we shall return to our families. I have had an open vision, in which I saw mother kneeling under an apple tree; and she is even now asking God, in tears, to spare our lives, that she may again behold us in the flesh. The Spirit testifies, that her prayers, united with ours, will be answered."

"Oh, my mother!" said Joseph, "how often have your prayers been the means of assisting us when the shadows of death encompassed us."

William was also taken sick of the same disease; but one of the sisters took him to her house, and nursed him so faithfully that he soon recovered. Jesse Smith, my nephew, was seized so violently that nothing could be done for him, and he died im[202]mediately. Brother Thayre was also taken with the cholera: he went to the river and commenced dipping himself, and finding that it helped him, he continued until he was quite restored. His example was followed by several others, and with the same effect.

After hearing this recital, I took Joseph and Hyrum with me, and showed them the new meetinghouse, with which they were highly pleased, and they approved of all that I had done relative to the matter.

CHAPTER 44

THE LORD'S HOUSE AT KIRTLAND COMMENCED—A LETTER FROM THE PROPHET TO HIS UNCLE SILAS

THE summer ensuing Joseph's return from Missouri, the brethren called a council with the view of investigating the subject of building a new meeting-house, as the first was now too small to accommodate the increased congregation.

In this council, Joseph requested that each of the brethren should give his views with regard to the house; and when they had all got through, he would then give his opinion concerning the matter. They all complied with his request. Some were in favour of building a frame house, but the majority were of a mind to put up another log house. Joseph reminded them that they were not building a house for man, but for God; "and shall we, brethren," said he, "build a house for our God, of logs? No, I have a better plan than that. I have a plan of the house of the Lord, given by Himself; and you will soon see by this, the difference between our calculations and His idea of things." [203]

He then gave them a full pattern of the house of the Lord at Kirtland, with which the brethren were highly delighted, particularly Hyrum, who was much more animated than if it were designed for himself.

After the close of the meeting, Joseph took the brethren with him, for the purpose of selecting a spot for the building to stand upon. The place which they made choice of was situated in the north-west corner of a field of wheat, which was sown by my sons the fall previous, on the farm upon which we were then living. In a few minutes the fence was removed, and the standing grain was levelled, in order to prepare a place for the building, and Hyrum commenced digging a trench for the wall, he having declared that he would strike the first blow upon the house.

This was Saturday night. On the following Monday the brethren went to work at the house with great ambition; and although but thirty families now remained in Kirtland, they never suffered the work to stop until it was accomplished. They had to endure great fatigue and privation, in consequence of the opposition they met with from their enemies, and which was so great, that they were compelled to keep a guard upon the walls every night after they were commenced, until they were completed. They "gave no sleep to their eyes, nor slumber to their eyelids, until they found a place for the Lord, a habitation for the mighty God of Jacob."

Mary Bailey and Agnes Coolbrith were then boarding with me; they devoted their whole time to making and mending clothes for the men who were employed on the house. There was but one mainspring to all our thoughts and actions, and that was, the building of the Lord's house.

I often wonder, when I hear brethren and sisters complain at the trifling inconveniences which they have to suffer in these days, and I think to myself that salvation is worth as much now as it was in the [204] commencement of the work. But "all like the purchase, few the price would pay." How often I have parted every bed in the house for the accommodation of the brethren, and then laid a single blanket on the floor for my husband and myself, while Joseph and Emma slept upon the same floor, with nothing but their cloaks for both bed and bedding. At this time, John Smith, my husband's brother, although he was unable to stand upon his feet without assistance, he resolved upon being baptized, which was accordingly done, and he was immediately healed. In a short time he moved his family to Kirtland, where he settled himself with the Church. Not long after brother John arrived, my oldest daughter, Sophronia Stodard, was taken sick. Her symptoms soon became so alarming, that her husband sent for a physician, who, after attending upon her for some time, pronounced her beyond the reach of medicine, and therefore discontinued his visits. As she did not speak, nor turn herself in bed, many supposed that she was dying. When she was in this situation, Jared Carter, together with my husband and our sons, administered to her in the name of the Lord, and in half an hour she spoke to me, saying, "Mother, I shall get well—not suddenly, but the Lord will heal me gradually." The same day she sat up half an hour, and in three days she walked across the street.

We were still living on the farm, and labouring with our might to make the droves of company which were constantly coming in, as comfortable as possible. Joseph saw how we were situated, and that it would not answer for us to keep a public house, at free cost, any longer; and, by his request, we moved into an upper room of his own house, where we lived very comfortably for a season. About this time, Joseph wrote a letter to his uncle Silas, which I think would be interesting to my readers, and shall therefore give it insertion in this place:— **[205]**

"Kirkland Mills, Ohio, September 26,1833.

"RESPECTED UNCLE SILAS,

"It is with feelings of deep interest for the welfare of mankind, which fill my mind on the reflection that all were formed by the hand of Him who will call the same to give an impartial account of all their works on that great day to which you and myself, in common with them, are bound, that I take up my pen and seat myself in an attitude to address a few, though imperfect, lines to you for your perusal.

"I have no doubt but that you will agree with me, that men will be held accountable for the things they have done, and not for the things they have not done. Or that all the light and intelligence communicated to them from their beneficent Creator, whether it is much or little, by the same they, in justice, will be judged. And that they are required to yield obedience, and improve upon that, and that only, which is given, for man is not to live by bread alone, but by every word that proceeds out of the mouth of the Lord.

"Seeing that the Lord has never given the world to understand, by anything heretofore revealed, that he had ceased for ever to speak to his creatures, when sought unto in a proper manner, why should it be thought a thing incredible, that he should be pleased to speak again in these last days for their salvation? Perhaps you may be surprised at this assertion, that I should say for the salvation of his creatures in these last days, since we have already in our possession a vast volume of his word, which he has previously given. But you will admit that the word spoken to Noah was not sufficient for Abraham, or it was not required of Abraham to leave the land of his nativity, and seek an inheritance in a strange country upon the word spoken to Noah, but, for himself he obtained promises at the hand of the Lord, and walked in that perfection, that he was called the friend of God. Isaac, the promised seed, was not required to rest his hope alone upon the promises made to his father Abraham, but was privileged with the assurance of his approbation, in the sight of Heaven, by the direct voice of the Lord to him. If one man can live upon the revelations given to another, might I not with propriety ask, why the necessity, then, of the Lord's speaking to Isaac as he did, as is recorded in the twenty-sixth chapter of Genesis? **[206]** For the Lord there repeats, or rather, promises again to perform the oath which he had previously sworn to Abraham; and why this repetition to Isaac? Why was not the first promise as sure for Isaac as it was for Abraham? Was not Isaac Abraham's son? and could he not place implicit confidence in the veracity of his father as being a man of God! Perhaps you may say that he was a very peculiar man, and different from men in these last days, consequently, the Lord favored him with blessings, peculiar and different, as he was different from men in this age. I admit that he was a peculiar man, and was not only peculiarly blessed, but greatly blessed. But all the peculiarity that I can discover in the man, or all the difference between him and men in this age, is, that he was more holy and more perfect before God, and came to him with a purer heart, and more faith than men in this day.

"The same might be said on the subject of Jacob's history. Why was it that the Lord spake to him concerning the same promise, after he had made it once to Abraham, and renewed it to Isaac? Why could not Jacob rest contented upon the word spoken to his fathers? When the time of the promise drew nigh for the deliverance of the children of Israel from the land of Egypt, why was it necessary that the Lord should begin to speak to them? The promise or word to Abraham, was, that his seed should serve in bondage, and be afflicted, four hundred years, and after that they should come out with great substance. Why did they not rely upon this promise, and when they had remained in Egypt, in bondage, four hundred years, come out, without waiting for further revelations, but act entirely upon the promise given to Abraham, that they should come out?

"Paul said to his Hebrew brethren, that God might more abundantly show unto the heirs of promise the immutability of his counsel, he confirmed it by an oath. He also exhorts them, who, through faith and patience inherit the promises.

"Notwithstanding, we (said Paul) have fled for refuge to lay hold upon the hope set before us, which hope we have as an anchor of the soul, both sure and stedfast, and which entereth into that within the vail, yet he was careful to press upon them the necessity of continuing on until they, as well as those who then inherited the [207] promises, might have the assurance of their salvation confirmed to them by an oath from the mouth of Him who could not lie; for that seemed to be the example anciently, and Paul holds it out to his Hebrew brethren as an object attainable in his day. And why not? I admit, that by reading the Scriptures of truth, the Saints, in the days of Paul, could learn, beyond the power of contradiction, that Abraham, Isaac, and Jacob, had the promise of eternal life confirmed to them by an oath of the Lord, but that promise or oath was no assurance to them of their salvation; but they could, by walking in the footsteps, continuing in the faith of their fathers, obtain, for themselves, an oath for confirmation that they were meet to be partakers of the inheritance with the Saints in light.

"If the Saints, in the days of the Apostles, were privileged to take the Saints for example, and lay hold of the same promises, and attain to the same exalted privileges of knowing that their names were written in the Lamb's Book of Life, and that they were sealed there as a perpetual memorial before the face of the Most High, will not the same faithfulness, the same purity of heart, and the same faith, bring the same assurance of eternal life, and that in the same manner to the children of men now, in this age of the world? I have no doubt, but that the holy Prophets, and Apostles, and Saints in ancient days were saved in the kingdom of God; neither do I doubt but that they held converse and communion with him while they were in the flesh, as Paul said to his Corinthian brethren, that the Lord Jesus showed himself to above five hundred Saints at one time after his resurrection. Job said that he knew that his Redeemer lived, and that he should see him in the flesh in the latter days. I may believe that Enoch walked with God, and by faith was translated. I may believe that Noah was a perfect man in his generation, and also walked with God. I may believe that Abraham communed with God, and conversed with angels. I may believe that Isaac obtained a renewal of the covenant made to Abraham by the direct voice of the Lord. I may believe that Jacob conversed with holy angels, and heard the word of his Maker, that he wrestled with the angel until he prevailed, and obtained a blessing. I may believe that Elijah was taken to Heaven in a chariot of fire with fiery horses. I may believe that the Saints saw the Lord, and conversed with him face to face after his resurrection. I may believe that the [208] Hebrew Church came to Mount Zion, and unto the city of the living God, the *Heavenly* Jerusalem, and to an innumerable company of angels. I may believe that they looked into eternity, and saw the Judge of all, and Jesus the Mediator of the New Covenant. But will all this purchase an assurance for me, and waft me to the regions of eternal day, with my garments spotless, pure, and white? Or, must I not rather obtain for myself, by my own faith and diligence in keeping the commandments of the Lord, an assurance of salvation for myself? And have I not an equal privilege with the ancient Saints? And will not the Lord hear my prayers, and listen to my cries as soon as he ever did to theirs, if I come to him in the manner they did! Or, is he a respecter of persons?

"I must now close this subject for the want of time; and, I may say, with propriety, at the beginning. We would be pleased to see you in Kirtland; and more pleased to have you embrace the New Covenant.

"I remain,

"Yours affectionately,

"JOSEPH SMITH, JUN."

Previous to the time of our going to live with Joseph, my attention had been chiefly taken up with business; I now concluded to devote the most of my time to the study of the Bible, Book of Mormon, and Doctrine and Covenants, but a circumstance occurred, which deprived me of the privilege. One day upon going down stairs to dinner, I incautiously set my foot upon a round stick, that lay near the top of the stairs. This, rolling under my foot, pitched me forward down the steps; my head was severely bruised in falling; however, I said but little about it, thinking I should be better soon.

In the afternoon I went with my husband to a blessing meeting; I took cold, and an inflammation settled in my eyes, which increased until I became entirely blind. The distress which I suffered for a few days, surpasses all description. Every effort was made by my friends to relieve me, but all in vain. I called upon the Elders, and requested them to pray to the Lord, that I might be able to see, so **[209]** as to be able to read without even wearing spectacles. They did so, and when they took their hands off my head, I read two lines in the Book of Mormon; and although I am now seventy years old, I have never worn glasses since.

CHAPTER 45

THE HOUSE OF THE LORD COMPLETED — A DIVISION IN THE CHURCH

THE house of the Lord went steadily forward, until it was completed, notwithstanding the threats of the mob. When this work was accomplished, there was much rejoicing in the Church, and great blessings were poured out upon the elders; but as I was not present at the endowment, I shall say but little about it.

Shortly after the completion of the house, Joseph and Martin Harris, took a short tour through the eastern country. When they arrived at Palmyra, on their return, Joseph had a vision, which lasted until he besought the Lord to take it from him; for it manifested to him things which were painful to contemplate. It was taken from before his eyes for a short time, but soon returned again, and remained until the whole scene was portrayed before him.

On his arrival at home, the brethren seemed greatly pleased to see him. The next day he preached a sermon, and the following are a part of his remarks: —

"Brethren, I am rejoiced to see you, and I have no doubt, but that you are glad to see me. We are now nearly as happy as we can be on earth. We have accomplished more than we had any reason to expect when we began. Our beautiful house is finished, and the Lord **[210]** has acknowledged it, by pouring out his Spirit upon us here, and revealing to us much of his will in regard to the work which he is about to perform. Furthermore, we have every thing that is necessary to our comfort and convenience, and, judging from appearances, one would not suppose that anything could occur which would break up our friendship for each other, or disturb our tranquillity. But brethren, beware; for I tell you in the name of the Lord, that there is an evil in this very congregation, which, if not repented of, will result in setting one-third of you, who are here this day, so much at enmity against me, that you will have a desire to take my life; and you even *would do it*, if God should permit the deed. But brethren, I now call upon you to repent, and cease all your hardness of heart, and turn from those principles of death and dishonesty which you are harbouring in your bosoms, before it is eternally too late, for there is yet room for repentance."

He continued to labour with them in this way, appealing to them in the most solemn manner, until almost every one in the house was in tears, and he was exhausted with speaking.

The following week was spent in surmises and speculations, as to who would be the traitors, and why they should be so, &c, &c.

Prior to this, a bank was established in Kirtland. Soon after the sermon, above mentioned, Joseph discovered that a large amount of money had been taken away by fraud, from this bank. He immediately demanded a search warrant of Esquire Williams, which was flatly refused. "I insist upon a warrant," said Joseph, "for if you will give me one, I can get the money, and if you do not, I will break you of your office." "Well, break it is then," said Williams, "and we will strike hands upon it." "Very well," said Joseph, "from henceforth I drop you from my quorum, in the name of the Lord."

Williams, in wrath, replied, "Amen." Joseph entered a complaint against him, for neglect of duty, as an officer of justice; in consequence of which the magistracy was taken from him, and given to Oliver Cowdery. [211]

Joseph then went to Cleveland, in order to transact some business pertaining to the bank; and as he was absent the ensuing Sunday, my husband preached to the people. In speaking of the bank affair, he reflected somewhat sharply upon Warren Parrish. Although the reflection was just, Parrish was highly incensed, and made an attempt to drag him out of the stand. My husband appealed to Oliver Cowdery, who was justice of the peace, to have him brought to order; but Oliver never moved from his seat. William, seeing the abuse which his father was receiving, sprang forward and caught Parrish, and carried him in his arms nearly out of the house. At this John Boynton stepped forward, and drawing a sword from his cane, presented it to William's breast, and said, "if you advance one step further, I will run you through." Before William had time to turn himself, several gathered around him, threatening to handle him severely, if he should lay the weight of his finger upon Parrish again. At this juncture of affairs, I left the house, not only terrified at the scene, but likewise sick at heart, to see that the apostacy of which Joseph had prophecied, was so near at hand.

At this time a certain young woman, who was living at David Whitmer's, uttered a prophecy, which she said was given her, by looking through a black stone that she had found. This prophecy gave some altogether a new idea of things. She said, the reason why one-third of the

Church would turn away from Joseph, was because that he was in transgression himself; that he would fall from his office on account of the same; that David Whitmer or Martin Harris would fill Joseph's place; and that the one who did not succeed him, would be the Counsellor to the one that did.

This girl soon became an object of great attention among those who were disaffected. Dr. Williams, the ex-justice of the peace, became her scribe, and wrote her revelations for her. Jared Carter, who lived in the same house with David Whitmer, soon [212] imbibed the same spirit, and I was informed, that he said in one of their meetings, that he had power to raise "Joe Smith" to the highest heavens, or sink him down to the lowest hell.

Shortly after this, Jared came to our house, and I questioned him relative to what he had said concerning Joseph. Not having mentioned the matter to my husband, he did not understand what I meant at first; but after a little explanation, he warned Jared to repent of the injudicious course that he was taking, and speedily confess his sins to the Church, or the judgments of God would overtake him. Jared received this admonition, and acknowledging his fault, agreed to confess to the brethren the first opportunity. The next morning he was seized with a violent pain in his eyes, and continued in great distress for two days. On the evening of the second day, he arose from his bed, and, kneeling down, besought the Lord to heal him, covenanting to make a full confession to the Church at meeting the next Sunday.

Accordingly, the next Sabbath he arose and stated to the brethren, that he had done wrong; and, asking their forgiveness, begged to be received again into their confidence. He did not, however, state what he had done that was wrong; nevertheless his confession was received, and he was forgiven. But the rest of his party continued obstinate. They still held their secret meetings at David Whitmer's, and when the young woman, who was their instructress, was through giving what revelations she intended for the evening, she would jump out of her chair and dance over the floor, boasting of her power, until she was perfectly exhausted. Her proselytes would also, in the most vehement manner, proclaim their purity and holiness, and the mighty power which they were going to have.

They made a standing appointment for meetings to be held every Thursday, by the pure Church in the house of the Lord. They also circulated a paper, in order to ascertain how many would follow them, [213] and it was found, that a great proportion of the Church were decidedly in favour of the new party. In this spirit they went to Missouri, and contaminated the minds of many of the brethren against Joseph, in order to destroy his influence. This made it more necessary than ever, to keep a strict guard at the houses of those who were the chief objects of their vengeance.

———

CHAPTER 46

JOSEPH SMITH, SENIOR, AND HIS BROTHER JOHN, GO ON A MISSION TO THE EAST—THE DEATH OF JERUSHA SMITH

IN the year 1836, my husband and his brother John were sent on a short mission to New Portage. While there, they administered patriarchal blessings, and baptized sixteen persons.

Soon after they left for New Portage, their aged mother arrived in Kirtland from New York, after travelling the distance of five hundred miles. We sent immediately for my husband and his brother, who returned as speedily as possible, and found the old lady in good health and excellent spirits. She rejoiced to meet so many of her children, grand-children, and great grand-children, whom she expected never to see.

In two days after, her sons, John and Joseph, arrived, she was taken sick, and survived but one week; at the end of which she died, firm in the faith of the Gospel, although she had never yielded obedience to any of its ordinances. Her age was ninety-three years.

In a short time after her death, my husband and his brother John took a journey to visit all the Churches, and the following is a sketch from the journal of John Smith, of this tour:— **[214]**

"As we travelled through New Hampshire, we visited Daniel Mack, who was Joseph's brother-in-law. He treated us very kindly, but was unwilling to hear the Gospel. We travelled thence up the Connecticut river to Grafton. Here we found an own sister, whom we had not seen for twenty years. Her prejudice had become so strong against 'Mormonism,' that she was unwilling to treat us even decently. From this place we went to Vermont, through Windsor and Orange counties, and found many of our relatives, who treated us kindly, but would not receive the Gospel. We next crossed the Green Mountains to Middlebury. Here we found our oldest sister, who was very much pleased to see us, and received our testimony. We staid with her over night, and the next day set out for St. Lawrence county, New York, where we had one brother and a sister. Having arrived at this brother's (who was Jesse Smith), we spent one day with him. He treated us very ill. Leaving him, we went to see our sister Susan. I had business about ten miles on one side, and during my absence, Jesse pursued Joseph to Potsdam, with a warrant, on a pretended debt of twelve dollars, and took him back to Stockholm. Not satisfied with this, he abused him most shamefully, in the presence of strangers; and he exacted fifty dollars of him, which Joseph borrowed of brother Silas, who happened to be there just at that time from Kirtland, and paid Jesse this sum, in order to save further trouble.

"The meekness manifested by brother Joseph upon this occasion, won upon the feelings of many, who said that Jesse had disgraced himself so much, that he would never be able to redeem his character.

"From Potsdam we went to Ogdensburg, when to our joy we found Heber C. Kimball, who had raised up a small branch in that place. These were the first Latter-day Saints we had seen in travelling three hundred miles. On the tenth of October we returned home."

About one year after my husband returned from this mission, a calamity happened to our family that wrung our hearts with more than common grief. Jerusha, Hyrum's wife, was taken sick, and, after an illness of, perhaps, two weeks, died, while her husband was absent on a mission to Missouri. She was a woman whom everybody loved that was acquainted with her, for she was every way worthy. **[215]** The family were so warmly attached to her, that, had she been our own sister, they could not have been more afflicted by her death.

CHAPTER 47

THE PERSECUTION REVIVES—DON CARLOS AND HIS FATHER FLY
FROM THEIR ENEMIES—JOSEPH MOVES TO MISSOURI

SOON after the division that took place in the Church, our enemies without began again to trouble us. Having seen our prosperity in everything to which we had set our hands previous to this, they became discouraged, and ceased their operations; but, suddenly discovering that there was a division in our midst, their fruitful imaginations were aroused to the utmost, to invent new schemes to accomplish our destruction.

Their first movement was to sue Joseph for debt, and, with this pretence, seize upon every piece of property belonging to any of the family. Joseph then had in his possession four Egyptian mummies, with some ancient records that accompanied them. These the mob swore they would take from the meeting-house, and then burn every one of them. Accordingly, they levied an execution upon them for an unjust debt of fifty dollars; but, by various stratagems, we succeeded in keeping them out of their hands.

The persecution finally became so violent, that Joseph regarded it as unsafe to remain any longer in Kirtland, and began to make arrangements to move to Missouri. One evening, before finishing his preparations for the contemplated journey, he sat in council with the brethren at our house. After giving **[216]** them directions as to what he desired them to do, while he was absent from them, and, as he was about leaving the room, he said, "Well, brethren, I do not recollect anything more, but one thing, brethren, is certain, I shall see you again, let what will happen, for I have a promise of life five years, and they cannot kill me until that time is expired."

That night he was warned by the Spirit to make his escape, with his family, as speedily as possible; he therefore arose from his bed, and took his family, with barely beds and clothing sufficient for them, and left Kirtland in the dead hour of the night. The day following, the constable, Luke Johnson, an apostate, served a summons upon my husband, telling him that no harm was intended, and desired him to go immediately to the office.

I begged Johnson not to drag my husband away among our enemies, for I knew, by sad experience, the direful consequences of these civil suits. Johnson paid no attention to what I said, but hurried my husband away to the office. He was taken for marrying a couple; and as Esquire Cowdery, and the mob, did not consider that he was a minister of the Gospel, they disputed his having the right to perform this ceremony, and so fined him the sum of three thousand dollars, and, in case he should fail to pay this amount forthwith, he was sentenced to go to the penitentiary. Luke Johnson bustled about, pretending to be very much engaged in preparing to draw writings for the money, and making other arrangements, such as were required of him by the party to which he belonged. The first opportunity that offered itself, he went to Hyrum, and told him to take his father into a room, which he pointed out to him, and, said Johnson, "I will manage to get the window out, which will set him at liberty to jump out, and go where he pleases." Mr. Smith and Hyrum, who had been together all the time, then retired from the company, who were kept from following them by Luke Johnson, who told the mob, that the prisoner had gone to consult about raising **[217]** the money. In this way they were stilled, until Mr. Smith, by the help of Hyrum and John Boynton, escaped from the window.

My husband, after travelling about four miles, stopped with brother Snow, who was father to Eliza Snow, the poetess. The old man told Mr. Smith that he would secrete him, and, calling his family together, he forbade them telling any one of his being there.

When Johnson supposed that my husband was out of their reach, he started up and ran into the room where he had left him, saying, that he must see after the prisoner, and finding the room empty, he made a great outcry, and ran, hunting in every direction for the fugitive. He came to me and inquired if Mr. Smith had returned home. This frightened me very much, and I exclaimed, "Luke, you have killed my husband." He denied it, but gave no further explanation. In a short time I found out where he was, and sent him both money and clothes to travel with, so that in a few days, he started with Don Carlos and brother Wilber. By this time, hand-bills were stuck up, on every public, as well as private road, offering a reward for him, and describing his person, in order, if possible, to prevent his escape. Runners were also sent throughout the country to watch for him, with authority to bring him back, in case he should be found; but, in spite of all their diligence, he succeeded in making his escape, and getting to New Portage, where he stopped with brother Taylor. Don Carlos, having accompanied his father to the above-named place, returned home again to his family; but, immediately discovering that the mob contemplated taking him for the same offence, he moved with his family to New Portage, and was there with his father, until the rest of the family were ready to remove to Missouri. Hyrum had already moved there with his family.

Shortly after they left, a man by the name of Edward Woolley came to Kirtland to see Mr. Smith; not finding him there, he went to New Portage, and persuaded my husband to accompany him home. **[218]**

After Mr. Smith had been at this gentleman's residence about two weeks, we became very uneasy about him; and, as we did not know at that time whither he had gone, William set out in pursuit of him, in order to learn, if possible, whether he had met with friends, and was well provided for, or had fallen into the hands of his enemies, and been murdered, for we had as much reason to apprehend the latter calamity, as to hope for the former good fortune.

It was some time after William arrived at New Portage, before he could ascertain where my husband had gone. But as soon as he did receive the desired information he proceeded to Edward Woolley's, where he found his father in good health, but extremely anxious about the family.

On hearing that William was in the place, many of the inhabitants were desirous that he should preach, and he agreed to do so; but a few declared, that if he did, they would tar and feather him. One of these was Mr. Bear, a man of unusual size and strength; besides him there were three others. These men came into the house, just as William was taking his text, which was, "The poor deluded Mormons." The singularity of this text excited their curiosity, and they stopped in the doorway, saying, wait a little, let us see what he will do with his text; and they waited so long, that they either forgot what they came for, or changed their minds, for they made no further moves towards using their tar and feathers. After meeting, Mr. Bear frankly acknowledged his conviction of the truth, and was baptized.

Immediately after this, William returned home, and his father went again to New Portage. Here he remained with Don Carlos, until we were ready to start to Missouri. **[219]**

CHAPTER 48

JOSEPH SMITH, SENIOR, MOVES WITH HIS FAMILY TO MISSOURI —
COMMENCEMENT OF THE PERSECUTION IN CALDWELL

WHEN we were ready to start on our journey, I went to New Portage, and brought my husband to his family, and we all proceeded together on our journey, highly delighted to enjoy each other's society again, after so long a separation.

As soon as we had got fairly started, our sons began to have calls to preach, and they directly discovered, that if they should yield to every solicitation, our journey would be a preaching mission of no inconsiderable length, which was quite inconsistent with the number and situation of our family. They therefore stopped preaching, while on their journey, and we proceeded as fast as possible, under the disadvantageous circumstances with which we were frequently surrounded. Sometimes we lay in our tents, through driving storms; at other times, we were travelling on foot through marshes and quagmires. Once in particular, we lay all night exposed to the rain, which fell in torrents, so that when I arose in the morning, I found that my clothing was perfectly saturated with the rain. However, I could not mend the matter by a change of dress, for the rain was still falling rapidly, and I wore my clothes in this situation, three days; inconsequence of which, I took a severe cold, so that when we arrived at the Mississippi river, I was unable to walk or sit up. After crossing this river, we stopped at a negro hut, a most unlovely place, yet the best shelter we could find. This hut was the birth-place of Catharine's daughter.

The next day, my husband succeeded in getting a comfortable place, about four miles distant, for Catharine and her infant daughter, and they were **[220]** carried thither, on a lumber waggon, the same day. We then agreed that Sophronia, and her second husband, Mc Lerrey, should stop and take care of Catharine; while Mr. Smith and the remainder of the party, should take me, and make what speed they could to Huntsville.

Our progress was but slow, for I was unable to travel more than four miles a day, on account of a violent cough with which I was afflicted; however, we at length arrived there, and succeeded in getting a place where we could stay for some considerable length of time, if we should think proper to do so.

The next morning after our arrival, the family being absent I seized the opportunity to make an effort to get far enough from the house to pray without interruption. Accordingly, I took a staff in each hand, and, by the assistance which they afforded me, I was enabled to reach a dense thicket, which lay some distance from the house. As soon as I was sufficiently rested to speak with ease, I commenced calling upon the Lord, beseeching him to restore me to health, as well as my daughter Catharine. I urged every claim which is afforded us by the Scriptures, and continued praying faithfully for three hours, at the end of which time, I was relieved from every kind of pain, my cough left me, and I was well.

At one o'clock, Wilkins J. Salisbury, Catharine's husband, came to Huntsville, and informed us that Catharine was so much better, that, if she had a carriage to ride in, she could proceed on her journey.

After getting a carriage, Salisbury returned to his wife, who was forty miles from Huntsville, and the first day she travelled, she rode thirty miles. The second day, it commenced raining quite early in the morning, and continued to rain all day. However, this did not stop Catherine; she started about eight o'clock and arrived at the above-named place, a little before noon. When she got to Huntsville she was wet and cold. We put her immediately into a dry bed, and goon after she had an ague fit. The Elders [221] were called to lay hands upon her, after which she seemed better, but continued weak and inclined to chills and fever sometime.

The day following I washed a quantity of clothes, and then we proceeded on our journey, and met with no further difficulty until we arrived at Far West.

We moved into a small log house, having but one room, a very inconvenient place for so large a family. Joseph saw how uncomfortably we were situated, and proposed that we should take a large tavern house, which he had recently purchased of brother Gilbert. We took the tavern, and moved into it. Samuel, previous to this, had moved to a place called Marrowbone. William had moved thirty miles in another direction. We were all now quite comfortable. But this state of affairs was of short duration, for it was not long before our peace was again disturbed by the mob. An election took place at Gallatin, the county seat of Davies county; the brethren went to the poll as usual, but, on attempting to vote, they were forbidden by the mob. They, however, paid no attention to this, but proceeded to vote; upon which, one of the mob struck brother John Butler a heavy blow, which was returned by the latter, with a force that brought his antagonist to the ground. Four others came to the assistance of the fallen man, and shared the same fate. The mob saw the discomfiture of their champions with shame and disappointment, and not choosing to render them any present help, they waited till evening, when, procuring the assistance of the judge of the election, they wrote letters to all the adjoining counties, begging their assistance against the "Mormons." They stated that Joseph Smith had, himself, killed seven men, at the election the day previous, and that the inhabitants had every reason to expect that he would collect his people together, as soon as possible, and murder all that did not belong to his Church.

These letters were extensively circulated, and as widely believed.

A few days subsequent to this, Joseph was at our **[222]** house writing a letter. While he was thus engaged, I stepped to the door, and looking towards the prairie, I beheld a large company of armed men advancing towards the city, but, as I supposed it to be training day, said nothing about it.

Presently the main body came to a halt. The officers dismounting, eight of them came into the house. Thinking that they had come for some refreshment, I offered them chairs, but they refused to be seated, and, placing themselves in a line across the floor, continued standing. I again requested them to sit, but they replied, "We do not choose to sit down; we have come here to kill Joe Smith and all the Mormons."

"Ah," said I, "what has Joseph Smith done, that you should want to kill him?"

"He has killed seven men in Davies county," replied the foremost, "and we have come to kill him, and all his Church."

"He has not been in Davies county," I answered, "consequently the report must be false. Furthermore, if you should see him, you would not want to kill him."

"There is no doubt but that the report is perfectly correct," rejoined the officer; "it came straight to us, and I believe it; and we were sent to kill the Prophet and all who believe in him, and I'll be d—d if I don't execute my orders."

"I suppose," said I, "you intend to kill me, with the rest?"

"Yes, we do," returned the officer.

"Very well," I continued, "I want you to act the gentleman about it, and do the job quick. Just shoot me down at once, then I shall be at rest; but I should not like to be murdered by inches."

"There it is again," said he. "You tell a Mormon that you will kill him, and they will always tell you, 'that is nothing—if you kill us, we shall be happy.'"

Joseph, just at this moment, finished his letter, and, seeing that he was at liberty, I said, "Gentle[223]men, suffer me to make you acquainted with Joseph Smith, the Prophet." They stared at him as if he were a spectre. He smiled, and, stepping towards them, gave each of them his hand, in a manner which convinced them that he was neither a guilty criminal nor yet a hypocrite.

Joseph then sat down, and explained to them the views, feelings, &c., of the Church, and what their course had been; besides the treatment which they had received from their enemies since the first. He also argued, that if any of the brethren had broken the law, they ought to be tried by the law, before any one else was molested. After talking with them some time in this way, he said, "Mother, I believe I will go home now—Emma will be expecting me." At this two of the men sprang to their feet, and declared that he should not go alone, as it would be unsafe—that they would go with him, in order to protect him. Accordingly, the three left together, and, during their absence, I overheard the following conversation among the officers, who remained at the door:—

1st Officer. "Did you not feel strangely when Smith took you by the hand? I never felt so in my life."

2nd Officer. "I could not move. I would not harm a hair of that man's head for the whole world."

3rd Officer. "This is the last time you will catch me coming to kill Joe Smith, or the Mormons either."

1st Officer. "I guess this is about my last expedition against this place. I never saw a more harmless, innocent appearing man, than that Mormon Prophet."

2nd Officer. "That story about his killing them men is all a d—d lie—there is no doubt of it; and we have had all this trouble for nothing; but they will never fool me in this way again, I'll warrant them."

The men who went home with my son promised [224] to disband the militia under them, and go home, which they accordingly did, and we supposed that peace was again restored. After they were gone, Joseph and Hyrum went to Davies county, and, receiving the strongest assurances from the civil officers of that county, that equal rights should be administered to all parties, they returned, hoping that all would be well.

About this time, we heard that William and his wife were very sick. Samuel, who was then at Far West, set out with a carriage to bring them to our house, and, in a few days, returned with them. They were very low when they arrived; however, by great care and close attention, they soon began to recover.

Soon after Samuel brought William and Caroline to our house, there was born unto Samuel a son, whom he called by his own name. When the child was three days old, his father was compelled to leave, and, on the fourth day of its existence, his mother was informed that she must leave home forthwith, and take a journey of thirty miles to Far West. One of the neighbours offered to furnish her a team, and a small boy to drive it, if she would start immediately. To this she agreed. A lumber waggon was brought, and she, with her bed, her children, and very little clothing either for them or herself, was put into it, and sent to Far West, under the care of a boy of eleven years of age.

The day following, Samuel started home from Far West, although the rain was falling fast, and had been all the night previous. He had proceeded but ten miles when he met his wife and children, exposed to the inclemency of the weather, and dripping with wet. He returned with them to Far West, where they arrived in about thirty-six hours after they left Marrowbone, without having taken any nourishment from the time they left home. She was entirely speechless and stiff with the cold. We laid her on a bed, and my husband and sons administered to her by the lay[225]ing on of hands. We then changed her clothing, and put her into warm blankets, and, after pouring a little wine and water into her mouth, she was administered to again. This time she opened her eyes, and seemed to revive a little. I continued to employ every means that lay in my power for her recovery, and in this I was much assisted by Emma and my daughters.

My children soon began to mend, and I felt to rejoice at the prospect of returning health.

When William began to sit up a little, he told me that he had a vision during his sickness, in which he saw a tremendous army of men coming into Far West, and that it was his impression that the time would not be long before he should see it fulfilled. I was soon convinced, by the circumstances which afterwards transpired, that he was not mistaken in his opinion.

———

CHAPTER 49

TESTIMONY OF HYRUM SMITH

HERE I shall introduce a brief history of our troubles in Missouri, given by my son Hyrum, before the Municipal Court, at Nauvoo, June 30, 1843, when Joseph was tried for treason against the state of Missouri: —

"HYRUM SMITH, sworn:—Said that the defendant now in court is his
brother, and that his name is not Joseph Smith, junior, but his name is
Joseph Smith, senior, and has been for more than two years past. I have
been acquainted with him ever since he was born, which was
thirty-seven years in December last, and I have not been absent from
him at any one time, not even the space of [226] six months, since his
birth, to my recollection; and have been intimately acquainted with all
his sayings, doings, business transactions, and movements, as much as
any one man could be acquainted with any other man's business, up to
the present time, and do know that he has not committed treason against
any state in the Union, by any overt act, or by levying war, or by aiding
and abetting, or assisting an enemy, in any state in the Union. And that
the said Joseph Smith, senior, has not committed treason in the state of
Missouri, nor violated any law or rule of said state, I being personally
acquainted with the transactions and doings of said Smith, whilst he
resided in said state, which was for about six months in the year 1838;
I being also a resident in said state, during the same period of time. And
I do know that said Joseph Smith, senior, never was subject to military
duty in any state, neither was he in the state of Missouri, he being
exempt by the amputation or extraction of a bone from his leg, and by
his having a license to preach the Gospel, or being in other words, a
minister of the Gospel. And I do know that said Smith never bore arms
as a military man, in any capacity whatever, whilst in the state of
Missouri, or previous to that time; neither has he given any orders, or
assumed any command, in any capacity whatever. But I do know that
whilst he was in the state of Missouri, that the people commonly called
'Mormons,' were threatened with violence and extermination, and on or
about the first Monday in August 1838, at the election at Gallatin, the
county seat in Davies county, the citizens who were commonly called
'Mormons,' were forbidden to exercise the rights of franchise, and from
that unhallowed circumstance an affray commenced, and a fight ensued
among the citizens of that place, and from that time a mob commenced
gathering in that county, threatening the extermination of the
'Mormons.' The said Smith and myself, upon hearing that mobs were
collecting together, and that they had also murdered two of the citizens
of the same place, and would not suffer them to be buried, the said
Smith and myself went over to Davies county to learn the particulars of
the affray; but upon our arrival at Diahman, we learned that none were
killed, but several were wounded. We tarried all night at Col. Lyman
Wight's. The next morning the weather being very [227] warm, and
having been very dry for some time previous, the springs and wells in
that region were dried up. On mounting our horses to return, we rode
up to Mr. Black's, who was then an acting justice of the peace, to obtain
some water for ourselves and horses. Some few of the citizens
accompanied us there, and after obtaining the refreshment of water, Mr.
Black was asked, by said Joseph Smith, senior, if he would use his
influence to see that the laws were faithfully executed, and to put down

mob violence, and he gave us a paper written by his own hand stating that he would do so. He also requested him, (Mr. Black) to call together the most influential men of the county the next day, that we might have an interview with them; to this he acquiesced, and accordingly, the next day they assembled at the house of Col. Wight, and entered into a mutual covenant of peace to put down mob violence, and to protect each other in the enjoyment of their rights. After this we all parted with the best of feelings, and each man returned to his own home. This mutual agreement of peace, however, did not last long; for but a few days afterwards the mob began to collect again, until several hundreds rendezvoused at Millport, a few miles distant from Diahman. They immediately commenced making aggressions upon the citizens called 'Mormons,' taking away their hogs and cattle, and threatening them with extermination, or utter destruction; saying that they had a cannon, and there should be no compromise only at its mouth; frequently taking men, women, and children prisoners, whipping them and lacerating their bodies with hickory withes, and tying them to trees, and depriving them of food until they were compelled to gnaw the bark from the trees to which they were bound, in order to sustain life, treating them in the most cruel manner they could invent or think of, and doing everything they could to excite the indignation of the 'Mormon' people to rescue them, in order that they might make that a pretext for an accusation for the breach of the law, and that they might the better excite the prejudice of the populace, and thereby get aid and assistance to carry out their hellish purposes of extermination. Immediately on the authentication of these facts, messengers were despatched from Far West to Austin A. King, judge of the fifth judicial district of the state of Missouri, and also to Major-Gen. Atchison, Commander-[228]in-Chief of that division, and Brigadier-General Doniphan, giving them information of the existing facts, and demanding immediate assistance. General Atchison returned with the messengers, and went immediately to Diahman, and from thence to Millport, and he found the facts were true as reported to him; that the citizens of that county were assembled together in a hostile attitude, to the amount of two or three hundred men, threatening the utter extermination of the 'Mormons.' He immediately returned to Clay county, and ordered out a suffcient military force to quell the mob. Immediately after they were dispersed, and the army returned, the mob commenced collecting again; soon after, we again applied for military aid, when General Doniphan came out with a force of sixty armed men to Far West; but they were in such a state of insubordination, that he said he could not control them, and it was thought advisable by Colonel Hinkle, Mr. Rigdon, and others, that they should return home. General Doniphan ordered Colonel Hinkle to call out the Militia of Caldwell, and defend the town against the mob, for, said he, you have great reason to be alarmed; for, he said, Neil Gillum, from the Platte Country, had come down with two hundred armed men, and had taken up their station at Hunter's Mill, a place distant about seventeen or eighteen miles north-west of the town of Far West, and, also, that an armed force had collected again at Millport; in Davies county, consisting of several hundred men, and that another armed force had collected at De Witt, in Carroll county, about fifty miles south-east of Far West, where about seventy families of the 'Mormon' people had settled, upon the bank of the Missouri River, at a little town called De Witt. Immediately a messenger, whilst he was yet talking, came in from De Witt, stating, that three or four hundred men had assembled together at that place, armed *cap-a-pie*, and that they threatened the utter extinction of the citizens of that place, if they did not leave the place immediately, and that they had also surrounded the town and cut off all supplies of food, so that many of them were suffering with hunger. General Doniphan seemed to be very much alarmed, and appeared to be willing to do all he could to assist, and to relieve the sufferings of the 'Mormon' people. He advised that a petition be immediately got up and sent to the Gover[229]nor. A petition was accordingly prepared, and a messenger immediately despatched to the Governor, and another petition was sent to Judge King. The 'Mormon' people throughout the country were in a great state of alarm, and also in great distress. They saw themselves completely surrounded with armed forces, on the north, and on the north-west, and on the south, and also Bogard, who was a Methodist preacher, and who was then a Captain over a Militia company of fifty soldiers, but who had added to his number, out of the surrounding counties, about a hundred more, which made his force about one hundred and fifty strong, was stationed at Crooked Creek, sending out his scouting parties, taking men, women, and children prisoners, driving off cattle, hogs, and horses, entering into every house on Log and Long Creeks, rifling their houses of their most precious articles, such as money, bedding, and clothing, taking all their old muskets and their rifles or military implements, threatening the people with instant death if they did not deliver up all their precious things, and enter into a covenant to leave the state or go into the city of Far West by the next morning, saying that 'they calculated to drive the people into Far West, and then drive them to hell.' Gillum also was doing the same on the north-west side of Far West; and Sashiel Woods, a Presbyterian Minister, was the leader of the mob in Davies county, and a very noted man, of the same society, was the leader of the mob in Carroll county; and they were also sending out their scouting parties, robbing and pillaging houses, driving away hogs, horses, and cattle, taking men, women, and children, and carrying them off, threatening their lives, and subjecting them to all manner of abuses that they could invent or think of.

"Under this state of alarm, excitement, and distress, the messengers returned from the Governor, and from the other authorities, bringing the fatal news that the 'Mormons' could have no assistance. They stated that the Governor said, 'that the Mormons had got into a difficulty with the citizens, and they might fight it out, for all what he cared, he could not render them any assistance.'

"The people of De Witt were obliged to leave their homes and go into Far West; but did not until many of them had starved to death for want of proper sustenance, [230] and several died on the road there, and were buried by the way side, without a coffin or a funeral ceremony, and the distress, sufferings, and privations of the people cannot be expressed. All the scattered families of the 'Mormon' people, in all the counties except Davies, were driven into Far West, with but few exceptions.

"This only increased their distress, for many thousands who were driven there had no habitations or houses to shelter them, and were huddled together, some in tents, and others under blankets, while others had no shelter from the inclemency of the weather. Nearly two months the people had been in this awful state of consternation, many of them had been killed, whilst others had been whipped until they had to swathe up their bowels to prevent them from falling out. About this time, General Parks came out from Richmond, Ray county, who was one of the commissioned officers who was sent out to Diahman, and I, myself, and my brother Joseph Smith, senior, went out at the same time.

"On the evening that General Parks arrived at Diahman, the wife of the late Don Carlos Smith, my brother, came in to Colonel Wight's, about eleven o'clock at night, bringing her two children along with her, one about two years and a half old, the other a babe in her arms. She came in on foot, a distance of three miles, and waded Grand River, and the water was then about waist deep, and the snow about three inches deep. She stated that a party of the mob, a gang of ruffians, had turned her out of doors, had taken her household goods, and had burnt up her house, and she had escaped by the skin of her teeth. Her husband at that time was in Virginia, and she was living alone. This cruel transaction excited the feelings of the people in Diahman, especially Col. Wight, and he asked Gen. Parks, in my hearing, *how long we had got to suffer such base violence?* Gen. Parks said he did not know how long. Col. Wight then asked him what should be done? Gen. Parks told him, 'he should take a company of men, well armed, and go and disperse the mob wherever he should find any collected together, and take away their arms.' Col. Wight did so precisely, according to the orders of Gen. Parks, and my brother Joseph Smith, senior, made no words about it. And after Col. Wight had dispersed the mob, and put a stop to their burning houses belonging to the 'Mormon' people [231] and turning women and children out of doors, which they had done up to that time, to the amount of eight or ten houses, which were consumed to ashes. After being cut short in their intended designs, the mob started up a new plan. They went to work, and moved their families out of the county, and set fire to their houses, and not being able to incense the 'Mormons' to commit crimes, they had recourse to this stratagem—to set their houses on fire, and send runners into all the counties adjacent, to declare to the people, that the 'Mormons' had burnt up their houses, and destroyed their fields; and if the people would not believe them, they would tell them to go and see if what they had said was not true. Many people came to see—they saw the houses burning, and being filled with prejudice, they could not be made to believe, but that the 'Mormons' set them on fire; which deed was most diabolical and of the blackest kind, for indeed the 'Mormons' did not set them on fire, nor meddle with their houses or their fields. And the houses that were burnt, together with the pre-emption rights, and the corn in the fields, had all been previously purchased by the 'Mormons,' of the people, and paid for in money, and with waggons and horses, and with other property, about two weeks before; but they had not taken possession of the premises; but this wicked transaction was for the purpose of clandestinely exciting the minds of a prejudiced populace and the Executive, that they might get an order, that they could the more easily carry out their hellish purposes, in expulsion or extermination, or utter extinction of the 'Mormon' people. After witnessing the distressed situation of the people in Diahman, my brother Joseph Smith, senior, and myself, returned back to the city of Far West, and immediately despatched a messenger, with written documents, to General Atchison, stating the facts as they did then exist, praying for assistance, if possible, and requesting the editor of the "Far West," to insert the same in his newspaper, but he utterly refused to do so. We still believed that we should get assistance from the Governor, and again petitioned him, praying for assistance, setting forth our distressed situation. And in the mean time, the presiding judge of the county court issued orders, upon affidavits made to him by the citizens, to the sheriff of the county, to order out the militia of the county, to stand in constant readiness, night and day, to prevent the citizens from being massacred, which fearful [232] situation they were exposed to every moment. Every thing was very portentous and alarming. Notwithstanding all this, there was a ray of hope yet existing in the minds of the people, that the Governor would render us assistance. And whilst the people were waiting anxiously for deliverance—men, women, and children frightened, praying and weeping, we beheld at a distance, crossing the prairies, and approaching the town, a large army in military array, brandishing their glittering swords in the sunshine, and we could not but feel joyful for a moment, thinking that probably the Governor had sent an armed force to our relief, notwithstanding the awful forebodings that pervaded our breasts. But to our great surprise, when the army arrived, they came up and formed a line in double file, in one half mile on the east of the city of Far West, and despatched three messengers with a white flag to come to the city. They were met by Captain Morey, with a few other individuals, whose names I do not now recollect. I was, myself, standing close by, and could very distinctly hear every word they said. Being filled with anxiety, I rushed forward to the spot, expecting to hear good news, but, alas! and heart-thrilling to every soul that heard them—they demanded three persons to be brought out of the city, before they should massacre the rest. The names of the persons they demanded, were Adam

Lightner, John Cleminson, and his wife. Immediately the three persons were brought forth to hold an interview with the officers who had made the demand, and the officers told them, they had, now a chance to save their lives, for they calculated to destroy the people, and lay the city in ashes. They replied to the officers, and said, 'If the people must be destroyed, and the city burned to ashes, they would remain in the city and die with them.' The officers immediately returned, and the army retreated, and encamped about a mile and a half from the city. A messenger was immediately despatched with a white flag, from the colonel of the militia of Far West, requesting an interview with General Atchison, and General Doniphan; but, as the messenger approached the camp, he was shot at by Bogard, the Methodist preacher. The name of the messenger was Charles C. Rich, who is now Brigadier-General in the Nauvoo Legion. However, he gained permission to see General Doniphan. He also requested an interview with General Atchison. General Doniphan said, that General Atchison had been dis[233]mounted by a special order of the Governor, a few miles back, and had been sent back to Liberty, Clay county. He also stated, that the reason was, that he (Atchison), was too merciful unto the 'Mormons,' and Boggs would not let him have the command, but had given it to General Lucas, who was from Jackson county, and whose heart had become hardened by his former acts of rapine and bloodshed, he being one of the leaders in murdering, driving, plundering, and burning some two or three hundred houses belonging to the 'Mormon' people in that county, in the years 1833 and 1834.

"Mr. Rich requested General Doniphan to spare the people, and not suffer them to be massacred until the next morning, it then being evening. He coolly agreed that he would not, and also said, that, 'he had not as yet received the Governor's order, but expected it every hour, and should not make any further move until he had received it; but he would not make any promises so far as regarded Neil Gillum's army,' (he having arrived a few minutes previously, and joined the main body of the army, he knowing well, at what hour to form a junction with the main body). Mr. Rich then returned to the city, giving this information. The colonel immediately despatched a second messenger with a white flag, to request another interview with General Doniphan, in order to touch his sympathy and compassion, and if it were possible, for him to use his best endeavours to preserve the lives of the people. On the return of this messenger, we learned that several persons had been killed by some of the soldiers, who were under the command of General Lucas. One Mr. Carey had his brains knocked out by the breech of a gun, and he lay bleeding several hours, but his family were not permitted to approach him, nor any one else allowed to administer relief to him whilst he lay upon the ground in the agonies of death. Mr. Carey had just arrived in the country, from the state of Ohio, only a few hours previous to the arrival of the army. He had a family consisting of a wife and several small children. He was buried by Lucius N. Scovil, who is now the senior warden of the Nauvoo Lodge. Another man, of the name of John Tanner, was knocked on the head at the same time, and his skull laid bare the width of a man's hand, and he lay, to all appearance, in the agonies of death for several hours; but by the permission of General Doniphan, his friends brought him out of the [234] camp, and with good nursing he slowly recovered, and is now living. There was another man, whose name is Powell, who was beat on the head with the breech of a gun until his skull was fractured, and his brains ran out in two or three places. He is now alive, and resides in this county, but has lost the use of his senses; several persons of his family were also left for dead, but have since recovered. These acts of barbarity were also committed by the soldiers under the command of General Lucas, previous to having received the Governor's order of extermination.

"It was on the evening of the thirtieth of October, according to the best of my recollection, that the army arrived at Far West, the sun about half an hour high. In a few moments afterwards, Cornelius Gillum arrived with his army and formed a junction. This Gillum had been stationed at Hunter's Mills for about two months previous to that time—committing depredations upon the inhabitants, capturing men, women, and children, and carrying them off as prisoners, lacerating their bodies with hickory withes. The army of *Gillum* were painted like Indians, some of them were more conspicuous than were others, designated by red spots, and he also was painted in a similar manner, with red spots marked on his face, and styled himself the *"Delaware chief."* They would whoop, and hollow, and yell, as nearly like Indians as they could, and continued to do so all that night. In the morning early the Colonel of militia, sent a messenger into the camp, with a white flag, to have another interview with Gen. Doniphan. On his return he informed us that the Governor's order had arrived. General Doniphan said, 'that the order of the Governor was, to exterminate the Mormons by God, but he would be d—d if *he* obeyed *that order,* but General Lucas might do what he pleased.' We immediately learned from General Doniphan, that the Governor's order that had arrived was only a copy of the original, and that the original order was in the hands of Major General Clark, who was on his way to Far West, with an additional army of six thousand men.' Immediately after this there came into the city a messenger from Haun's Mill, bringing the intelligence of an awful massacre of the people who were residing in that place, and that a force of two or three hundred, detached from the main body of the army, under the superior command of Colonel Ashley, but [235] under the immediate command of Captain Nehemiah Comstock, who, the day previous, had promised them peace and protection, but on receiving a copy of the Governor's order, *'to exterminate or to expel,'* from the hands of Colonel Ashley, he returned upon them the following day, and surprised and massacred the whole population of the town, and then came on to the town of Far West, and entered into conjunction with the main body of the army. The messenger informed us, that he, himself, with a few others, fled into the thickets, which preserved them from the massacre, and on the following morning they returned, and collected the dead bodies of the people, and cast them into a well; and there were upwards of twenty, who were dead, or mortally wounded, and there are several of the wounded, who are now living in this city. One of the name of Yocum, has lately had his leg amputated, in consequence of wounds he then received. He had a ball shot through his head, which entered near his eye and came out at the back part of his head, and another bail passed through one of his arms.

"The army during all the while they had been encamped in Far West, continued to lay waste fields of corn, making hogs, sheep, and cattle common plunder, and shooting them down for sport. One man shot a cow, and took a strip of her skin, the width of his hand, from her head to her tail, and tied it around a tree to slip his halter into to tie his horse to. The city was surrounded with a strong guard, and no man, woman, or child, was permitted to go out or come in, under the penalty of death. Many of the citizens were shot, in attempting to go out to obtain sustenance for themselves and families. There was one field fenced in, consisting of twelve-hundred acres, mostly covered with corn. It was entirely laid waste by the horses of the army, and the next day after the arrival of the army, towards evening, Col. Hinkle came up from the camp, requesting to see my brother Joseph, Parley P. Pratt, Sidney Rigdon, Lyman Wight, and George W. Robinson, stating that the officers of the army wanted a mutual consultation with those men, also stating that Generals Doniphan, Lucas, Wilson, and Graham, (however, General Graham is an honourable exception: he did all he could to preserve the lives of the people, contrary to the order of the Governor,) he (Hinkle) assured them that these generals had pledged [236] their sacred honour, that they should not be abused or insulted; but should be guarded back in safety in the morning, or so soon as the consultation was over. My brother Joseph replied, that he did not know what good he could do in any consultation, as he was only a private individual; however, he said that he was always willing to do all the good he could, and would obey every law of the land, and then leave the event with God. They immediately started with Col. Hinkle to go down into the camp. As they were going down, about half way to the camp, they met General Lucas, with a phalanx of men, with a wing to the right and to the left, and a four-pounder in the centre. They supposed he was coming with this strong force to guard them into the camp in safety; but, to their surprise, when they came up to General Lucas, he ordered his men to surround them, and Hinkle stepped up to the General and said, 'These are the prisoners I agreed to deliver up.' General Lucas drew his sword, and said, 'Gentlemen, you are my prisoners,' and about that time the main army were on their march to meet them. They came up in two divisions, and opened to the right and left, and my brother and his friends were marched down through their lines, with a strong guard in front, and the cannon in the rear to the camp, amidst the whoopings, hollowings, yellings, and shoutings of the army, which were so horrid and terrific, that they frightened the inhabitants of the city. It is impossible to describe the feelings of horror and distress of the people. After being thus betrayed, they were placed under a strong guard of thirty men, armed *cap-a-pie*, which were relieved every two hours. There they were compelled to lie on the cold ground that night, and were told in plain language that they need never to expect their liberties again. So far for their honours pledged. However, this was as much as could be expected from a mob under the garb of military and executive authority in the state of Missouri. On the next day, the soldiers were permitted to patrol the streets, to abuse and insult the people at their leisure, and enter into houses and pillage them, and ravish the women, taking away every gun, and every other kind of arms or military implements. And about twelve o'clock that day, Col. Hinkle came to my house with an armed force, opened the door, and called me out of doors and delivered me up as a prisoner unto that force. They [237] surrounded me and commanded me to march into the camp. I told them that I could not go, my family were sick, and I was sick myself, and could not leave home. They said, they did not care for that, I must and should go. I asked when they would permit me to return. They made me no answer, but forced me along with the point of the bayonet into the camp, and put me under the same guard with my brother Joseph; and within about half an hour afterwards, Amasa Lyman was also brought, and placed under the same guard. There we were compelled to stay all that night, and lie on the ground; but along some time in the same night, Col. Hinkle came to me and told me, that he had been pleading my case before the court-martial, but he was afraid he should not succeed. He said there was a court-martial then in session, consisting of thirteen or fourteen officers, Circuit Judge A. A. King; and Mr. Birch, District Attorney, also Sashiel Woods, Presbyterian priest, and about twenty other priests of the different religious denominations in that county. He said they were determined to shoot us on the next morning in the public square in Far West. I made him no reply. On the next morning about sunrise, Gen. Doniphan ordered his brigade to take up the line of march, and leave the camp. He came to us where we were under guard, to shake hands with us, and bid us farewell. His first salutation was, 'By God, you have been sentenced by the court-martial to be shot this morning; but I will be d—d if I will have any of the honour of it, or any of the disgrace of it; therefore I have ordered my brigade to take up the line of march, and to leave the camp, for I consider it to be cold blooded murder, and I bid you farewell,' and he went away. This movement of General Doniphan, made considerable excitement in the army, and there were considerable whisperings amongst the officers. We listened very attentively, and frequently heard it mentioned by the guard, that the d—d 'Mormons' would not be shot this time. In a few moments the guard was relieved with a new set; one of the new guard said, that the d—d 'Mormons' would not be shot this time, for the movement of General Doniphan had frustrated the whole plan, and that the officers had called another court-martial, and had ordered us to be taken to Jackson county, and there to be executed. And in a few moments two large waggons drove up, and **[238]** we were ordered to get into them. While we were getting into them, there came up four or five men armed with guns, who drew up, and snapped their guns at us, in order to kill us. Some flashed in the pan, and others only snapped, but none of their guns went off. They were immediately arrested by several officers, and their guns taken from them, and the drivers drove off. We requested of General Lucas, to let us go to our houses, and get some clothing. In order to do this we had to be driven up into the city. It was with much difficulty that we could get his permission to go and see our families, and get some clothing; but, after considerable consultation, we were permitted to go under a strong guard of five or six men to each of us, and we were not permitted to speak to any one of our families, under the pain of death. The guard that went with me ordered my wife to get me some clothes immediately — within two minutes; and if she did not do it, I should go off without them. I was obliged to submit to their tyrannical orders, however painful it was, with my wife and children clinging to my arms and to the skirts of my garments, and was not permitted to utter to them a word of consolation, and in a moment was hurried away from them at the point of the bayonet. We were hurried back to the waggons and ordered into them, all in about the same space of time. In the mean while, our father, and mother, and sisters, had forced their way to the waggons to get permission to see us, but were forbidden to speak to us, and we were immediately driven off for Jackson county. We travelled about twelve miles that evening, and encamped for the night. The same strong guard was kept around us, and was relieved every two hours, and we were permitted to sleep on the ground. The nights were then cold, with considerable snow on the ground, and for the want of covering and clothing we suffered extremely with the cold. That night was the commencement of a fit of sickness from which I have not wholly recovered unto this day, in consequence of my exposure to the inclemency of the weather. Our provision was fresh beef, roasted in the fire on a stick; the army having no bread, in consequence of the want of mills to grind the grain. In the morning, at the dawn of day, we were forced on our journey, and were exhibited to the inhabitants along the road, the same as they exhibit a caravan of elephants or camels. We were examined from head to foot by **[239]** men, women, and children, only I believe they did not make us open our mouths to look at our teeth. This treatment was continued incessantly, until we arrived at Independence, in Jackson county. After our arrival at Independence, we were driven all through the town for inspection, and then we were ordered into an old log house, and there kept under guard as usual, until supper, which was served up to us, as we sat upon the floor, or on billets of wood, and we were compelled to stay in that house all that night and the next day. They continued to exhibit us to the public, by letting the people come in and examine us, and then go away and give place for others alternately, all that day and the next night; but on the morning of the following day, we were all permitted to go to the tavern to eat and to sleep, but afterwards they made us pay our own expenses for board, lodging, and attendance, and for which they made a most exorbitant charge. We remained in the tavern about two days and two nights, when an officer arrived with authority from General Clark to take us back to Richmond, Ray county, where the General had arrived with his army to await our arrival there; but on the morning of our start for Richmond, we were informed by General Wilson, that it was expected by the soldiers that we would be hung up by the necks on the road, while on the march to that place, and that it was prevented by a demand made for us by General Clark, who had the command in consequence of seniority, and, that it was his prerogative to execute us himself, and he should give us up into the hands of the officer, who would take us to General Clark, and he might do with us as he pleased. During our stay at Independence, the officers informed us that there were eight or ten horses in that place belonging to the 'Mormon' people, which had been stolen by the soldiers, and that we might have two of them to ride upon, if we would cause them to be sent back to the owners after our arrival at Richmond. We accepted of them, and they were rode to Richmond, and the owners came there and got them. We started in the morning under our new officer, Colonel Price, of Keytsville, Chariton county, Mo., with several other men to guard us over. We arrived there on Friday evening, the ninth day of November, and were thrust into an old log house, with a strong guard placed over us. After we had been there for the space of half an hour, there came in a **[240]** man, who was said to have some notoriety in the penitentiary, bringing in his hands a quantity of chains and padlocks. He said he was commanded by General Clark to put us in chains. Immediately the soldiers rose up, and pointing their guns at us, placed their thumb on the cock, and their finger on the trigger, and the state's prison keeper went to work putting a chain around the leg of each man, and fastening it on with a padlock, until we were all chained together, seven of us.

"In a few moments came in General Clarke. We requested to know of him what was the cause of all this harsh and cruel treatment. He refused to give us any information at that time, but said he would in a few days; so we were compelled to continue in that situation—camping on the floor, all chained together, without any chance or means to be made comfortable, having to eat our victuals as they were served up to us, using our fingers and teeth instead of knives and forks. Whilst we were in this situation, a young man, of the name of Grant, brother-in-law to my brother, William Smith, came to see us, and put up at the tavern where General Clark made his quarters. He happened to come in time to see General Clark make choice of his men to shoot us on Monday morning, the twelfth day of November; he saw them make choice of their rifles, and load them with two balls in each; and after they had prepared their guns, General Clark saluted them by saying, *'Gentlemen, you shall have the honour of shooting the Mormon leaders, on Monday morning, at eight o'clock!'* But in consequence of the influence of our friends, the heathen General was intimidated, so that he durst not carry his murderous design into execution, and sent a messenger immediately to Fort Leavenworth, to obtain the military code of laws. After the messenger's return, the General was employed, nearly a whole week, examining the laws, so Monday passed away without our being shot. However, it seemed like foolishness to me, for so great a man as General Clark pretended to be, should have to search the military law to find out whether preachers of the Gospel, who never did military duty, could be subject to court-martial. However, the General seemed to learn that fact after searching the military code, and came into the old log cabin, where we were under guard and in chains, and told us he had concluded to deliver us over to the authorities, as persons guilty of treason, murder, arson, **[241]** larceny, theft, and stealing. The poor, deluded General did not know the difference between theft, larceny, and stealing. Accordingly, we were handed over to the pretended civil authorities, and the next morning our chains were taken off, and we were guarded to the Court-house, where there was a pretended court in session; Austin A. King being the judge, and Mr. Birch, the District Attorney, the two extremely, and very honourable gentlemen, who sat on the court-martial when we were sentenced to be shot. Witnesses were called up and sworn, at the point of the bayonet, and if they would not swear to the things they were told to do, they were threatened with instant death; and I do know, positively, that the evidence given in by those men, whilst under duress, was false. This state of things was continued twelve or fourteen days, and after that, we were ordered by the judge, to introduce some rebutting evidence, saying, if we did not do it, we would be thrust into prison. I could hardly understand what the judge meant, for I considered we were in prison already, and could not think of anything but the persecutions of the days Nero, knowing that it was a religious persecution, and the court an inquisition; however, we gave him the names of forty persons, who were acquainted with all the persecutions and sufferings of the people. The judge made out a subpoena, and inserted the names of those men, and caused it to be placed in the hands of Bogard, the notorious Methodist minister, and he took fifty armed soldiers, and started for Far West. I saw the subpoena given to him and his company, when they started. In the course of a few days they returned with most all those forty men, whose names were inserted in the subpoena, and thrust them into jail, and we were not permitted to bring one of them before the court; but the judge turned upon us, with an air of indignation, and said 'Gentlemen, you must get your witnesses, or you shall be committed to jail immediately, for we are not going to hold the court open, on expense, much longer for you, anyhow.' We felt very much distressed and oppressed at that time. Colonel Wight said, 'What shall we do? Our witnesses are all thrust into prison, and probably will be, and we have no power to do anything, of course we must submit to this tyranny and oppression; we cannot help ourselves.' Several others made similar expressions, in the agony of their souls, but my brother Joseph did not say anything, **[242]** he being sick at that time with the tooth-ache, and ague in his face, in consequence of a severe cold brought on by being exposed to the severity of the weather. However, it was considered best by General Doniphan and Lawyer Reese, that we should try to get some witnesses, before the pretended court. Accordingly, I myself gave the names of about twenty other persons; the judge inserted them in a subpoena, and caused it to be placed in the hands of Bogard the Methodist priest, and he again started off with his fifty soldiers, to take those men prisoners, as he had done to the forty others. The judge sat and laughed at the good opportunity of getting the names, that they might the more easily capture them, and so bring them down to be thrust into prison, in order to prevent us from getting the truth before the pretended court, of which himself was the chief inquisitor or conspirator. Bogard returned from his second expedition, with one prisoner only, whom he also thrust into prison.

"The people at Far West had learned the intrigue, and had left the state, having been made acquainted with the treatment of the former witnesses. But we, on learning that we could not obtain witnesses, whilst privately consulting with each other what we should do, discovered a Mr. Allen, standing by the window on the outside of the house; we beckoned to him as though we would have him come in. He immediately came in. At that time Judge King retorted upon us again, saying, 'Gentlemen, are you not going to introduce some witnesses; also, saying it was the last day he should hold the court open for us, and if we did not rebut the testimony that had been given against us, he should have to commit us to jail. I had then got Mr. Allen into the house, and before the court, so called. I told the judge we had one witness, if he would be so good as to put him under oath; he seemed unwilling to do so, but after a few moments consultation the state's attorney arose and said, he should object to that witness being sworn, and, that he should object to that witness giving in his evidence at all; stating that this was not a court to try the case, but only a court of investigation on the part of the state. Upon this, General Doniphan arose, and said, 'He would be God d—d, if the witness should not be sworn, and that it was a damned shame, that these defendants should be treated in this manner; that they could not be permitted to get one witness before the court, whilst all their witnesses, even **[243]** forty at a time, have been taken by force of arms, and thrust into the *bull pen*—in order to prevent them from giving their testimony.' After Doniphan sat down, the judge permitted the witness to be sworn, and enter upon his testimony. But so soon as he began to speak, a man by the name of Cook, who was a brother-in-law to priest Bogard, the Methodist, and who was a lieutenant, and whose place at that time was to superintend the guard, stepped in before the pretended court, and took him by the nape of his neck, and jammed his head down under the pole or log of wood that was placed up around the place where the inquisition was sitting, to keep the by-standers from intruding upon the majesty of the inquisitors, and jammed him along to the door, and kicked him out of doors. He instantly turned to some soldiers, who were standing by him, and said to them, 'go and shoot him, d—n him, shoot him, d—n him.'

"The soldiers ran after the man to shoot him—he fled for his life, and with great difficulty made his escape. The pretended court immediately arose, and we were ordered to be carried to Liberty, Clay county, and there to be thrust into jail. We endeavoured to find out for what cause, but, all that we could learn was, because we were 'Mormons.' The next morning a large waggon drove up to the door, and a blacksmith came into the house with some chains and handcuffs. He said his orders from the judge were to handcuff us, and chain us together. He informed us that the judge had made out a mittimus, and sentenced us to jail for treason; he also said, the judge had done this, that we might not get bail; he also said the judge stated his intention to keep us in jail, until all the 'Mormons' were driven out of the state; he also said that the judge had further stated, that if he let us out before the 'Mormons' had left the state, that we would not let them leave, and there would be another d—d fuss kicked up. I also heard the judge say myself, whilst he was sitting in his pretended court, that there was no law for us, nor the 'Mormons' in the state of Missouri; that he had sworn to see them exterminated, and to see the Governor's order executed to the very letter, and that he would do so; however, the blacksmith proceeded, and put the irons upon us, and we were ordered into the waggon, and were driven off for Clay county, and as we journeyed along on the road, we were exhibited to the inhabitants. And this course was adopted all the way, [244] thus making a public exhibition of us, until we arrived at Liberty, Clay county. There we were thrust into prison again, and locked up, and were held there in close confinement for the space of six months, and our place of lodging was the square side of a hewed white oak log, and our food was anything but good and decent. Poison was administered to us three or four times; the effect it had upon our system, was, that it vomited us almost to death, and then we would lay some two or three days in a torpid, stupid state, not even caring or wishing for life. The poison being administered in too large doses, or it would inevitably have proved fatal, had not the power of Jehovah interposed on our behalf, to save us from their wicked purpose. We were also subjected to the necessity of eating human flesh for the space of five days, or go without food, except a little coffee, or a little corn bread—the latter I chose in preference to the former. We none of us partook of the flesh, except Lyman Wight. We also heard the guard which was placed over us, making sport of us, saying, that they had fed us upon 'Mormon beef.' I have described the appearance of this flesh to several experienced physicians, and they have decided that it was human flesh.

We learned afterwards, by one of the guard, that it was supposed, that that act of savage cannibalism, in feeding us with human flesh, would be considered a popular deed of notoriety, but the people, on learning that it would not take, tried to keep it secret; but the fact was noised abroad before they took that precaution. Whilst we were incarcerated in prison, we petitioned the supreme court of the state of Missouri, for habeas corpus, twice; but were refused both times, by Judge Reynolds, who is now the Governor of that state. We also petitioned one of the county judges for a writ of habeas corpus, which was granted in about three weeks afterwards, but were not permitted to have any trial—we were only taken out of jail, and kept out for a few hours, and then remanded back again. In the course of three or four days after that time, Judge Turnham came into the jail in the evening, and said, he had permitted Mr. Rigdon to get bail, but said he had to do it in the night, and had also to get away in the night, and unknown to any of the citizens, or they would kill him, for they had sworn to kill him if they could find him. And as to the rest of us, he dared not let us go, for fear of his own life, as well as ours. He [245] said it was d—d hard to be confined under such circumstances; for he knew we were innocent men! and he said the people also knew it; and that it was only a persecution and treachery, and the scenes of Jackson county acted over again, for fear that we would become too numerous in that upper country. He said the plan was concocted from the Governor, down to the lowest judge; and, that that Baptist priest, Riley, was riding into town every day to watch the people, stirring up the minds of the people against us all he could, exciting them, and stirring up their religious prejudices against us, for fear they would let us go. Mr. Rigdon, however, got bail, and made his escape to Illinois. The jailor, Samuel Tillery, Esq., told us also, that the whole plan was concocted by the Governor, down to the lowest judge, in that upper country, early in the previous spring, and that the plan was more fully carried out at the time that General Atchison went down to Jefferson city with Generals Wilson, Lucas, and Gillum, the self styled 'DELAWARE CHIEF.' This was sometime in the month of September, when the mob were collected at De Witt, in Carroll county. He also told us that the Governor was now ashamed enough of the whole transaction, and would be glad to set us at liberty if he dared to do it; but, said he, you need not be concerned, for the governor has laid a plan for your release. He also said that Esquire Birch, the state's attorney, was appointed to be circuit judge, on the circuit passing through Davies county, and that he (Birch) was instructed to fix the papers, so that we would be sure to be clear of any incumbrance in a very short time.

"Some time in April we were taken to Davies county, as they said, to have a trial; but when we arrived at that place, instead of finding a court or jury, we found another inquisition, and Birch, who was the district attorney—the same man who was one of the court-martial when we were sentenced to death—was now the circuit judge of that pretended court, and the grand jury that was empannelled were all at the massacre at Haun's Mill, and lively actors in that awful, solemn, disgraceful, cool-blooded murder; and all the pretence they made of excuse was, they had done it, because the Governor ordered them to do it. The same jury sat as a jury in the day time, and were placed over us as a guard in the night time; they tantalized and boasted over us of their great achievements at Haun's Mill and other **[246]** places, telling us how many houses they had burned, and how many sheep, cattle, and hogs they had driven off, belonging to the 'Mormons,' and how many rapes they had committed, and what kicking and squealing there was among the d—d bitches, saying that they lashed one woman upon one of the d—d 'Mormon' meeting benches, tying her hands and her feet fast, and sixteen of them abused her as much as they had a mind to, and then left her bound and exposed in that distressed condition. These fiends of the lower region boasted of these acts of barbarity, and tantalized our feelings with them for ten days. We had heard of these acts of cruelty previous to this time, but were slow to believe that such acts of cruelty had been perpetrated. The lady who was the subject of their brutality did not recover her health, to be able to help herself, for more than three months afterwards. This grand jury constantly celebrated their achievements with grog and glass in hand, like the Indian warriors at their dances, singing and telling each other of their exploits, in murdering the 'Mormons,' in plundering their houses, and carrying off their property. At the end of every song, they would bring in the chorus, 'God d—n God, God d—n Jesus Christ, God d—n the Presbyterians, God d—n the Baptists, God d—n the Methodists!' reiterating one sect after another in the same manner, until they came to the 'Mormons:' to them it was, 'God d—n, the God d—n Mormons! we have sent them to hell.' Then they would slap their hands and shout, 'Hosannah, hosannah, glory to God!' and fall down on their backs, and kick with their feet a few moments; then they would pretend to have swooned away in a glorious trance, in order to imitate some of the transactions at camp meetings. Then they would pretend to come out of their trance, and would shout, and again slap their hands, and jump up, while one would take a bottle of whiskey and a tumbler, and turn it out full of whiskey, and pour it down each other's necks, crying 'D—n it, take it, you must take it;' and if any one refused to drink the whiskey, others would clinch him, while another poured it down his neck, and what did not go down the inside went down the outside. This is a part of the farce acted out by the grand jury of Davies county, while they stood over us as guards for ten nights successively. And all this in the presence of the *great Judge Birch!* who had previously said in our hearing that there was no law for 'Mormons' in the state of **[247]** Missouri. His brother was then acting as district attorney in that circuit, and, if anything, was a greater cannibal than the judge. After all these ten days of drunkenness, we were informed that we were indicted for *treason, murder, arson, larceny, theft, and stealing.* We asked for a change of venue from that county to Marion county, but they would not grant it; but they gave us a change of venue from Davies to Boon county, and a mittimus was made out by the pretended Judge Birch, without date, name, or place. They fitted us out with a two-horse waggon and horses, and four men, besides the sheriff, to be our guard. There were five of us. We started from Gallatin, the sun about two hours high, P.M., and went as far as Diahman that evening, and staid till morning. There we bought two horses of the guard, and paid for one of them in our clothing which we had with us, and for the other we gave our note. We went down that day as far as Judge Morin's, a distance of some four or five miles. There we staid until the morning, when we started on our journey to Boon county, and travelled on the road about twenty miles distance. There we bought a jug of whiskey, with which we treated the company, and while there the sheriff showed us the mittimus before referred to, without date or signature, and said that Judge Birch told him never to carry us to Boon county, and never to show the mittimus, 'and,' said he, 'I shall take a good drink of grog, and go to bed, you may do as you have a mind to.' Three others of the guard drank pretty freely of whiskey, sweetened with honey; they also went to bed, and were soon asleep, and the other guard went along with us and helped to saddle the horses. Two of us mounted the horses, and the other three started on foot, and we took our change of venue for the state of Illinois, and, in the course of nine or ten days, we arrived in Quincy, Adam's county, [Illinois,] where we found our families in a state of poverty, although in good health, they having been driven out of the state previously, by the murderous militia, under the exterminating order of the Executive of Missouri. And now the people of that state, a portion of them, would be glad to make the people of this state believe that my brother Joseph has committed treason, for the purpose of keeping up their murderous and hellish persecution; and they seem to be unrelenting, and thirsting for the blood of innocence, for I do know, most posi[248]tively, that my brother Joseph has not committed treason, nor violated one solitary item of law or rule in the state of Missouri.

"But I do know that the 'Mormon' people, *en masse*, were driven out of that state after being robbed of all they had, and they barely escaped with their lives, as well as my brother Joseph, who barely escaped with his life. His family also were robbed of all they had, and barely escaped with the skin of their teeth, and all of this in consequence of the exterminating order of Governor Boggs, the same being confirmed by the Legislature of that state. And I do know, so does this court, and every rational man who is acquainted with the circumstances, and every man who shall hereafter become acquainted with the particulars thereof will know, that Governor Boggs, and Generals Clark, Lucas, Wilson, and Gillum, also Austin A. King, have committed treason upon the citizens of Missouri, and did violate the constitution of the United States, and also the constitution and laws of the state of Missouri, and did exile and expel, at the point of the bayonet, some twelve or fourteen thousand inhabitants from the state; and did murder some three or four hundreds of men, women, and children, in cold blood, and in the most horrid and cruel manner possible; and the whole of it was caused by religious bigotry and persecution, because the 'Mormons' dared to worship Almighty God according to the dictates of their own consciences, and agreeable to his divine will, as revealed in the Scriptures of eternal truth, and had turned away from following the vain traditions of their fathers, and would not worship according to the dogmas and commandments of those men who preach for hire and divine for money, and teach for doctrine the precepts of men, expecting that the constitution of the United States would have protected them therein. But notwithstanding the 'Mormon' people had purchased upwards of *two hundred thousand dollars worth of land*, most of which was entered and paid for at the land office of the United States, in the state of Missouri; and although the President of the United States has been made acquainted with these facts, and the particulars of our persecutions and oppressions, by petition to him and to Congress, yet they have not even attempted to restore the 'Mormons' to their rights, or given any assurance that we may hereafter expect redress from them. And I do also know most positively and assuredly, that my brother Joseph **[249]** Smith, senior, has not been in the state of Missouri since the spring of the year 1839. And further this deponent saith not.[1]

"HYRUM SMITH."

CHAPTER 50

REMOVAL OF THE SMITH FAMILY TO ILLINOIS

AT the time when Joseph went into the enemy's camp, Mr. Smith and myself stood in the door of the house in which we were then living, and could distinctly hear their horrid yellings. Not knowing the cause, we supposed they were murdering him. Soon after the screaming commenced, five or six guns were discharged. At this, Mr. Smith, folding his arms tight across his heart, cried out, "Oh, my God! my God! they have killed my son! they have murdered him! and I must die, for I cannot live without him!"

I had no word of consolation to give him, for my heart was broken within me—my agony was unutterable. I assisted him to the bed, and he fell back upon it helpless as a child, for he had not strength to stand upon his feet. The shrieking continued; no tongue can describe the sound which was conveyed to our ears; no heart can imagine the sensations of our breasts, as we listened to those *awful* screams. Had the army been composed of so many blood-hounds, wolves, and panthers, they could not have made a sound more terrible.

My husband was immediately taken sick, and never afterwards entirely recovered, yet he lived about two years, and was occasionally

---

[1] *Times and Seasons*, vol. 4, p. 246-256.

quite comfortable, and able to attend meetings. **[250]**

It will be seen by the testimony of Hyrum, that he was taken by the officers the next day after he arrived at the camp, and that he was seated with Joseph on a log, which was placed there for the purpose before he was taken. The soldiers crowded around them, and swearing that they would shoot them, snapped several guns at them, before any one interfered for their protection. At length Captain Martin ordered his men to surround the prisoners with drawn swords and loaded muskets, "and now," continued he, (drawing his own sword,) "I swear by God, that if any man attempts to harm a hair of their heads, I'll cut his d—d head off the minute he does it. Do you (speaking to his men) protect them, and if any man attempts to lift his gun to his face to shoot those prisoners, cut him down instantly, for they are innocent men, I know they are innocent—look at them, they show it plainly in their very countenances."

This man was but a captain, yet he assumed the responsibility of protecting my sons. And for two nights and a day, he stood constantly on guard, keeping his men to their posts; he neither slept himself, nor suffered his company to rest, until Joseph and Hyrum were removed from the place.

When they were about starting from Far West, a messenger came and told us, that if we ever saw our sons alive, we must go immediately to them, for they were in a waggon that would start in a few minutes for Independence, and in all probability they would never return alive. Receiving this intimation, Lucy and myself set out directly for the place. On coming within about four hundred yards of the waggon, we were compelled to stop, for we could press no further through the crowd. I therefore appealed to those around me, exclaiming, "I am the mother of the Prophet—is there not a gentleman here, who will assist me to that waggon, that I may take a last look at my children, and speak to them once more before I die?" Upon this, one individual volunteered to make a pathway through the **[251]** army, and we passed on, threatened with death at every step, till at length we arrived at the waggon. The man who led us through the crowd spoke to Hyrum, who was sitting in front, and, telling him that his mother had come to see him, requested that he should reach his hand to me. He did so, but I was not allowed to see him: the cover was of strong cloth, and nailed down so close, that he could barely get his hand through. We had merely shaken hands with him, when we were ordered away by the mob, who forbade any conversation between us, and, threatening to shoot us, they ordered the teamster to drive over us. Our friend then conducted us to the back part of the waggon, where Joseph sat, and said, "Mr. Smith, your mother and sister are here, and wish to shake hands with you." Joseph crowded his hand through between the cover and waggon, and we caught hold of it; but he spoke not to either of us, until I said, "Joseph, do speak to your poor mother once more—I cannot bear to go till I hear your voice." "God bless you, mother!" he sobbed out. Then a cry was raised, and the waggon dashed off, tearing him from us just as Lucy was pressing his hand to her lips, to bestow upon it a sister's last kiss—for he was then sentenced to be shot.

For some time our house was filled with mourning, lamentation, and woe; but, in the midst of my grief, I found consolation that surpassed all earthly comfort. I was filled with the Spirit of God, and received the following by the gift of prophecy:—"Let your heart be comforted concerning your children, they shall not be harmed by their enemies; and, in less than four years, Joseph shall speak before the judges and great men of the land, for his voice shall be heard in their councils. And in five years from this time he will have power over all his enemies." This relieved my mind, and I was prepared to comfort my children. I told them what had been revealed to me, which greatly consoled them.

As soon as William was able to stir about a little [252] he besought his father to move to Illinois, but Mr. Smith would not consent to this, for he was in hopes that our sons would be liberated, and peace again be restored. William continued to expostulate with him, but to no effect, as Mr. Smith declared that he would not leave Far West, except by revelation. William said that he had revelation; that he himself knew that we would have to leave Far West. Mr. Smith finally said that the family might get ready to move, and then, if we were obliged to go, there would be nothing to hinder us.

Our business in Far West had been trading in corn and wheat, as well as keeping a boarding house. When the mob came in, we had considerable grain on hand, but very little flour or meal, therefore we sent a man who was living with us to mill with fourteen sacks of grain; but the miller considered it unsafe to allow the brethren to remain about his premises, as the mob were near at hand, and he was afraid they would burn his buildings. Consequently, the young man returned without his grain, and, for bread-stuff, we were for a long time obliged to pound corn in a samp-mortar. Many subsisted altogether upon parched corn for some length of time.

The brethren were all driven in from the country. There was an acre of ground in front of our house, completely covered with beds, lying in the open sun, where families were compelled to sleep, exposed to all kinds of weather; these were the last who came into the city, and, as the houses were all full, they could not find a shelter. It was enough to make the heart ache to see the children, sick with colds, and crying around their mothers for food, whilst their parents were destitute of the means of making them comfortable.

It may be said that, if Joseph Smith had been a Prophet, he would have foreseen the evil, and provided against it. To this I reply, he did all that was in his power to prevail upon his brethren to move into Far West, before the difficulty commenced, [253] and at a meeting, three weeks previous, he urged the brethren to make all possible haste in moving both their houses and their provisions into the city. But this counsel appeared to them unreasonable and inconsistent, therefore they did not heed it. If the brethren at Haun's Mill had hearkened to counsel, it would, without doubt, have saved their lives; but, as the consequences of their negligence are already published, and as my mind is loth to dwell upon these days of sorrow, I shall only give those facts which have not been published.

While the mob was in the city, William went out one day to feed his horse, but the horse was gone. It was not long, however, before a soldier, who had been absent on a despatch, rode him into the yard. William took the horse by the bridle, and ordered the soldier to dismount, which he did, and left the horse in William's hands again.

Soon after this the brethren were compelled to lay down their arms, and sign away their property. This was done quite near our house, so that I could distinctly hear General Clark's notable speech on this occasion; and, without any great degree of alarm, I heard him declare, concerning Joseph and Hyrum, that "their die was cast, their doom was fixed, and their fate was sealed."

Not long after Hyrum left home, Joseph, his youngest son, was born. This was Mary's first child. She never saw her husband but once after she became a mother before leaving the state. She suffered beyond description in her sickness, but, in all her afflictions, her sister, Mrs. Thompson, stood by her to nurse and comfort her, and, by the best of attention, she gained sufficient strength to accompany Emma to the prison once before she left the state.

At this time, my husband sent to Joseph to know if it was the will of the Lord that we should leave the state. Whereupon Joseph sent him a revelation which he had received while in prison, which satis[254]tied my husband's mind, and he was willing to remove to Illinois as soon as possible.

After this, William took his own family, without further delay, to Quincy, thence to Plymouth, where he settled himself, and afterwards sent back the team for his father's family.

Just as we got our goods into the waggon, a man came to us and said, that Sidney Rigdon's family were ready to start, and must have the waggon immediately. Accordingly, our goods were taken out, and we were compelled to wait until the team could come after us again. We put our goods into the waggon a second time, but the waggon was wanted for Emma and her family, so our goods we're again taken out. However, we succeeded, after a long time, in getting one single waggon to convey beds, clothing, and provisions for our family, Salisbury's family, and Mr. M'Lerry's family, besides considerable luggage for Don Carlos, who, with his family and the remainder of his baggage, was crowded into a buggy,[1] and went in the same company with us.

For the want of teams, we were compelled to leave most of our provisions and furniture. Another inconvenience which we suffered was, the horses were wind-broken, consequently we were obliged to walk much of the way, especially up all the hills, which was very tiresome.

The first day we arrived at a place called Tinney's Grove, where we lodged, over night, in an old log house, which was very uncomfortable. Half of the succeeding day I travelled on foot. That night we stayed at the house of one Mr. Thomas, who was then a member of the Church. On the third day, in the afternoon, it began to rain. At night we stopped at a house, and asked permission to stay till morning. The man to whom we applied showed us a miserable out-house, which was filthy enough to [255] sicken the stomach, and told us, if we would clean this place, and haul our own wood and water, we might lodge there. To this we agreed, and, with much trouble, we succeeded in making a place for our beds. For the use of this loathsome hovel, he charged us seventy-five cents. We travelled all the next day in a pouring rain. We asked for shelter at many places, but were refused. At last we came to a place, quite like the one where we spent the previous night. Here we spent the night without fire. On the fifth day, just before arriving at Palmyra, in Missouri, Don Carlos called to Mr. Smith, and said, "Father, this exposure is too bad, and I will not bear it any longer; the first place that I come to that looks comfortable, I shall drive up and go into the house, and do you follow me."

We soon came to a farm house, surrounded with every appearance of plenty. The house was but a short distance from the road, having in front of it a large gate. Through this Don Carlos drove, without hesitating to ask the privilege, and, after assisting us through, he started to the house, and, meeting the landlord, he said, "I do not know but that I am trespassing, but I have with me an aged father, who is sick, besides my mother, and a number of women, with small children. We have

---

[1] A light vehicle, drawn by one horse.

travelled two days and a half in this rain, and if we are compelled to go much further, we shall all of us die. If you will allow us to stay with you over night, we will pay you almost any price for our accommodation."

"Why, what do you mean, sir!" said the gentleman, "Do you not consider us human beings! Do you think that we would turn anything that is flesh and blood from our door, in such a time as this! Drive up to the house and help your wife and children out: I'll attend to your father and mother and the rest of them." The landlord then assisted Mr. Smith and myself into the room in which his lady was sitting, but as she was rather ill, and he feared that the dampness of our clothing would cause her to take cold, he ordered a black servant to make a fire for her in another [256] room. He then assisted each of our family into the house, and hung up our cloaks and shawls to dry.

At this house we had every thing which could conduce to comfort. The gentleman, who was Esquire Mann, brought us milk for our children, hauled us water to wash with, and furnished us good beds to sleep in.

In the evening, he remarked that he was sent by his county, the year before, to the House of Representatives, where he met one Mr. Carroll, who was sent from the county in which the 'Mormons' resided; "and if ever," said Esquire Mann, "I felt like fighting any man, it was him. He never once raised his voice, nor even his hand, in behalf of that abused people, once while the House was in session. I was never a member of the House before, and had not sufficient confidence to take a stand upon the floor in their behalf, as I should have done, had I been a man of a little more experience."

After spending the night with this good man, we proceeded on our journey, although it continued raining, for we were obliged to travel through mud and rain to avoid being detained by high water. When we came within six miles of the Mississippi river, the weather grew colder, and, in the place of rain, we had snow and hail; and the ground between us and the river was so low and swampy, that a person on foot would sink in over his ancles at every step, yet we were all of us forced to walk, or rather wade, the whole six miles.

On reaching the Mississippi, we found that we could not cross that night, nor yet find a shelter, for many Saints were there before us, waiting to go over into Quincy. The snow was now six inches deep, and still falling. We made our beds upon it, and went to rest with what comfort we might under such circumstances. The next morning our beds were covered with snow, and much of the bedding under which we lay was frozen. We rose and tried to light a lire, but, finding it impossible, we resigned ourselves to our comfortless situation. [257]

Soon after this, Samuel came over from Quincy, and he, with the assistance of Seymour Branson, obtained permission of the ferryman for us to cross that day. About sunset, we landed in Quincy. Here Samuel had hired a house, and we moved into it, with four other families.

CHAPTER 51

JOSEPH AND HYRUM ESCAPE FROM THEIR PERSECUTORS, AND RETURN TO THEIR FAMILIES

WE spent the evening after we arrived in Quincy in relating our adventures and escapes, while making our exit from the land of Missouri, and the following circumstance, during our evening's conversation, was related by Samuel, who, in company with a number of others, fled for his life before the enemy: —

He said that they travelled the most secluded route that they could find, as they considered it unsafe to be seen by the inhabitants of the country. Game being very scarce, they soon lacked for provisions, and finally ran out altogether; yet they pursued their journey, until they became so weak that they could proceed no further. They then held a council, in which Samuel was appointed to receive the word of the Lord, and they united in prayer to God, that he would make known to them the means and time of their deliverance.

After a short supplication, it was manifested to Samuel that they might obtain sustenance by travelling a short distance in a certain direction. This he made known to the company, and immediately set out with two others in quest of the promised food. After travelling a short time, they came to [258] an Indian wigwam, and made known to the Indians by signs that they wore hungry. Upon this the squaw, with all possible speed, baked them some cakes, and gave each of them two; after which she sent the same number to those who remained in the woods, giving them to understand that she would send more, but she had very little flour, and her papooses[1] would be hungry.

From this time onward, the brethren succeeded in getting food sufficient to sustain them, so that none of them perished.

In a few days, Samuel moved his family into another house, and we were then less crowded. Soon after he left, Lucy was taken violently ill, and for several days she refused to take any kind of nourishment whatever. I had not long the privilege of taking care of her, as I was shortly seized with the cholera myself, and, although I suffered

---

[1] Children.

dreadfully with the cramp, which usually attends this disease, it was nothing in comparison to another pain, which operated upon the marrow of my bones. It seemed sometimes as though it would almost burst the bones themselves asunder.

Everything that could be obtained which was considered good for such diseases was administered in my case, but without effect. At length we applied to a young botanic physician, who gave me some herb tea that relieved me immediately.

During my sickness, Samuel brought Lucy down stairs several times in his arms to see me, as they did not expect me to live any length of time, and they were willing that she should be gratified. When I recovered, I found that she had taken nothing but ice water while I was sick, but her fever was broken, and, by careful nursing, she was soon able to walk about.

Whilst we were sick, the ladies of Quincy sent us every delicacy which the city afforded; in fact, we were surrounded with the kindest of neighbours. One Mr. Messer and family, in particular, sought [259] every opportunity to oblige us while we remained in the place.

Previous to our sickness in Quincy, my husband sent brother Lamoreaux to Missouri, under strict injunctions to see Joseph and Hyrum, or find out where they were before he should return. About the time that Lucy began to walk about a little, brother Partridge and brother Morley came to our house from Lima, to see if brother Lamoreaux had either written or returned. When they came we had heard nothing of him, but while they were with us he arrived in Quincy, and sent us word that he had seen neither Joseph nor Hyrum. At this information brother Partridge was in despair, and said that, when another messenger was to be sent, he would go himself, as it was hardly possible to find a man that would do as he was instructed. I listened to him some time in silence; at last the Spirit, which had so often comforted my heart, again spoke peace to my soul, and gave me an assurance that I should see my sons before the night should again close over my head. "Brother Partridge," I exclaimed, in tears of joy, "I shall see Joseph and Hyrum before to-morrow night." "No, mother Smith," said he, "I am perfectly discouraged; I don't believe we shall ever see them again in the world. At any rate, do not flatter yourself that they will be here as soon as that, for I tell you that you will be disappointed. I have always believed you before, but I cannot see any prospect of this prophecy being fulfilled, but, if it is so, I will never dispute your word again." I asked him if he would stay in town long enough to prove my sayings, whether they were true or false. He promised to do so. Brothers Partridge and Morley soon afterwards left the house, in order to get further information upon the subject.

After falling asleep that night, I saw my sons in vision. They were upon the prairie travelling, and seemed very tired and hungry. They had but one horse. I saw them stop and tie him to the stump of a burnt sapling, then lie down upon the ground to [260] rest themselves; and they looked so pale and faint that it distressed me. I sprang up, and said to my husband, "Oh, Mr. Smith, I can see Joseph and Hyrum, and they are so weak they can hardly stand. Now they are lying asleep on the cold ground! Oh, how I wish that I could give them something to eat!"

Mr. Smith begged me to be quiet, saying that I was nervous; but it was impossible for me to rest—they were still before my eyes—I saw them lie there full two hours; then one of them went away to get something to eat, but not succeeding, they travelled on. This time, Hyrum rode and Joseph walked by his side, holding himself up by the stirrup leather. I saw him reel with weakness, but could render him no assistance. My soul was grieved, I rose from my bed, and spent the remainder of the night in walking the floor.

The next day I made preparations to receive my sons, confident that the poor, afflicted wanderers would arrive at home before sunset. Sometime in the afternoon, Lucy and I were coming down stairs—she was before me. When she came to the bottom of the steps she sprang forward, and exclaimed, "There is brother Baldwin. My brothers—where are they?" This was Caleb Baldwin, who was imprisoned with them. He told us that Joseph and Hyrum were then crossing the river, and would soon be in Quincy. Lucy, hearing this, ran to carry the tidings to Hyrum's family, but the excitement was not sufficient to keep up her strength. When she came to the door she fell prostrate. After recovering a little, she communicated the welcome news.

When Hyrum and Joseph landed, they went immediately to see their families, and the next day, they, together with their wives and the rest of our connexions, visited us. The Quincy Grays also came to our house, and saluted my sons in the most polite manner. During the afternoon, I asked Joseph and Hyrum, in the presence of the company, if they were not on the prairie the night [261] previous in the situation which I have already related. They replied in the affirmative. I then asked brother Partridge if he believed what I told him two days before. He answered that he would for ever after that time acknowledge me to be a true prophetess. The day passed pleasantly, and my sons returned to their homes, happy in their freedom and the society of their friends.

In a short time after Joseph and Hyrum landed in Illinois, George Miller, who is now the second Bishop of the Church, came and informed us that he had a quantity of land in his possession; also, that upon this land were a number of log houses, which the brethren might occupy if they chose, and that he would charge them nothing for the use of them, unless it would be to repair them a little, as they needed something of this kind.

My sons were pleased with his offer, and Samuel, Don Carlos, and W. J. Salisbury, renting some land of him, moved upon his premises as soon as preparations could be made for their families.

CHAPTER 52

A PURCHASE MADE IN THE TOWN OF COMMERCE—JOSEPH THE PROPHET GOES TO WASHINGTON—THE DEATH OF JOSEPH SMITH, SENIOR

IN the spring of 1839, Joseph and Hyrum made a purchase of a tract of land in Commerce, of one Mr. White, and, after moving their families thither, sent brother Jacob Bigler back for Mr. Smith and myself.

When our good friend, Mr. Messer, learned that we were about leaving Quincy, he came and spent a whole day with us. The next day we set out for [262] Commerce. After proceeding about ten miles, our carriage broke down, and, although my husband was quite sick, we were compelled to remain in the sun at least three hours before another vehicle could be procured. After this we started on, and soon arrived at Bear Creek, below Lima. We found this stream so high that it was dangerous to ford, especially for those who were unacquainted with the crossing place, but, fortunately, we took the right direction, and, with much difficulty, succeeded in getting across. That night we stayed with sister Lawrence, and the next day arrived in Commerce, where we found our children in good health.

We moved into a small room attached to the house in which Joseph was living. Here we might have enjoyed ourselves, but Mr. Smith continued to sink, his health constantly failing, until we found that medicine was of no benefit to him.

As the season advanced the brethren began to feel the effects of the hardships which they had endured, as also the unhealthiness of the climate in which we were then situated. They came down with agues and bilious fevers to such an extent, that there were whole families in which not one was able to help himself to a drink of cold water. Among the sick were Hyrum and his family, also my daughter Lucy. Joseph and Emma, seeing the distress, commenced taking the sick into their own house, with the view of taking care of them, and making them more comfortable. This they continued to do, until their house became so crowded that they were compelled to spread a tent for that part of the family who were still on their feet, in order to make room in the house for the sick. During this time of distress, Silas Smith, my husband's brother, came up from Pike county, Illinois, to consult with Mr. Smith in relation to some Church business, and returned with the intention of bringing his family hither, but was taken sick and died before he could accomplish it, and we never saw him again. My son William also came from Plymouth about this time, and informed **[263]** us that he had sent to Missouri for our provisions and furniture, and that all had been destroyed by the mob. When he returned home, he took Lovina, Hyrum's eldest daughter, with him, hoping, as she was sick, that the ride would be a benefit to her. In this he was disappointed, for she grew worse instead of better, so that in a short time he considered it necessary to send for her father, as she was not expected to live. As her father was not able to sit up when the messenger arrived, myself and Lucy went in his stead. On our arrival at Plymouth, we found Lovina better, and she continued to mend until she regained her health. But the ague took a fresh hold on Lucy, and she remained completely under the power of the disease until the sickness in Commerce had so abated that Joseph was able to make us a visit.

When he arrived, Lucy was lying up stairs in a high fever. Upon hearing his voice below, she sprang from her bed and flew down stairs, as though she was altogether well, and was so rejoiced to hear that her relatives were all still living, and in better health than when she left them, that the excitement performed an entire cure. She soon regained her strength, and we returned home.

It now became necessary for Joseph to take a journey to the city of Washington, for he had been commanded of the Lord, while in prison, to pray for redress at the feet of the President, as well as of Congress, when his family should be so situated that he could leave home.

Accordingly, Joseph started, in company with Sidney Rigdon, Elias Higbee, Dr. Foster, and Porter Rockwell, to fulfil this injunction. After arriving in Washington, Joseph and Sidney waited upon his Excellency Martin Van Buren, but it was some time before they had an opportunity of laying their grievances before him; however, they at length succeeded in getting his attention. After listening to the entire history of the oppression and abuse, which we had received at the hands of our enemies, he **[264]** replied, "GENTLEMEN, YOUR CAUSE IS JUST; BUT I CAN DO NOTHING FOR YOU!"

The matter was, however, laid before Congress. They, too, concluded that our cause was just, but that they could do nothing for us, as Missouri was a sovereign, independent state; and that the 'Mormons' might appeal to her for redress, for, in their opinion, she neither wanted the power nor lacked the disposition to redress the wrongs of her own citizens.

During Joseph's absence, Mr. Smith was at times very weak, and coughed dreadfully, so that some nights I had to lift him out of bed. On one occasion of this kind, he expressed a fear that he should die with me alone. I told him this would not be the case, for it was impressed upon my mind that, when he died, he would have his children around him. This comforted him much, for he was very anxious to live until Joseph should return, that he might bless him again before he should die.

This was in the winter of 1840. Before spring he got some better, so that he was able to walk about a little, and attend a few blessing meetings, in one of which he blessed Mrs. Page, the wife of one of the Twelve, and a young woman whom brother Page had baptized and confirmed on Bear Creek but a few days previous. In blessing the latter, Mr. Smith repeated a prophecy which had been pronounced upon her head in her confirmation, as precisely as though he had been present when it was uttered, stating that the Spirit testified that these things had been predicted upon her head in her confirmation, which very much surprised her, as she knew that he had not received any intimation of the same, except by the Spirit of God.

In March, 1840, Joseph returned from the city of Washington. At this time Mr. Smith had suffered a relapse, and was confined to his bed. On Joseph's arrival, he administered to him, and, for a short time, my husband was better. In the ensuing April a Conference was held in Nauvoo (formerly Com[265]merce), during which the result of Joseph's mission to Washington was made known to the brethren; who, after hearing that their petition was rejected, concluded, as they had now tried every court which was accessible to them on earth, to lay their case before the Court of Heaven, and leave it in the hands of the great God.

Joseph, soon after his arrival, had a house built for us, near his own, and one that was more commodious than that which we previously occupied.

When the heat of the ensuing summer came on, my husband's health began to decline more rapidly than before. This was perhaps caused, in part, by the renewal of the Missouri persecutions, for our sons were now demanded of the authorities of Illinois, as fugitives from justice. In consequence of which, they were compelled to absent themselves from the city, until the writs which were issued for their arrest, were returned.

About this time, John C. Bennett came into the city, and undertook to devise a scheme whereby Joseph and Hyrum, besides other brethren who were persecuted in like manner, might remain at home in peace. I do not know what he did, I only know that he seemed to be engaged in the law, as well as the Gospel. My heart was then too full of anxiety about my husband, for me to inquire much into matters which I did not understand, however, the result was, Joseph returned from Iowa.

On the evening of his return, my husband commenced vomiting blood. I sent immediately for Joseph and Hyrum, who, as soon as they came, gave him something that alleviated his distress. This was on Saturday night. The next morning Joseph came in and told his father, that he should not be troubled any more for the present with the Missourians; "and," said he, "I can now stay with you as much as you wish." After which he informed his father, that it was then the privilege of the Saints to be baptized for the dead. These two facts Mr. Smith was delighted to hear, and requested, that **[266]** Joseph should be baptized for Alvin immediately; and, as he expected to live but a short time, desired that his children would stay with him, as much as they could consistently.

They were all with him, except Catharine, who was detained from coming by a sick husband. Mr. Smith being apprised of this, sent Arthur Miliken, who, but a short time previous was married to our youngest daughter, after Catharine and her children; but, before he went, my husband blessed him, fearing that it would be too late, when he returned. He took Arthur by the hand, and said:—

"My son, I have given you my youngest darling child, and will you be kind to her?" "Yes, father," he replied, "I will." "Arthur," he continued, "you shall be blessed, and you shall be great in the eyes of the Lord; and if you will be faithful, you shall have all the desires of your heart in righteousness. Now, I want you to go after my daughter Catharine, for I know, that because of the faithfulness of your heart, you will not come back without her."

Arthur then left, and my husband next addressed himself to me:—

"Mother, do you not know, that you are the mother of as great a family, as ever lived upon the earth. The world loves its own, but it does not love us. It hates us because we are not of the world; therefore, all their malice is poured out upon us, and they seek to take away our lives. When I look upon my children, and realize, that although they were raised up to do the Lord's work, yet they must pass through scenes of trouble and affliction as long as they live upon the earth; and I dread to leave them surrounded by enemies."

At this Hyrum bent over his father, and said: — "Father, if you are taken away, will you not intercede for us at the throne of grace, that our enemies may not have so much power over us?" He then laid his hands upon Hyrum's head, and said: —

"My son, Hyrum, I seal upon your head your patriarchal blessing, which I placed upon your head before, for that shall be verified. In addition to this, I now give [267] you my dying blessing. You shall have a season of peace, so that you shall have sufficient rest to accomplish the work which God has given you to do. You shall be as firm as the pillars of heaven unto the end of your days. I now seal upon your head the patriarchal power, and you shall bless the people. This is my dying blessing upon your head in the name of Jesus. Amen."

To Joseph he said: —

"Joseph, my son, you are called to a high and holy calling. You are even called to do the work of the Lord. Hold out faithful, and you shall be blessed, and your children after you. You shall even live to finish your work." At this Joseph cried out, weeping, "Oh! my father, shall I." "Yes," said his father, "you shall live to lay out the plan of all the work which God has given you to do. This is my dying blessing on your head in the name of Jesus. I also confirm your former blessing upon your head; for it shall be fulfilled. Even so. Amen."

To Samuel he said: —

"Samuel, you have been a faithful and obedient son. By your faithfulness you have brought many into the Church. The Lord has seen your diligence, and you are blessed, in that he has never chastised you, but has called you home to rest; and there is a crown laid up for you, which shall grow brighter and brighter unto the perfect day.

"When the Lord called you, he said, 'Samuel, I have seen thy sufferings, have heard thy cries, and beheld thy faithfulness; thy skirts are clear from the blood of this generation.' Because of these things, I seal upon your head all the blessings which I have heretofore pronounced upon you; and this my dying blessing, I now seal upon you. Even so. Amen."

To William he said: —

"William, my son, thou hast been faithful in declaring the word, even before the Church was organized. Thou hast been sick, yet thou hast travelled to warn the people. And when thou couldst not walk, thou didst sit by the way side, and call upon the Lord, until he provided a way for thee to be carried. Thou wast sick and afflicted, when thou wast away from thy father's house, [268] and no ono knew it, to assist thee in thy afflictions; but the Lord did see the honesty of thine heart, and thou wast blessed in thy mission. William, thou shalt be blest, and thy voice shall be heard in distant lands, from place to place, and they shall regard thy teachings. Thou shalt be like a roaring lion in the forest, for they shall hearken and hear thee. And thou shalt be the means of bringing many sheaves to Zion, and thou shalt be great in the eyes of many, and they shall call thee blessed, and I will bless thee, and thy children after thee. And the blessings which I sealed upon thy head before, I now confirm again, and thy days shall be many, thou shalt do a great work, and live as long as thou desirest life. Even so. Amen."

To Don Carlos he said: —

"Carlos, my darling son, when I blessed you, your blessing was never written, and I could not get it done, but now I want you to get my book, which contains the blessings of my family. Take your pen and fill out all those parts of your blessing which were not written. You shall have the Spirit of the Lord, and be able to fill up all the vacancies which were left by Oliver when he wrote it. You shall be great in the sight of the Lord, for he sees and knows the integrity of your heart, and you shall be blessed; all that know you shall bless you. Your wife and your children shall also be blessed, and you shall live to fulfil all that the Lord has sent you to do. Even so. Amen."

To Sophronia he said: —

"Sophronia, my oldest daughter, thou hadst sickness when thou wast young, and thy parents did cry over thee, to have the Lord spare thy life. Thou didst see trouble and sorrow, but thy troubles shall be lessened, for thou hast been faithful in helping thy father and thy mother, in the work of the Lord. And thou shalt be blessed, and the blessings of heaven shall rest down upon thee. Thy last days shall be thy best. Although thou shalt see trouble, sorrow, and mourning, thou shalt be comforted, and the Lord will lift thee up, and bless thee and thy family, and thou shalt live as long as thou desirest life. This dying blessing I pronounce and seal upon thy head, with thine other blessings. Even so. Amen."
[269]

After this he rested some time, and then said: —

"Catherine has been a sorrowful child, trouble has she seen, the Lord has looked down upon her and seen her patience, and has heard her cries. She shall be comforted when her days of sorrow are ended, then shall the Lord look down upon her, and she shall have the comforts of life, and the good things of this world, then shall she rise up, and defend her cause. She shall live to raise up her family; and in time her sufferings shall be over, for the day is coming when the patient shall receive their reward. Then she shall rise over her enemies, and shall have horses and land, and things round her to make her heart glad. I, in this dying blessing, confirm her patriarchal blessing upon her head, and she shall receive eternal life. Even so. Amen."

To Lucy he said:—

"Lucy, thou art my youngest child, my darling. And the Lord gave thee unto us to be a comfort and a blessing to us in our old age, therefore, thou must take good care of thy mother. Thou art innocent, and thy heart is right before the Lord. Thou hast been with us through all the persecution; thou hast seen nothing but persecution, sickness, and trouble, except when the Lord hath cheered our hearts. If thou wilt continue faithful, thou shalt be blessed with a house and land; thou shalt have food and raiment, and no more be persecuted and driven, as thou hast hitherto been. Now continue faithful, and thou shalt live long and be blessed, and thou shalt receive a reward in heaven. This dying blessing, and also thy patriarchal blessing, I seal upon thy head in the name of Jesus. Even so. Amen."

After this he spoke to me again, and said:—

"Mother, do you not know, that you are one of the most singular women in the world?" "No," I replied, "I do not," "Well, I do," he continued, "you have brought up my children for me by the fireside, and, when I was gone from home, you comforted them. You have brought up all my children, and could always comfort them when I could not. We have often wished that we might both die at the same time, but you must not desire to die when I do, for you must stay to comfort the children when I am gone. So do not mourn, but try [270] to be comforted. Your last days shall be your best days, as to being driven, for you shall have more power over your enemies than you have had. Again I say, be comforted."

He then paused for some time, being exhausted. After which he said, in a tone of surprise, "I can see and hear, as well as ever I could." [*A second pause, of considerable length.*] "I see Alvin." [*Third pause.*] "I shall live seven or eight minutes." Then straightening himself, he laid his hands together; after which he began to breathe shorter, and, in about eight minutes, his breath stopped, without even a struggle or a sigh, and his spirit took its flight for the regions where the justified ones rest from their labours. He departed so calmly, that, for some time, we could not believe but that he would breathe again.

Catherine did not arrive until the evening of the second day; still we were compelled to attend to his obsequies the day after his decease, or run the risk of seeing Joseph and Hyrum torn from their father's corpse before it was interred, and carried away by their enemies to prison. After we had deposited his last remains in their narrow house, my sons fled from the city, and I returned to my desolate home; and I then thought, that the greatest grief which it was possible for me to feel, had fallen upon me in the death of my beloved husband. Although that portion of my life, which lay before me, seemed to be a lonesome, trackless waste, yet I did not think that I could possibly find, in travelling over it, a sorrow more searching, or a calamity more dreadful, than the present. But, as I hasten to the end of my story, the reader will be able to form an opinion with regard to the correctness of my conclusion. **[271]**

CHAPTER 53

JOSEPH ARRESTED AT QUINCY—DISCHARGED AT MONMOUTH— JOSEPH CHARGED WITH AN ATTEMPT TO ASSASSINATE EX-GOVERNOR BOGGS

IN the month of December, 1840, we received for Nauvoo, a city charter, with extensive privileges; and in February of the same winter, charters were also received for the Nauvoo Legion, and for the University of the City of Nauvoo.

Not long after this the office of Lieutenant-General was conferred upon Joseph, by the vote of the people and a commission from the Governor of the state. In the early part of the same winter, I made brother Knowlton a visit on Bear-Creek. While there I had the misfortune to sprain one of my knees, in getting out of a waggon, and, a cold settling in the injured part, rheumatism succeeded. Soon after I returned home, I was confined to my bed, and for six weeks I had watchers every night. Sophronia was then with me, her husband being absent on a mission, and she assisted Lucy and Arthur in taking care of me. They were indefatigable in their attentions, and by their faithful care I was enabled, after a long season of helplessness, to stand upon my feet again.

On the twenty-fifth of January, 1841, Mary Smith, Samuel's wife, died, in consequence of her exposures in Missouri.

On the fifth of June the same year, Joseph went, in company with several others, on a visit to Quincy. As he was returning, Governor Carlin sent one of the Missouri writs after him, and had him arrested for murder, treason, &c., &c. Joseph choosing to be tried at Monmouth, Warren county, the officers brought him to Nauvoo, and, after procuring witnesses, they proceeded to Monmouth. Esquire Browning spoke in Joseph's defence, and was moved **[272]** upon by the spirit that was given him, in answer to the prayers of the Saints; and, suffice it to say, he gained the case. The opposing attorney tried his utmost to convict Joseph of the crimes mentioned in the writ, but before he had spoken many minutes, he turned sick, and vomited at the feet of the Judge; which, joined to the circumstance of his advocating the case of the Missourians, who are called *pukes* by their countrymen, obtained for him the same appellation, and was a source of much amusement to the court.

When Joseph returned, the Church was greatly rejoiced, and besought him never again to leave the city.

About the first of August, Don Carlos was taken sick, and on the seventh he died. The particulars of his death will be given hereafter.

On the first day of September, Robert B. Thompson, who was Hyrum's brother-in-law, and partner to Don Carlos in publishing the *Times and Seasons*, died of the same disease which carried Carlos out of the world—supposed to be quick consumption.

On the fifteenth of September Joseph's youngest child died: he was named Don Carlos, after his uncle.

On the twenty-eighth of September, Hyrum's second son, named Hyrum, died of a fever.

The succeeding winter we were left to mourn over the ravages which death had made in our family, without interruption; but sickness ceased from among us, and the mob retired to their homes.

On the sixth of May, 1842, Lilburn W. Boggs, ex-Governor of Missouri, was said to have been shot by an assassin. And, in consequence of the injuries which we had received, suspicion immediately fastened itself upon Joseph, who was accused of having committed the crime. But, as he was on that day at an officers' drill in Nauvoo, several hundred miles from where Boggs resided, and was seen by hundreds, and, on the day following, at a public training, where thousands of witnesses [273] beheld him, we supposed that the crime, being charged upon him, was such an outrage upon common sense, that, when his persecutors became apprised of these facts, they would cease to accuse him. But in this we were disappointed, for when they found it impossible to sustain the charge in this shape, they preferred it in another, in order to make it more probable. They now accused my son of sending O. P. Rockwell into Missouri, with orders to shoot the ex-Governor; and, from this time, they pursued both Joseph and Porter, with all diligence, till they succeeded in getting the latter into jail, in Missouri.

Joseph, not choosing to fall into their hands, fled from the city, and secreted himself, sometimes in one place, sometimes in another. He generally kept some friend with him, in whom he had confidence, who came frequently to the city. Thus communication was kept up between Joseph, his family, and the Church. At this time, brother John Taylor lay very sick of the fever, and was so reduced that he was not able to stand upon his feet. Joseph visited him, and, after telling him that he wished to start that night on a journey of fifty miles, requested brother Taylor to accompany him, saying, if he would do so, he would be able to ride the whole way. Brother Taylor believing this, they set out together, and performed the journey with ease. This time Joseph remained away two weeks; then made his family and myself a short visit, after which he again left us. In this way he lived, hiding first in one place, and then in another, until the sitting of the Legislature, when, by the advice of Governor Ford, he went to Springfield, and was tried before Judge Pope for the crime alleged against him; namely, that of being accessory to the attempted assassination of ex-Governor Boggs. He was again discharged, and, when he returned home, there was a jubilee held throughout the city. The remainder of the winter, and the next spring, we spent in peace. [274]

About the middle of June, 1843, Joseph went with his wife to visit Mrs. Wasson, who was his wife's sister. Whilst there, an attempt was made to kidnap him, and take him into Missouri, by J. H. Reynolds, from that state, and Harmon Wilson, of Carthage, Hancock county, Illinois, who was a Missourian in principle. You have read Hyrum's testimony, and can judge of the treatment which Joseph received at their hands. Suffice to say, he was shamefully abused. Wilson had authority from the Governor of Illinois to take Joseph Smith, junior, and deliver him into the hands of the before named Reynolds; but as neither of them showed any authority save a brace of pistols, Joseph took them for false imprisonment. He then obtained a writ of Habeas Corpus of the Master in Chancery of Lee county, returnable before the nearest court authorized to determine upon such writs; and the Municipal Court of Nauvoo being the nearest one invested with this power, an examination was had before said court, when it was made to appear that the writ was defective and void; furthermore, that he was innocent of the charges therein alleged against him. It was in this case that Hyrum's testimony was given, which is rehearsed in a preceding chapter.

Not long after this I broke up house-keeping, and at Joseph's request, I took up my residence at his house. Soon after which I was taken very sick, and was brought nigh unto death. For five nights Emma never left me, but stood at my bed-side all the night long, at the end of which time, she was overcome with fatigue, and taken sick herself. Joseph then took her place, and watched with me the five succeeding nights, as faithfully as Emma had done. About this time I began to recover, and, in the course of a few weeks, I was able to walk about the house a little, and sit up during the day. I have hardly been able to go on foot further than across the street since. [275]

On the third day of October, 1843, Sophronia, second daughter of Don Carlos, died of the scarlet fever, leaving her widowed mother doubly desolate.

CHAPTER 54

JOSEPH AND HYRUM ASSASSINATED

ABOUT the time that John C. Bennett left Nauvoo, an election was held for the office of Mayor, and Joseph, being one of the candidates, was elected to that office. I mention this fact, in order to explain a circumstance that took place in the winter of 1843 and 1844, which was as follows. Joseph, in organizing the city police, remarked, that, "were it not for enemies within the city, there would be no danger from foes without," adding, "if it were not for a Brutus, I might live as long as Cæsar would have lived."

Some one, who suspected that Joseph alluded to William Law, went to the latter, and informed him that Joseph regarded him as a Brutus; and, that it was his own opinion, that he (Law) was in imminent danger. Law, on hearing this tale, went immediately to Joseph, who straightway called a council, and had all that knew anything concerning the matter brought together, and thus succeeded in satisfying Law, that he intended no evil in what he had said.

About this time, a man by the name of Joseph Jackson, who had been in the city several months, being desirous to marry Lovina Smith, Hyrum's oldest daughter, asked her father if he was willing to receive him as a son-in-law. Being answered in the negative, he went and requested Joseph to use his influence in his favour. As Joseph refused to do so, he next applied to Law, who was our secret enemy, for assistance in stealing Lovina from her [276] father, and, from this time forth, he continued seeking out our enemies, till he succeeded in getting a number to join him in a conspiracy to murder the whole Smith family. They commenced holding secret meetings, one of which was attended by a man named Eaton, who was our friend, and he exposed the plot.

This man declared that the Higbees, Laws, and Fosters, were all connected with Jackson in his operations. There was also another individual, named Augustine Spencer, a dissolute character, (although a member of an excellent family,) who, I believe, was concerned in this conspiracy. About the time of Eaton's disclosures, this man went to the house of his brother Orson, and abused my sons and the Church at such a rate, that Orson finally told him that he must either stop or leave the house. Augustine refused, and they grappled. In the contest, Orson was considerably injured. He went immediately to Joseph, and, stating the case, asked for a warrant. Joseph advised him to go to Dr. Foster, who was a justice of the peace. Accordingly, he went and demanded a warrant of Foster, but was refused. On account of this refusal, Foster was brought before Esquire Wells, and tried for nonperformance of duty. At this trial Joseph met Charles Foster, the doctor's brother, who attempted to shoot him, as soon as they met, but was hindered by Joseph's catching his hands, and holding him by main force, in which way Joseph was compelled to confine him above an hour, in order to preserve his own life.

Jackson and the apostates continued to gather strength, till, finally, they established a printing press in our midst. Through this organ they belched forth the most intolerable, and the blackest lies that were ever palmed upon a community. Being advised, by men of influence and standing, to have this scandalous press removed, the city council took the matter into consideration, and, finding that the law would allow them to do so, they declared it a nuisance, and had it treated accordingly. [277]

At this the apostates left the city, in a great rage, swearing vengeance against Joseph and the city council, and, in fact, the whole city. They went forthwith to Carthage, and got out writs for Joseph, and all those who were in any wise concerned in the destruction of the press. But, having no hopes of justice in that place, the brethren took out a writ of Habeas Corpus, and were tried before Esquire Wells, at Nauvoo. With this the apostates were not satisfied. They then called upon one Levi Williams, who was a bitter enemy to us, whenever he was sufficiently sober to know his own sentiments, for he is a drunken, ignorant, illiterate brute, that never had a particle of character or influence, until he began to call mob meetings, and placed himself at the head of a rabble like unto himself, to drive the "Mormons," at which time he was joined by certain unmentionable ones in Warsaw and Carthage; and for his zeal in promoting mobocracy, he became the intimate acquaintance and confidential friend of some certain preachers, lawyers, and representatives, and, finally, of Joseph Jackson and the apostates. He, as Colonel Levi Williams, commands the militia (alias mob) of Hancock county. On this man, I say, they called for assistance to drag Joseph and Hyrum, with the rest of the council, to Carthage. Williams swore it should be done, and gathered his band together. Joseph, not choosing to fall into the hands of wolves or tigers, called upon the Legion to be in readiness to defend the city and its chartered rights. Just at this crisis, Governor Ford arrived in Quincy. The apostates then appealed from the mob to the Governor. At this he came into the midst of the mob, and asked them if they would stand by him in executing and defending the law. They said they would; and so he organized them into militia, and then demanded the brethren for trial upon the warrant issued by Smith; (as he did not choose to recognize the right of Habeas Corpus granted us in the city charter). At the same time he pledged the faith of the state, that the brethren [278] should be protected from mob violence. Those called for in the warrant, made their appearance at Carthage, June 24, 1844. On the morning of the twenty-fifth, Joseph and Hyrum were arrested for treason, by a warrant founded upon the oaths of A. O. Norton and Augustine Spencer.

I will not dwell upon the awful scene which succeeded. My heart is thrilled with grief and indignation, and my blood curdles in my veins whenever I speak of it.

My sons were thrown into jail, where they remained three days, in company with brothers Richards, Taylor, and Markham. At the end of this time, the Governor disbanded most of the men, but left a guard of eight of our bitterest enemies over the jail, and sixty more of the same character about a hundred yards distant. He then came into Nauvoo with a guard of fifty or sixty men, made a short speech, and returned immediately. During his absence from Carthage, the guard rushed brother Markham out of the place at the point of the bayonet. Soon after this, two hundred of those discharged in the morning rushed into Carthage, armed, and painted black, red, and yellow, and in ten minutes fled again, leaving my sons murdered and mangled corpses!!

In leaving the place, a few of them found Samuel coming into Carthage, alone, on horseback, and, finding that he was one of our family, they attempted to shoot him, but he escaped out of their hands, although they pursued him at the top of their speed for more than two hours. He succeeded the next day in getting to Nauvoo in season to go out and meet the procession with the bodies of Hyrum and Joseph, as the mob had the *kindness* to allow us the privilege of bringing them home, and burying them in Nauvoo, notwithstanding the immense reward which was offered by the Missourians for Joseph's head.

Their bodies were attended home by only two persons, save those that went from this place. These were brother Willard Richards, and a Mr. Hamilton; [279] brother John Taylor having been shot in prison, and nearly killed, he could not be moved until some time afterwards.

After the corpses were washed, and dressed in their burial clothes, we were allowed to see them. I had for a long time braced every nerve, roused every energy of my soul, and called upon God to strengthen me; but when I entered the room, and saw my murdered sons extended both at once before my eyes, and heard the sobs and groans of my family, and the cries of "Father! Husband! Brothers!" from the lips of their wives, children, brother, and sisters, it was too much, I sank back, crying to the Lord, in the agony of my soul, "My God, my God, why hast thou forsaken this family!" A voice replied, "I have taken them to myself, that they might have rest." Emma was carried back to her room almost in a state of insensibility. Her oldest son approached the corpse, and dropped upon his knees, and laying his cheek against his father's, and kissing him, exclaimed, "Oh, my father! my father!" As for myself, I was swallowed up in the depth of my afflictions; and though my soul was filled with horror past imagination, yet I was dumb, until I arose again to contemplate the spectacle before me. Oh! at that moment how my mind flew through every scene of sorrow and distress which we had passed together, in which they had shown the innocence and sympathy which filled their guileless hearts. As I looked upon their peaceful, smiling countenances, I seemed almost to hear them say,— "Mother, weep not for us, we have overcome the world by love; we carried to them the Gospel, that their souls might be saved; they slew us for our testimony, and thus placed us beyond their power; their ascendancy is for a moment, ours is an eternal triumph."

I then thought upon the promise which I had received in Missouri, that in five years Joseph should have power over all his enemies. The time had elapsed, and the promise was fulfilled. **[280]**

I left the scene and returned to my room, to ponder upon the calamities of my family. Soon after this, Samuel said, "Mother, I have had a dreadful distress in my side ever since I was chased by the mob, and I think I have received some injury which is going to make me sick." And indeed he was then not able to sit up, as he had been broken of his rest, besides being dreadfully fatigued in the chase, which, joined to the shock occasioned by the death of his brothers, brought on a disease that never was removed.

On the following day the funeral rites of the murdered ones were attended to, in the midst of terror and alarm, for the mob had made their arrangements to burn the city that night, but by the diligence of the brethren, they were kept at bay until they became discouraged, and returned to their homes.

In a short time Samuel, who continued unwell, was confined to his bed, and lingering till the thirtieth of July, his spirit forsook its earthly tabernacle, and went to join his brothers, and the ancient martyrs, in the Paradise of God.

At this time, William was absent on a mission to the Eastern States. And he had taken his family with him, in consequence of his wife being afflicted with the dropsy, hoping that the journey might be a benefit to her. Thus was I left desolate in my distress. I had reared six sons to manhood, and of them all, one only remained, and he was too far distant to speak one consoling word to me in this trying hour. It would have been some satisfaction to me, if I had expected his immediate return, but his wife was lying at the point of death, which compelled him to remain where he was. His case was, if it were possible, worse than mine, for he had to bear all his grief alone in a land of strangers, confined to the side of his dying wife, and absent from those who felt the deepest interest in his welfare; whilst I was surrounded with friends, being in the midst of the Church; my daughters, [281] too, were with me, and from their society I derived great comfort.

The Church at this time was in a state of gloomy suspense. Not knowing who was to take the place of Joseph, the people were greatly wrought upon with anxiety, lest an impostor should arise and deceive many. Suddenly, Sidney Rigdon made his appearance from Pittsburgh, and rather insinuated that the Church ought to make choice of him, not as President, but as guardian; for "Joseph," said he, "is still President, and the Church must be built up unto him." But before he could carry his measures into effect, the Twelve, who had also been absent, arrived, and assuming their proper places, all was set to rights.

William, however, did not return till the spring of 1845, when, with great difficulty, he got his wife to Nauvoo. She survived but a short time after her arrival, for in about two weeks, to complete the sum of William's afflictions, he followed her to the grave. Her disease was brought on by her exposures in Missouri, so that she was what might be termed an indirect martyr to the cause of Christ, which makes the sum of martyrs in our family no less than six in number.

Shortly after William's return from the east, he was ordained Patriarch of the Church, in the place of Hyrum, who held the keys of that Priesthood previous to his death.

Here ends the history of my life, as well as that of my family, as far as I intend carrying it for the present. And I shall leave the world to judge, as seemeth them good, concerning what I have written. But this much I will say, that the testimony which I have given is true, and will stand for ever; and the same will be my testimony in the day of God Almighty, when I shall meet them, concerning whom I have testified, before angels, and the spirits of the just made perfect, before Archangels and Seraphims, Cherubims and Gods; where the brief authority of the unjust man will shrink to nothing[282]ness before Him, who is the Lord of lords, and God of gods; and where the righteousness of the just shall exalt them in the scale, wherein God weigheth the hearts of men. And now having, in common with the Saints, appealed in vain for justice, to

Lilburn W. Boggs, Thomas Carlin, Martin Van Buren, and Thomas Ford, I bid them a last farewell, until I shall appear with them before Him who is the judge of both the quick and dead; to whom I solemnly appeal in the name of Jesus Christ. Amen. **[283]**

———————

APPENDIX

A JOURNAL KEPT BY DON C. SMITH, WHILE ON A MISSION WITH
GEORGE A. SMITH, HIS COUSIN

AT a meeting of the High Council held in Adam-ondi-Ahman, I was
appointed, in company with my cousin George A. Smith, Lorenzo D.
Barnes, and Harrison Sagers, to take a mission to the east and south, for
the purpose of raising means to buy out the mobbers in Davies County,
Missouri; also to effect an exchange of farms between the brethren in the
east, and the mobbers in our immediate neighbourhood.

On the twenty-sixth of September 1838, we took leave of our friends,
and started on our mission, in company with brother Earl, who
proposed taking us in his waggon as far as Richmond, a distance of
seventy miles. We stopped at Far West to see brother Joseph. He
sanctioned our mission, and bid us God speed. On our way to
Richmond we stayed over night with Captain Alpheus Cutler, formerly
of the United States' army. He and his family treated us with much
kindness. We also called on John Goodson, who a few days previous
had shared freely in the hospitality of my uncle's house, yet he had not
the politeness to ask either cousin George or myself to take breakfast
with him.

When we got to the landing, we found the river very low, and but
one boat up, which was the *Kansas*. Whilst waiting for this boat we had
an interview with David Whitmer. He had not confidence to look us in
the face, for he had become our enemy; yet, when we parted, he shook
hands with us quite cordially, and wished us success.

On the thirtieth of September, we went on board the *Kansas;* this was
a very slow conveyance, for one of the wheels was broken; besides the
river being very low, and full of snags and sand bars, we got along but
slowly on our journey. Here we travelled in company with [284] General
Wilson, and Samuel Lucas, besides many others who had taken an active
part in the expulsion of the Saints from Jackson County, in 1833. General
Atchison was also on board. On arriving at De Witt, we found about
seventy of the brethren with their families, surrounded by a mob of two
hundred men. When the boat landed, the women and children were
much frightened, supposing that we also were mob. We would have
stopped, and assisted them what we could, but we were unarmed, and,
upon consulting together, it was thought advisable for us to fulfil our
mission, so we returned to the boat, and proceeded on our journey.
From this onward, the "Mormons" were the only subject of
conversation, and nothing was heard but the most bitter imprecations
against them. Gen. Wilson related many of his deeds of noble daring in

the Jackson mob, one of which was the following: "I went, in company with forty others, to the house of one Hiram Page, who was a Mormon, in Jackson county. We got logs and broke in every door and window at the same instant; and, pointing our rifles at the family, we told them, we would be God d—d if we did'nt shoot every one of them, if Page did not come out. At that, a tall woman made her appearance, with a child in her arms. I told the boys, she was too d—d tall. In a moment the boys stripped her, and found it was Page. I told them to give him a d—d good one. We gave him sixty or seventy lashes with hickory withes which we had prepared. Then, after pulling the roof off this house, we went to the next d—d Mormon's house, and whipped him in like manner. We continued until we whipped ten or fifteen of the God d—d Mormons, and demolished their houses that night. If the Carroll boys would do that way, they might conquer; but it is no use to think of driving them without about four to one. I wish I could stay, I would help drive the d—d Mormons to hell, old Joe, and all the rest."

At this I looked the General sternly in the face, and told him, that he was neither a republican nor a gentleman, but a savage, without a single principle of honour. "If," said I, "the 'Mormons' have broken the law, let it be strictly executed against them; but such anti-republican, and unconstitutional acts as these related by you, are below the brutes." We were upon the hurricane deck, [285] and a large company present were listening to the conversation. When I ceased speaking, the General placed his hand upon his pistol, but I felt safe, for cousin George stood by his side, watching every move the General made, and would have knocked him into the river instantly, had he attempted to draw a deadly weapon. But General Atchison saved him the trouble, by saying, "I'll be God d—d, if Smith aint right." At this, Wilson left the company, rather crest-fallen. In the course of the conversation Wilson said, that the best plan was, to rush into the "Mormon" Settlement, murder the men, make slaves of the children, take possession of the property, and use the women as they pleased.

There was a gentleman present from Baltimore, Maryland; he said, he never was among such a pack of d—d savages before; that he had passed through Far West, and saw nothing among the "Mormons" but good order. Then, drawing his pistols, he discharged them; and re-loading, he said, "If God spares my life till I get out of Upper Missouri, I will never be found associating with such devils again."

Shortly after this we were invited to preach on board. Elder Barnes gave them a good lecture, and I bore testimony. The rest of the way we were treated more civilly, but being deck passengers, and having very little money, we suffered much for food. On one occasion we paid twelve and a half cents for one dozen ears of [Indian] corn; and after grating it, we paid a woman twelve and a half cents more for baking it into bread, although it was badly done, being neither sifted, nor the whole kernels taken out; but we were so hungry that we were glad to get it.

We continued our journey together through every species of hardship and fatigue, until the eleventh of October, when Elder Barnes and H. Sagers left us, after our giving them all the money we had; they starting for Cincinnati, and we, to visit the Churches in West Tennessee. Soon after this, Julian Moses, who had fallen in company with us on the way, gave us a five franc piece, and bade us farewell. This left cousin George and myself alone, and in a strange land; and we soon found that the mob spirit was here, as well as in Missouri, for it was not long before we were mobbed by near twenty men, who surrounded the house in the night, and terrified the family very much; however, we succeeded in driving them away. [286]

After which, we continued our journey until we arrived at brother Utley's, in Benton county, a neighbourhood where brothers Patten and Woodruff were mobbed some years ago. We soon made our business known to all the Saints, who said they would use every effort to be on hand with their money and means—some in the fall, others in the spring. We received from brother West twenty-eight dollars to bear our expenses; and also from others, acts of kindness which will never be forgotten.

About this time our minds were seized with an awful foreboding—horror seemed to have laid his grasp upon us—we lay awake night after night, for we could not sleep. Our forebodings increased, and we felt sure that all was not right; yet we continued preaching, until the Lord showed us that the Saints would be driven from Missouri. We then started home, and, on arriving at Wyatt's Mills, which was on our return, we were told, that, if we preached there it should cost us our lives. We gave out an appointment at the house of sister Foster, a wealthy widow. She advised us to give it up; but, as she had no fears for herself, her property, or family, we concluded to fulfil our appointment. The hour of meeting came, and many attended. Cousin George preached about an hour; during which time, a man, named Fitch, came in at the head of twelve other mobbers, who had large hickory clubs, and they sat down with their hats on. When cousin George took his seat, I arose and addressed them for an hour and a half, during which time, I told them that I was a patriot—that I was free—that I loved my country—that I loved liberty—that I despised both mobs and mobbers—that no gentleman, or Christian at heart, would ever be guilty of such things, or countenance them. At last the mob pulled off their hats, laid down their clubs, and listened with almost breathless attention.

After meeting, Mr. Fitch came to us and said that he was ashamed of his conduct, and would never do the like again, that he had been misinformed about us by some religious bigots.

We continued our journey until we reached the town of Columbus, Hickman county, Kentucky. Here we put up with Captain Robinson, formerly an officer in the army, who treated us very kindly, assuring us that we were welcome to stay at his house until a boat should come, if it were three months. While here, a company [287] of thirteen hundred Cherokee Indians encamped on the bank of the river to wait for ferry privileges. They felt deeply wounded at leaving their native country for the west. They said they were leaving a fine country, rich in minerals, but the whites knew very little of its value. This excited our sympathies very much; little did I think that my own wife and helpless babes were objects of greater sympathy than these.

At length a boat came along, and we went on board. We had to pay all our money (five dollars) for fare, and eat and lie among negroes, as we took a deck passage. About ninety miles from St. Louis our boat got aground, where it lay for three days. During this time we had nothing to eat but a little parched corn. They finally gave up the boat and left her. We went to the clerk and got two dollars of our money back, after which we went on board of a little boat that landed us in St. Louis the next morning. Here we found Elder Orson Pratt; he told us that Joseph was a prisoner with many others, and that David Patten was killed, giving us a long and sorrowful account of the sufferings of the Saints, which filled our hearts with sorrow.

The next morning, we started again on our journey. When we arrived at Huntsville, we stopped at the house of George Lyman to rest, he being uncle to cousin George, whose feet had now become very sore with travelling. Here we heard dreadful tales concerning our friends in Davies county, that they were all murdered, and that my brothers, Joseph and Hyrum, were shot with a hundred balls.

We had not been long in Huntsville till the mob made a rally to use us up with the rest of the Smiths, and, at the earnest request of our friends, we thought best to push on. The wind was in our faces, the ground was slippery, it was night, and very dark, nevertheless we proceeded on our journey. Travelling twenty-two miles, we came to the Chariton river, which we found frozen over, but the ice too weak to bear us, and the boat on the west side of the river. We went to the next ferry. Finding that there was no boat here, and that in the next neighbourhood a man's brains were beat out for being a "Mormon," we returned to the first ferry, and tried by hallooing to raise the ferryman on the opposite side of the river, but were not able to awake him. We were [288] almost benumbed with the cold, and to warm ourselves we commenced scuffling and jumping, we then beat our feet upon the logs and stumps, in order to start a circulation of blood; but at last cousin George became so cold and sleepy that he said he could not stand it any longer, and lay down. I told him he was freezing to death; I rolled him on the ground, pounded and thumped him; I then cut a stick and said I would thrash him. At this he got up and undertook to thrash me, this stirred his blood a little, but he soon lay down again; however, the ferryman in a short time came over, and set us on our own side of the river. We then travelled on until about breakfast time, when we stopped at the house of a man, who, we afterwards learned, was Senator Ashby, that commanded the mob at Haun's Mill. That night we stayed at one of the bitterest of mobocrats, by the name of Fox, and started the next morning without breakfast. Our route lay through a wild prairie, where there was but very little track, and only one house in forty miles. The north-west wind blew fiercely in our faces, and the ground was so slippery that we could scarcely keep our feet, and when the night came on, to add to our perplexity, we lost our way. Soon after which, I became so cold that it was with great difficulty I could keep from freezing. We also became extremely thirsty; however, we found a remedy for this by cutting through ice three inches thick. While we were drinking we heard a cow bell, this caused our hearts to leap for joy, and we arose and steered our course towards the sound. We soon entered a grove, which sheltered us from the wind, and we felt more comfortable. In a short time we came to a house, where George was well acquainted, here we were made welcome and kindly entertained. We laid down to rest about two o'clock in the morning, after having travelled one hundred and ten miles in two days and two nights. After breakfast I set out for Far West, leaving George sick with our hospitable friend. When I arrived I was fortunate enough to find my family alive, and in tolerable health, which was more than I could have expected, considering the scenes of persecution through which they had passed. **[289]**

LETTERS OF DON C. SMITH TO HIS WIFE, AGNES

Cohocton, Yates Co., June 25, 1836.

DEAR COMPANION,

I received your letter bearing date June 15, which I perused with eagerness, being the first I had received from you during my absence. I was rejoiced to hear that you were as well as you expressed, but grieved that your rest should be disturbed by the nervous affection of which you speak. You say that you are willing to submit to the will of the Lord in all things, this also is a source of great consolation to me; for, if these be your feelings, even when deprived of my society, in order to the prosperity of the kingdom of God (as nothing else would tear me from you), I feel that the Lord will bless, keep, preserve, and uphold you, so let your faith fail not, and your prayers cease not, and you shall be healed of your nervous complaint, and all other afflictions. For God is willing, and abundantly able, to raise you up and give you all the righteous desires of your heart, for he has said, "Ask and ye shall receive," and he has never lied, and I can truly say that he has been my help in every time of need.

When I left home I set my face, like a flint, towards Boston, until I found that it was my duty to return home. On arriving at Seneca Falls, I laid the matter before Samuel and Wilber, and we united our hearts in prayer before the Lord, who signified, by the voice of his Spirit, to Samuel, that he should continue his journey, but that we should return, after a short time, to our families; so tell Mary that we have not forsaken him; no, nor ever will, for he is as faithful as the sun—the Lord will not forsake him, and angels will bear him up, and bring him off triumphant and victorious. I heard of the death of grandmother, while at Aven, I could not help weeping, for her, although she has gone to rest. When I left Kirtland, I called at uncle John's—grandmother was asleep—I laid my hand on her head, and asked the Lord to spare her, that I might see her again in the flesh. But when I left, I felt as though she would be taken before I returned, which caused me to feel sorrowful; but I do not desire to call her back to this world of trouble. I must close **[290]** by saying, that I expect to labour in the vineyard, until I start for home. And, if the Lord will, I shall see you as soon as the last of July, then I shall finish this letter.

Yours, till death,

AGNES M. SMITH,   DON. C. S MITH

In the month of June, 1839, Don Carlos came from Mc Donough county to Commerce, for the purpose of making preparations to establish a printing press. As the press and type had been buried during the Missouri troubles, and were considerably injured by the dampness which they had gathered, it was necessary to get them into use as soon as possible; and in order to this, Carlos was under the necessity of cleaning out a cellar, through which a spring was constantly flowing, for there was no other place at liberty where he could put up the press. The dampness of the place, together with his labour, caused him to take a severe cold, with which he was sick some time; nevertheless, he continued his labour, until he got the press into operation, and issued one number of the paper. He then went to Mc Donough, and visited his family; after which, he returned to Commerce, but found the distress so great that no business could be done. Upon his arrival in Commerce, he wrote to his wife the following letter, which shows the situation of the Church at that time, as well as his affectionate disposition, which was breathed in every word he spoke to his family, and stamped upon every line he wrote to them when absent.

Commerce, July 25, 1839.

BELOVED,

I am in tolerable health, and have just risen from imploring the Throne of Grace, in behalf of you and our children, that God would preserve you all in health, and give you every needed blessing, and protect you by day and by night. When I arrived here nothing had been done in the office, as brother Robinson had been sick every day, since I left. And I have done **[291]** but little labour since I returned, except struggling against the destroyer, and attending upon the sick—there are not well ones enough to take care of the sick—there has been but one death, however, since my return. Mc Lerry, Sophronia, and Clarinda, are very sick. Sister E. Robinson has been nigh unto death. Last Tuesday, I, in company with George A. Smith, administered to sixteen souls; some notable miracles were wrought under our hands. I never had so great power over disease, as I have had this week: for this let God be glorified. There is now between fifty and one hundred sick, but they are generally on the gain; I do not know of more than two or three who are considered dangerous. I send you some money that you may not be destitute, in case you should be sick, and need anything which you have not in the house. Agnes, the Lord being my helper, you shall not want, Elijah's God will bless you, and I will bless you, for you are entwined around my heart, with ties that are stronger than death, and time cannot sever them. Deprived of your society, and that of my prattling babes, life would be irksome. Oh! that we may all live, and enjoy health and prosperity, until the coming of the Son of Man, that we may be a comfort to each other, and instil into the tender and noble minds of our children, principles of truth and virtue, which shall abide with them for ever, is my constant prayer. From your husband, who will ever remain, devoted and affectionate, both in time and in eternity,

DON C. SMITH.

While Don Carlos was at work in the before mentioned cellar, he took a severe pain in his side, which was never altogether removed. About a fortnight prior to his death, his family were very sick; and in taking care of them, he caught a violent cold — a fever set in, and the pain in his side increased, and with all our exertions, we were unable to arrest the disease, which I have no doubt was consumption, brought on by working in a damp room, in which he printed his paper. **[292]**

ELEGY ON THE DEATH OF THE DEARLY BELOVED AND MUCH LAMENTED FATHER IN ISRAEL, JOSEPH SMITH, SENIOR, A PATRIARCH IN THE CHURCH OF JESUS CHRIST OF LATTER-DAY SAINTS, WHO DIED AT NAUVOO, SEPTEMBER 4, 1840

BY MISS E. R. SNOW

Zion's noblest sons are weeping;
　See her daughters bathed in tears,
Where the Patriarch is sleeping,
　Nature's sleep — the sleep of years.
Hushed is every note of gladness —
　Every minstrel bows full low —
Every heart is tuned to sadness —
　Every bosom feels the blow.

Zion's children loved him dearly;
　Zion was his daily care:
That his loss is felt sincerely,
　Thousand weeping Saints declare;

Thousands, who have shared his blessing,
    Thousands whom his service blessed,
By his faith and prayers suppressing
    Evils which their lives opprest.

Faith and works, most sweetly blended,
    Proved his steadfast heart sincere;
And the power of God attended
    His official labours here;
Long he stemmed the powers of darkness,
    Like an anchor in the flood:
Like an oak amid the tempest,
    Bold and fearlessly he stood.

Years have witnessed his devotions,
    By the love of God inspired,
When his spirit's pure emotions,
    Were with holy ardour fired.
Oft he wept for suffering Zion—
    All her sorrows were his own:
When she passed through grievous trials,
    Her oppressions weighed him down. [293]

Now he's gone, we'd not recall him
    Prom a paradise of bliss,
Where no evil can befal him,
    To a changing world like this.
His loved name will never perish,
    Nor his mem'ry crown the dust;
For the Saints of God will cherish
    The remembrance of the JUST.

Faith's sweet voice of consolation,
    Soothes our grief: His spirit's flown,
Upward to a holier station,
    Nearer the celestial throne;
There to plead the cause of Zion,
    In the council of the JUST—
In the court, the Saints rely on,
    Pending causes to ADJUST.

Though his earthly part is sleeping,
    Lowly 'neath the prairie sod;
Soon the grave will yield its keeping—
    Yield to life the man of God.
When the heav'ns and earth are shaken,
    When all things shall be restored—
When the trump of God shall waken
    Those that sleep in Christ the Lord.

LINES WRITTEN ON THE DEATH OF GEN. DON CARLOS SMITH

BY MISS E. R. SNOW

"Thy shaft flew thrice, and thrice my peace was slain."

The insatiate archer death, once more
Has bathed his shaft in human gore;
The pale-faced monarch's crimsoned bow,
Once more has laid a good man low.

If tears of love could ever save
A noble victim from the grave; **[294]**
If strong affection e'er had power
To rescue in the dying hour;
If kindred sympathy could hold
A jewel in its sacred fold;
If friendship could produce a charm,
The heartless tyrant to disarm;
If wide acknowledged worth could be
A screen from mortal destiny;
If pure integrity of heart
Could baffle death's malignant dart;
If usefulness and noble zeal,
Devotedness to Zion's weal,
A conduct graced with purposed aim,
A reputation free from blame,
Could save a mortal from the tomb,
And stamp with an eternal bloom;
He never would have bowed to death,
Or yielded up his mortal breath.

Ours is the sorrow, ours the loss,
For, through the triumphs of the Cross,
His noble part, by death set free,
On wings of immortality,
Tracing the steps the Saviour trod,
Has reached the paradise of God.
There he rejoins the ransomed choir,
There, there he hails his noble sire,
A Patriarch of these latter-days,
Whose goodness memory loves to trace
With reverence, gratitude, and love;
He left us for the courts above.
There with the spirits of the just,
Where Zion's welfare is discussed,
Once more their efforts to combine
In Zion's cause.—And shall we mourn
For those who have been upwards borne?
And shall the Legion's sorrow flow,

As if a Chieftain were laid low,
Who threw his frail escutcheon by,
To join the Legion formed on high?
Yes, mourn. — The loss is great to earth,
A loss of high exalted worth. **[295]**

THE ASSASSINATION OF JOSEPH AND HYRUM SMITH, FIRST PRESIDENTS OF THE CHURCH OF JESUS CHRIST OF LATTER-DAY SAINTS, WHO WERE MASSACRED BY A MOB IN CARTHAGE, HANCOCK COUNTY, ILL., ON JUNE 27, 1844

BY MISS E. R. SNOW

Ye heavens attend! Let all the earth give ear!
Let Gods and Seraphs, men and Angels hear —
The worlds on high — the universe shall know
What awful scenes are acted here below!
Had Nature's self a heart, her heart would bleed,
For never, since the Son of God was slain,
Has blood so noble flowed from human vein,
As that which now, on God, for vengeance calls
From "Freedom's ground" — from Carthage prison walls!

Oh! Illinois! thy soil has drank the blood
Of Prophets, martyred for the truth of God.
Once loved America! What can atone
For the pure blood of innocence thou'st sown?
Were all thy streams in teary torrents shed
To mourn the fate of those illustrious dead,
How vain the tribute, for the noblest worth
That graced thy surface, O degraded earth!

Oh! wretched murd'rers! fierce for human blood!
You've slain the Prophets of the living God,
Who've borne oppression from their early youth,
To plant on earth the principles of truth.

Shades of our patriotic fathers! Can it be?
Beneath your blood-stained flag of liberty!
The firm supporters of our country's cause,
Are butchered, while submissive to her laws!
Yes, blameless men, defamed by hellish lies,
Have thus been offer'd as a sacrifice
T' appease the ragings of a brutish clan,
That has defied the laws of God and man!
'Twas not for crime or guilt of theirs they fell;
Against the laws they never did rebel.
True to their country, yet her plighted faith **[296]**

Has proved an instrument of cruel death!
Where are thy far-famed laws, Columbia, where
Thy boasted freedom—thy protecting care?
Is this a land of rights? Stern Facts shall say,
If legal justice here maintains its sway,
The official powers of state are sheer pretence,
When they're exerted in the Saints' defence.

Great men have fallen, and mighty men have died;
Nations have mourned their fav'rites and their pride;
But Two, so wise, so virtuous, great, and good,
Before on earth, at once, have never stood
Since the creation. Men whom God ordained
To publish truth where error long had reigned,
Of whom the world, itself unworthy proved.
It knew them not, but men with hatred moved,
And with infernal spirits have combined
Against the best, the noblest, of mankind.

Oh! persecution! shall thy purple hand
Spread utter destruction through the land?
Shall freedom's banner be no more unfurled?
Has peace, indeed, been taken from the world?

Thou God of Jacob, in this trying hour
Help us to trust in thy Almighty power;
Support thy Saints beneath this awful stroke,
Make bare thine arm to break oppression's yoke.
We mourn thy Prophet, from whose lips have flowed
The words of life thy Spirit has bestowed;
A depth of thought no human art could reach,
From time to time rolled in sublimest speech,
From the celestial fountain, through his mind,
To purify and elevate mankind.
The rich intelligence by him brought forth,
Is like the sun-beam spreading o'er the earth.

Now Zion mourns, she mourns an earthly head;
The Prophet and the Patriarch are dead!
The blackest deed that men or devils know
Since Calvary's scene, has laid the brothers low.
One in their life, and one in death—they proved
How strong their friendship—how they truly loved;
True to their mission, until death they stood,
Then sealed their testimony with their blood. [297]

All hearts with sorrow bleed, and every eye
Is bathed in tears—each bosom heaves a sigh—
Heart-broken widows' agonising groans
Are mingled with the helpless orphans' moans!

Ye Saints! be still, and know that God is just,
With steadfast purpose in his promise trust.
Girded with sackcloth, own his mighty hand,
And wait his judgments on this guilty land!
The noble martyrs' now have gone to move
The cause of Zion in the courts above.

INDEX

221

Made in United States
Troutdale, OR
01/17/2025

28054285R00137